高校英语选修课系列教材

ENGLISH SOCIETY AND CULTURE

英国社会与文化

主　编　方　妍
副主编　周　玲　徐　鸿
　　　　周欣迓　唐加宁

清华大学出版社
北　京

内 容 简 介

本教材分为 10 章，重点介绍了英国的文学巨匠、历史事件、交际礼仪、新闻媒体、地理特点、文娱活动、政治制度、国民特征、教育体系、女性运动等经典的社会文化现象，选材考究、导向清晰、层次递进，横向介绍英国社会的方方面面，纵向追溯其发展历程和因果渊源。为满足多群体、多维度、多层面的不同需要，本教材兼容并蓄，具有较高的可读性、可教性和可参考性，方便教师开展形式多样的教学活动，有助于学习者拓宽国际视野，树立跨文化交际意识，增强英语综合运用能力、自主学习能力和批判性思维能力。

本教材既可作为英语专业本科教材，又可用于高校英语文化类选修课，也可供英国文化爱好者阅读参考；本教材还有配套慕课资源，教师可开展线上线下相结合的混合式教学实践。

版权所有，侵权必究。举报：010-62782989，beiqinquan@tup.tsinghua.edu.cn。

图书在版编目（CIP）数据

英国社会与文化 / 方妍主编. —北京：清华大学出版社，2023.3
高校英语选修课系列教材
ISBN 978-7-302-62489-9

Ⅰ.①英… Ⅱ.①方… Ⅲ.①英语—阅读教学—高等学校—教材②英国—概况 Ⅳ.① H319.37

中国国家版本馆 CIP 数据核字（2023）第 021986 号

责任编辑：刘　艳
封面设计：子　一
责任校对：王凤芝
责任印制：杨　艳

出版发行：清华大学出版社
　　　　网　　址：http://www.tup.com.cn, http://www.wqbook.com
　　　　地　　址：北京清华大学学研大厦 A 座　邮　编：100084
　　　　社 总 机：010-83470000　邮　购：010-62786544
　　　　投稿与读者服务：010-62776969, c-service@tup.tsinghua.edu.cn
　　　　质量反馈：010-62772015, zhiliang@tup.tsinghua.edu.cn
印 装 者：三河市科茂嘉荣印务有限公司
经　　销：全国新华书店
开　　本：185mm×260mm　　印　张：23.75　　字　数：502 千字
版　　次：2023 年 3 月第 1 版　　　　　印　次：2023 年 3 月第 1 次印刷
定　　价：88.00 元

产品编号：092631-01

前　言

随着国家推进"一带一路"建设，社会对大学生英语能力和跨文化交际能力的要求越来越高。了解西方社会与文化、开拓国际视野、去除文化交流障碍已成为英语学习者的基本需求。鉴于此，本教材以任务教学法和产出导向法为理论指导，倡导研究型学习，旨在深度解读英国独特的文明画卷和文化符号。教材依托学习者密切关注的英国社会文化内容，在扩大阅读输入、提高文本难度的同时，侧重于口语和写作的输出，组织学习者进行语言交际活动，既训练了语言技能，也丰富了跨文化知识，可谓一箭双雕、事半功倍。此外，教材还将价值塑造、知识传授和能力培养融为一体，可有效拓宽学习的广度和深度。

与同类教材相比，本教材具有以下特色：

1. 文化导入、能力导向

本教材分为 10 章，重点介绍了英国的文学巨匠和鸿篇巨著，重要历史人物和事件，交往的礼仪，广播、报纸和电视，地理知识和旅游景点，体育运动和流行影视，君主立宪制，国民习惯和性格特征，独特的教育体系和知名学府，女性运动和伟大的女领导人等经典的社会文化现象，旨在增强学习者的英语综合运用能力、自主学习能力和批判性思维能力，培养他们的跨文化交际意识。

2. 原版资料、原汁原味

本教材文章全部选自英文原版资料，通过提供高质量的语言输入，让学习者体会到英国文化的原汁原味，了解生动的案例和最新的社会动态。

3. 寓教于乐、精彩纷呈

本教材从大众的视角出发，选材兼顾知识点的实用性和内容的趣味性，寓教于乐。同时，文章中插入了相关的图片、表格等视觉材料，以活泼的表现手段和多种多样的呈现方式展现出生动直观的效果，让学习者既能深化对语言文化知识的理解，又能体验精彩纷呈的文化之旅。

4. 多元切入、包罗万象

本教材从多元的角度切入，选材涉及文化的各个层面，旨在加深学习者对英国的风俗习惯、国民性格、生活方式、思维模式、价值观念、标准取向和民族发展史的认知和理解，可满足不同学习者的阅读兴趣，便于他们丰富知识储备、开拓国际视野、提高文学素养、培养人文情怀。

5. 预设目标、启发思维

每章开篇进行了章节简介并预设了学习目标，导向清晰、层层递进，有助于不同水平的学习者掌握章节要点，把握文章脉络，进行知识整合，以便做到有的放矢地学习，实现全过程自我检测，并完善自我学习策略，从而提升学习效果。

6. 题型新颖、考查全面

本教材对题型和题目进行了精心设计，层次分明、环环相扣，不仅有对知识点和文化背景的考查，也有对词汇和词组搭配的测试，还有口语讨论和演讲输出，更有重点句子翻译和写作训练，形式多样。编者特意选取了较为真实的场景，设计了应用性强的任务，如头脑风暴、话题辩论、角色表演、主题陈述、故事编述等，既新颖有趣又有挑战性，能多维度提升学习者的英语阅读水平和语言运用能力，促使他们积极地思考、提问、探索、发现和批判。

7. 联想记忆、深度解析

本教材对文章中出现的重点词汇进行了黑体标注，并提供了词性和中文释义，帮助学习者扫除阅读障碍，更快更好地扩大词汇量；对于语言难点、历史人物、重大事件和典故知识，教材也通过二维码提供了注释和解析，以帮助学习者加深对文章的理解，把握相关知识点，并拓展对英国文化的认识。

8. 资源丰富、延伸拓展

为倡导研究型学习，本教材以二维码的形式延展专题。开篇以二维码的形式提供了拓展知识面的相关背景介绍，提纲挈领、分门别类地介绍了相关知识点。篇中二维码提供了文章中历史人物和重大事件的文化注释，并附有推荐的相关网址和影视资源，方便学习者学习、查阅，进而提升他们的自主学习能力、信息获取能力和语言运用能力。篇尾二维码提供了 Text Ⅱ 的相关习题，对学习者的学习能力进行进一步考查。

9. 横纵结合、兼容并蓄

本教材横向介绍英国社会的方方面面，纵向追溯其发展历程和因果渊源。为满足多群体、多维度、多层面的不同需要，本教材兼容并蓄，具有较高的可读性、可教性和可参考性，方便教师借助教材有条不紊地开展形式多样的教学活动，鼓励学习者自主获取知识、发现问题并解决问题。

10. 课程思政、文化自信

在材料选择和练习设计方面，本教材立足课程思政，旨在提升学习者的文化自信，使其能在中外文化交流的舞台上讲好中国故事，传播中国声音，在跨文化交际中探讨中外差异。

"英国社会与文化"慕课是武汉大学外国语言文学学院大学英语部五位青年骨干教师团队十几年授课成果的凝练和提升，自 2018 年在爱课程平台上线以来，已经运行了 10 轮，选课人数近 8 万人。2019 年该慕课荣获"湖北高校线上线下混合式金课教学大赛优秀教学改革案例"称号，2021 年被湖北省教育厅认定为湖北高校一流本科课程。

前言

  本教材是"英国社会与文化"慕课的配套教材，编者也是该慕课的制作者，有丰富的语言文化教学经验，深知涉外工作和文化交流中对英语语言和英语文化的需求。这样编写的教材有的放矢、针对性强，可以满足中高级阶段英语学习者的学习需求，适用于高等院校本科生、研究生培养以及教师继续教育。

  我们期待，不论是高校英语专业学生，还是英语水平较高的非英语专业学生，或是有一定英语基础准备出国深造的英语学习者，甚至是在高校教授西方文化课尤其是英国文化课的教师，都能从本教材中学有所获、学以致用，为学习、工作和生活提供实用有益的参考。教师也可以与慕课同步，开展线上线下相结合的混合式教学实践。我们也希望，在教材使用过程中，能得到更多院校师生的反馈意见和建议，以便我们不断完善教材，给学习者带来更好的学习体验。

编者
2023 年 1 月

Contents

Chapter 1 Literature—Literary Giants and Their Masterpieces 1

Unit 1 Shakespeare, The Greatest Dramatist: Appreciation of His Comedies and Tragedies 2
- Text I   Why Study Shakespeare? 3
- Text II On Shakespeare 9

Unit 2 Great Authors and Their Novels of the Victorian Period 13
- Text I   Gender Roles in the 19th Century 13
- Text II Charles Dickens' Gift of Giving 20

Unit 3 Notable Poets of Romanticism—Byron, Shelley and Keats 24
- Text I   Famous Last Words 25
- Text II The Later Romantics: Shelley, Keats, and Byron 30

Chapter 2 History—Figures and Events of Significance 33

Unit 1 King Arthur and William of Normandy: Early History of Britain and the French Influence 34
- Text I   King Arthur 35
- Text II The Emergence of the British State 41

Unit 2 King John and King Charles I: Is King's Right Divine? 44
- Text I   King John 45
- Text II Charles I 50

Unit 3 Spanish Armada and the Two World Wars:
The Empire on Which the Sun Never Sets 54

    Text I   Rivalry Between Britain and France 55

    Text II   The Battle of Britain 62

Chapter 3 Communication—Etiquette Here and There 67

Unit 1 English Weather-Speak:
How to Talk About the Weather with the English 68

    Text I   Is the British Weather Unique in the World? 68

    Text II   Rules of English Weather-Speak 73

Unit 2 Greetings and Goodbyes: How to Greet and Say Goodbye 76

    Text I   A Short Primer on British Social Etiquette 76

    Text II   English Etiquette 80

Unit 3 English Pubs—How to Engage in Non-verbal and Verbal
Communication 84

    Text I   Seven Differences Between American and British Pubs 84

    Text II   What Is Britain Without the Pub? 88

Chapter 4 British Media—Broadcasting, Newspapers and Television 93

Unit 1 The Broadcasting History of BBC 94

    Text I   The Growth of Alternative Media 95

    Text II   Swashbuckling Sounds: The History of Pirate Radio Stations 99

Unit 2 Britain's Big Three: Quality or Popular Papers 104

    Text I   A History of the Broadsheet Newspaper 105

    Text II   The Era of the Press Barons 110

Unit 3 Television: An Idiotic Thing? 114

    Text I   The Age of Show Business 115

    Text II   The Medium Is the Message 120

Chapter 5 A Country of Countries—Geography and Tourist Attractions 125

Unit 1 Geographical Divisions of United Kingdom 126

    Text I   The Differences Among the UK, Britain, Great Britain and England 126

    Text II   People and Language 131

Unit 2 Historical Heritage and Landscape 134

    Text I   Stonehenge-Era Pig Roasts United Ancient Britain, Scientists Say 135

    Text II   The White Cliffs of Dover—Things to See and Do 139

Unit 3 A Tour to Major Cities: Landmarks and Spectaculars 143

    Text I   Six of London's Best Small Museums and Why You Should Visit Them Now 144

    Text II   How to Experience Belfast's Cultural Scene like a Local 148

Chapter 6 Entertainment—Sports, Movies and TV Series 153

Unit 1 Sports: Widespread Participation 154

    Text I   Sports in the UK 155

    Text II   Association Football or Soccer 160

Unit 2 What's So Fascinating of British Films? 164

    Text I   The Highest-Grossing British Films of All Time 165

    Text II   British Film History 171

Unit 3 Charms of Popular TV Series—*Sherlock, Downton Abbey* and *Doctor Who* 175

    Text I   Best Films and TV Shows Based on the British Royal Family 176

    Text II   Do You Love British TV Series? Showmax Got You Covered 182

Unit 4 One City, Three Olympic Games 186

    Text I   London Olympic Games Then and Now: 1908 & 2012 187

    Text II   Legacies of Past Olympic Games 192

Chapter 7 Politics—Constitutional Monarchy......197

Unit 1 Constitution and Monarch:
How to Justify Britain's Support for Monarchy 198

    Text I   Elizabeth II 199

    Text II   Harry's Departure Could Do Britain's Royal Family a Favor..... 203

Unit 2 General Election: Who Would Become the
Winner of First-Past-the-Post 207

    Text I   How Winston Churchill Lost the 1945
British General Election 208

    Text II   Some Arguments Surrounding the
Debate over FPTP vs. PR 214

Unit 3 Separation of Powers:
Would Early Election Do Wonders for Theresa May 218

    Text I   Theresa May's Election Announcement: Full Statement 219

    Text II   British PM May Calls for Early Election to Strengthen
Brexit Hand 225

Unit 4 Product of Ballot and Root of Trouble:
Soft Brexit, Hard Brexit or No-Deal Brexit 229

    Text I   Britain and the European Union 230

    Text II   Brexit: Pros and Cons 235

Chapter 8 People—Habit Is Second Nature.........239

Unit 1 Queuing: Queuers and Queue-Jumpers 240

    Text I   Queuing: Is It Really the British Way? 240

    Text II   Coronavirus Has Ruined the Great, Orderly British Queue 245

Unit 2 Moaning: Workplace Moans and Restaurant Moans 249

    Text I   Top 50 Things British People Complain About 249

    Text II   Moaning Is Bad for Your Health 255

Unit 3 Humour: Understatement and Self-deprecation 259

    Text I   British Humour: What Exactly Is It and How Does It Work? 259

    Text II   The Differences Between American and British Humour 265

Unit 4 Sorry, ... Sorry, ... Sorry, ...What Does It Say About Englishness? 269

    Text I   Why Do the British Say "Sorry" So Much? 269

    Text II   Terribly Sorry—But Britain's Famed Politeness May Be a Myth ... 274

Chapter 9 Education—Distinct Educational System and Distinguished Schools 279

Unit 1 Understanding the UK Education System 280

    Text I   Academic Route vs. Vocational Route: Which Is Better? 280

    Text II   Western Norms of Critical Argumentation 286

Unit 2 Public Schools and Independent Schools 290

    Text I   British Education System—Grammar School 291

    Text II   Best of British as Elite Public Schools Tap up Chinese Pupils ... 295

Unit 3 How to Apply for a British University 300

    Text I   The Personal Statement that Got Me a Large Scholarship to Cambridge 300

    Text II   What Is a Collegiate University? 306

Unit 4 Different Types of British Universities and Their Strengths 309

    Text I   Differences Between Oxford and Cambridge 309

    Text II   Why Should You Study at a Russell Group University? 314

Chapter 10 Feminine Culture in Britain 319

Unit 1 Women's Movement in Britain 320

    Text I   The Lives of the Suffragettes 321

    Text II   Woman as Other 326

Unit 2 Great Women Leaders in British History 330

    Text I   Twilight of Splendor: The Court of Queen Victoria During Her Diamond Jubilee 331

    Text II   Slums in Late-Victorian London 337

Unit 3 The Crazy Hat 342

    Text I   Margaret Thatcher: Fashion Rebel? 343

	Text II	History of Women Wearing Men's Clothing	349
Unit 4		Weddings: The Carrier of British Culture	356
	Text I	Miss Brooke	357
	Text II	Marriage Therapy in the 1960s: Marriage as a Platform for Personal Growth	362

Chapter 1
Literature— Literary Giants and Their Masterpieces

Introduction

    When it comes to British literary giants, which prominent figure would come to your mind? William Shakespeare, the unparalleled dramatist and poet in Renaissance? William Thackeray, the master of satire who described the world with a critical view in his masterpiece *Vanity Fair*? Charles Dickens, the greatest representative of English critical realism? The brilliant Brontë sisters, the creators of *Jane Eyre*, *Wuthering Heights* and *Agnes Gray*? Or the notable poets of Romanticism like Byron, Shelley and Keats? The masterpieces of those literary giants transcend the limitation of time and space, escape the constraint of humanity, purify our souls and spirit, and bring about profound enlightenment for us. This chapter intends to introduce the charms of those prestigious playwrights, authors and poets, and lead you to appreciate their masterpieces with critical analysis.

Shakespeare, The Greatest Dramatist: Appreciation of His Comedies and Tragedies

Literature adds to reality; it does not simply describe it. It enriches the necessary competencies that daily life requires and provides; and in this respect, it irrigates the deserts that our lives have already become.

—Clive Staples Lewis

Test Your Knowledge

I. Search for the relevant information to answer the following questions.

1. Who would you think of when talking about British literature?
2. Could you make a list of William Shakespeare's famous comedies and tragedies?
3. What are the three different types of plays that Shakespeare wrote?
4. Who said that Shakespeare was not of an age, but for all time?
5. Why do we still study Shakespeare?

II. Categorize the following plays into different types.

1. *Richard II*
2. *Romeo and Juliet*
3. *The Taming of the Shrew*
4. *The Tempest*
5. *Antony and Cleopatra*
6. *Hamlet*
7. *King Lear*
8. *Twelfth Night*
9. *Julius Caesar*
10. *A Midsummer Night's Dream*
11. *Macbeth*
12. *Henry IV*
13. *Othello*
14. *As You Like It*
15. *All's Well That Ends Well*
16. *Much Ado About Nothing*

Comedies: _____
Tragedies: _____
Historical Plays: _____

Chapter 1 Literature—Literary Giants and Their Masterpieces

Intensive Reading

Text I Why Study Shakespeare?*
—The Reasons Behind Shakespeare's Influence and Popularity

Ben Jonson **anticipated** Shakespeare's **dazzling** future when he declared, "He was not of an age, but for all time!" in the preface to the first folio. While most people know that Shakespeare is, in fact, the most popular dramatist and poet the Western world has ever produced, students new to his works often wonder why this is so. The following are the top four reasons why Shakespeare has stood the test of time.

Illumination of the Human Experience

Shakespeare's ability to summarize the range of human emotions in simple yet profoundly **eloquent** verse is perhaps the greatest reason for his **enduring** popularity. If you cannot find words to express how you feel about love or music or growing older, Shakespeare can speak for you. No author in the Western world has penned more beloved passages. Shakespeare's works are the reason why John Bartlett compiled the first major book of familiar quotations.

Great Stories

Marchette Chute, in the Introduction to her famous retelling of Shakespeare's stories, summarizes one of the reasons for Shakespeare's **immeasurable** fame:

> William Shakespeare was the most remarkable storyteller that the world has ever known. Homer told of adventures and men at war, Sophocles and Tolstoy told of tragedies and of people in trouble. Terence and Mark Twain told comedic stories, Dickens told **melodramatic** ones, Plutarch told histories and Hand Christian Andersen told fairy tales. But Shakespeare told every kind of story—comedy, tragedy, history, melodrama, adventure, love stories and fairy tales—and each of them so well that they have become **immortal**. In all the world of storytelling he has become the greatest name.

> Shakespeare's stories **transcend** time and culture. Modern storytellers continue to adapt Shakespeare's tales to suit our modern world, whether it be the tale of Lear on a farm in Iowa, Romeo and Juliet on the mean streets of New York City, or Macbeth in **feudal** Japan.

---

* Retrieved from Shakespeare Online website.

英国社会与文化

Compelling Characters

Shakespeare invented his share of **stock** characters, but his truly great characters—particularly his tragic heroes—are **unequalled** in literature, **dwarfing** even the **sublime** creations of the Greek tragedians. Shakespeare's great characters have remained popular because of their complexity; for example, we can see ourselves as gentle Hamlet, forced against his better nature to seek murderous **revenge**. For this reason Shakespeare is deeply admired by actors, and many consider playing a Shakespearean character to be the most difficult and most **rewarding** role possible.

Ability to Turn a Phrase

Many of the common expressions now thought to be **clichés** were Shakespeare's creations. Chances are you use Shakespeare's expressions all the time even though you may not know it is the Bard you are quoting. You may think that fact is "neither here nor there", but that's "the short and the long of it". Bernard Levin said it best in the following quote about Shakespeare's impact on our language:

> If you cannot understand my argument, and declare "It's Greek to me", you are quoting Shakespeare; if you claim to be more sinned against than sinning, you are quoting Shakespeare; if you recall your salad days, you are quoting Shakespeare; if you act more in sorrow than in anger, if your wish is father to the thought, if your lost property has **vanished** into thin air, you are quoting Shakespeare; if you have ever refused to **budge** an inch or suffered from green-eyed jealousy, if you have played fast and loose, if you have been tongue-tied, a tower of strength, **hoodwinked** or in a pickle, if you have knitted your brows, made a virtue of necessity, insisted on fair play, slept not one wink, stood on ceremony, danced attendance (on your lord and master), laughed yourself into stitches, had short shrift, cold comfort or too much of a good thing, if you have seen better days or lived in a fool's paradise—why, be that as it may, the more fool you, for it is a foregone conclusion that you are (as good luck would have it) quoting Shakespeare; if you think it is early days and clear out bag and baggage, if you think it is high time and that is the long and short of it, if you believe that the game is up and that truth will out even if it involves your own flesh and blood, if you lie low till the crack of doom because you suspect foul play, if you have your teeth set on edge (at one fell swoop) without rhyme or reason, then—to give the devil his due—if the truth were known (for surely you have a tongue in your head), you are quoting Shakespeare; even if you bid me good riddance and send me packing, if you wish I were dead as a door-nail, if you think I am an eyesore, a laughing stock, the devil **incarnate**, a stony-hearted **villain**, bloody-minded or a

Chapter 1 Literature—Literary Giants and Their Masterpieces

blinking idiot, then—by Jove! O Lord! Tut, tut! For goodness' sake! What the dickens! But me no buts—it is all one to me, for you are quoting Shakespeare.

Vocabulary

anticipate	*v.*	预料
dazzling	*adj.*	令人印象深刻的
illumination	*n.*	启示，启迪
eloquent	*adj.*	雄辩的；流利的
enduring	*adj.*	持久的，耐久的
immeasurable	*adj.*	不可估量的
melodramatic	*adj.*	情节剧式的
immortal	*adj.*	流芳百世的，名垂千古的
transcend	*v.*	超出，超越（通常的界限）
feudal	*adj.*	封建（制度）的
compelling	*adj.*	激发兴趣的；引人注目的
stock	*adj.*	（文学、戏剧或电影角色）老套的，陈腐的
unequalled	*adj.*	（业绩、范围）无比的，无敌的
dwarf	*v.*	使相形见绌
sublime	*adj.*	令人赞叹的
revenge	*n.*	报复，报仇
rewarding	*adj.*	令人满意的；令人有收获的
cliché	*n.*	陈词滥调
vanish	*v.*	突然消失
budge	*v.*	轻微移动
hoodwink	*v.*	欺诈，欺骗
incarnate	*adj.*	化身的；拟人化的
villain	*n.*	（戏剧、小说中的）反派角色
blinking	*adj.*	讨厌的，可恶的

Exercises

I. Decide whether the following statements are true or false, and mark T or F accordingly.

_____ **1.** Marchette Chute complimented Shakespeare as the most popular dramatist and poet in the Western world, since his works have stood the test of time.

_____ 2. Shakespeare had the competence to describe human emotions in complicated and profound verse, which accounts for his charms and popularity.

_____ 3. Ben Jonson compiled the first major book of familiar quotations for Shakespeare's works.

_____ 4. Shakespeare's stories have been adapted by modern storytellers to suit the modern world.

_____ 5. Shakespeare is admired by actors because he simplified his stock characters to make it easier for the actors to play the roles.

II. **Choose the best option to answer each question or complete each statement.**

1. "He was not of an age, but for all time!" This statement shows that _____.

    A. William Shakespeare was of an old age
    B. William Shakespeare was the most popular dramatist and poet of his age
    C. Ben Jonson had doubts about William Shakespeare's reputation
    D. Ben Jonson sang high praise for William Shakespeare's achievements and contribution

2. Why is William Shakespeare regarded as the most popular dramatist and poet by most Western people?

    A. He used simple but eloquent words to describe the feelings of human beings.
    B. He was skillful in telling various kinds of stories well.
    C. The characters in his works are unprecedented in literature.
    D. All of the above.

3. Which of the following statements is **NOT** true according to the passage?

    A. Homer was a remarkable storyteller of adventures and men at war.
    B. Bernard Levin compiled the first major book of familiar quotations of William Shakespeare.
    C. William Shakespeare's stories are adapted to suit the modern world.
    D. Many expressions commonly used today were created by William Shakespeare, but we may not realize it.

Chapter 1 Literature—Literary Giants and Their Masterpieces

   4. "Shakespeare's stories transcend time and culture." This statement means that _____.
      A. William Shakespeare's works have been tested by time, and are still favored by people nowadays
      B. William Shakespeare's stories won him great popularity and reputation in his age
      C. William Shakespeare created great characters of his time for us to understand English literature
      D. the characters created by William Shakespeare are the most difficult roles for the actors to play
   5. The author quoted many expressions of William Shakespeare to show that _____.
      A. William Shakespeare's creations have become clichés nowadays
      B. those phrases have been out of date and won't be used in modern society any more
      C. William Shakespeare was a real language master
      D. those idioms were rather hard for people to understand

III. Match the authors in the left column with the genres of works in the right column.

   1. Homer   A. fairy tales
   2. Sophocles   B. comedic stories
   3. Mark Twain   C. adventures and men at war
   4. Dickens   D. melodramatic stories
   5. Plutarch   E. tragedies and people in trouble
   6. Hand Christian Andersen   F. histories

IV. Fill in the blanks with the appropriate forms of the words in the box.

anticipate	illuminate	eloquent	enduring
popular	immeasurable	melodramatic	compelling
unequalled	sublime	vanish	villain

   1. His ruthless ambition and drive for self-promotion have not made him _____ among his co-workers.
   2. While many in northern Norway explore the wilderness for fun, the

Sami, the Arctic north's most _____ human presence, do so as a way of life.

3. Go into the fields or the woods, spend a summer day by the sea or the mountains, and all your little perplexities and anxieties will _____.

4. If we feel something within ourselves drawing us in one direction but also something drawing us the other way, what exactly can philosophy do to offer us _____?

5. For some, Keynes is the hero who rescued the West from the Great Depression, for others the _____ to blame for the current mess.

6. She said that she left home a little earlier this year in _____ of heavy crowds at the station, but was pleased to see a relatively calm scene.

7. That vision of public education is a(n) _____ one, although America has often fallen short in its pursuit of the ideal.

8. To our great amazement, this country boasts a three-decade persistent economic growth, which is _____ elsewhere in the world.

9. His speech at Madrid was perhaps the most _____ the West had ever heard from a Palestinian: a plea for understanding, for sympathy and for territory.

10. Strong, violently emotional, somewhat _____, Jane Eyre brilliantly articulates the theme found in all Charlotte's works—the need of women for both love and independence.

11. If beauty is great and charismatic enough, it begins to take on attributes of the _____—the nobility, the majesty and awesomeness.

12. These tests are a somewhat more scientific way to measure something that is, in reality, _____.

V. Fill in the blanks with the appropriate forms of the phrases in the box.

fair play	much ado about nothing
the long and short of it	vanish into thin air
at one fell swoop	play fast and loose
in a pickle	short shrift

1. When you arrived there and saw the beautiful scenery, all your weariness would _____ straight away.

2. We can use "_____" to describe a situation in which there has been a lot of excitement about something that is not really important.

Chapter 1 **Literature—Literary Giants and Their Masterpieces**

3. The contestants agreed to observe the spirit of _____ in all of the games.
4. Only a foolish politician would promise to lower the rate of inflation and reduce unemployment _____.
5. Definition is important to us, and we're certainly not going to give it _____ in this course.
6. If you are _____, you are in trouble or a difficult situation.
7. If you think you're not able to observe these rules, you can move out anytime—that's _____!
8. While many period dramas _____ with history, this one has been praised for its realistic setting and respect for history and the source material.

VI. Based on your knowledge, how would you evaluate William Shakespeare's contribution to literature? Please illustrate with specific reasons and examples, and write no less than 200 words.

Further Reading

Text II On Shakespeare*

　　Of this Shakespeare of ours, perhaps the opinion one sometimes hears a little **idolatrously** expressed is, in fact, the right one; I think the best judgment not of this country only, but of Europe at large, is slowly pointing to the conclusion that Shakespeare is the chief of all poets **hitherto**; the greatest intellect who, in our recorded world, has left record of himself in the way of literature. On the whole, I know not such a power of vision, such a faculty of thought, if we take all the characters of it, in any other man. Such a calmness of depth; **placid** joyous strength; all things imaged in that great soul of his so true and clear, as in a tranquil **unfathomable** sea! It has been said, that in the constructing of Shakespeare's dramas there is, apart from all other "faculties" as they are called, an understanding manifested, equal to that in Bacon's *Novum Organum*. That is true, and it is not a truth that strikes every one. It would become more apparent if we tried, any of us for himself, how, out of Shakespeare's dramatic materials,

---

* Retrieved from WE Teach+ website.

we could fashion such a result! The built house seems all so fit, "every way as it should be, as if it came there by its own law and the nature of things", we forget the rude disorderly **quarry** it was shaped from. The very perfection of the house, as if Nature herself had made it, hides the builder's merit. Perfect, more perfect than any other man, we may call Shakespeare in this: He **discerns**, knows as by instinct, what condition he works under, what his materials are, what his own force and its relation to them is. It is not a **transitory** glance of insight that will suffice; it is **deliberate** illumination of the whole matter; it is a calmly seeing eye; a great intellect, in short. How a man, of some wide thing that he has witnessed, will construct a narrative, what kind of picture and **delineation** he will give of it, is the best measure you could get of what intellect is in the man. Which circumstance is vital and shall stand prominent; which unessential, fit to be suppressed; where is the true beginning, the true sequence and ending? To find out this, you task the whole force of insight that is in the man. He must understand the thing; according to the depth of his understanding, will the fitness of his answer be. You will try him so. Does like join itself to like; does the spirit of method stir in that confusion, so that its **embroilment** becomes order? Can the man say, "Fiat lux. Let there be light"; and out of **chaos** make a world? Precisely as there is light in himself, will he accomplish this.

Or indeed we may say again, it is in what I called portrait painting, delineating of men and things, especially of men, that Shakespeare is great. All the greatness of the man comes out decisively here. It is unexampled, I think, that calm creative **perspicacity** of Shakespeare. The thing he looks at reveals not this or that face of it, but its inmost heart, and **generic** secret: It **dissolves** itself as in light before him, so that he discerns the perfect structure of it. Creative, we said: poetic creation, what is this too but seeing the thing sufficiently? The word that will describe the thing, follows of itself from such clear intense sight of the thing. And is not Shakespeare's morality, his valor, candor, tolerance, truthfulness; his whole victorious strength and greatness, which can **triumph** over such **obstructions**, visible there too? Great as the world. No twisted, poor convex-concave mirror, reflecting all objects with its own convexities and concavities; a perfectly level mirror; that is to say withal, if we will understand it, a man justly related to all things and men, a good man. It is truly a lordly **spectacle** how this great soul takes in all kinds of men and objects, a Falstaff, an Othello, a Juliet, a Coriolanus; sets them all forth to us in their round completeness; loving, just, the equal brother of all. *Novum Organum*, and all the intellect you will find in Bacon, is of a quite secondary order; earthy, material, poor in comparison with this. Among modern men, one finds, in strictness, almost nothing of the same rank. Goethe alone, since the days of Shakespeare, reminds me of it. Of him too you say that he saw the object; you may say what he himself says of Shakespeare: "His characters are like watches with dial-plates of **transparent** crystal; they show you the hour like others, and the inward **mechanism** also is all visible."

If I say, therefore, that Shakespeare is the greatest of intellects, I have said all concerning him. But there is more in Shakespeare's intellect than we have yet seen. It is what I call an unconscious intellect; there is more virtue in it than he himself is aware of. Novalis beautifully remarks of him, that those dramas of his are products of Nature too, deep as Nature herself. I find a great truth in this saying. Shakespeare's art is not **artifice**; the noblest worth of it is not there by plan or pre-contrivance. It grows up from the deeps of Nature, through this noble sincere soul, who is a voice of Nature. The latest generations of men will find new meanings in Shakespeare, new **elucidations** of their own human being; "new harmonies with the infinite structure of the Universe; **concurrences** with later ideas, **affinities** with the higher powers and senses of man". This well deserves meditating. It is Nature's highest reward to a true simple great soul, that she gets thus to be a part of herself. Such a man's works, **whatsoever** he with utmost conscious exertion and forethought shall accomplish, grow up withal unconsciously, from the unknown deeps in him—as the oak-tree grows from the Earth's bosom, as the mountains and waters shape themselves; with a **symmetry** grounded on Nature's own laws, conformable to all truth whatsoever. How much in Shakespeare lies hid; his sorrows, his silent struggles known to himself; much that was not known at all, not speakable at all: like roots, like sap and forces working underground! Speech is great; but silence is greater.

Vocabulary

idolatrously	*adv.*	盲目崇拜地，崇拜偶像地
hitherto	*adv.*	迄今，至今
placid	*adj.*	平静的；宁静的
unfathomable	*adj.*	难以理解的；高深莫测的
quarry	*n.*	采石场；矿场
discern	*v.*	觉察出；识别
transitory	*adj.*	片刻的，转瞬即逝的
deliberate	*adj.*	故意的，蓄意的
delineation	*n.*	描述，描绘

embroilment	n.	混乱，搅乱
chaos	n.	混乱
perspicacity	n.	洞察力；睿智
generic	adj.	通用的
dissolve	v.	消散
triumph	v.	打败，战胜
obstruction	n.	障碍，阻碍
spectacle	n.	惊人的表演或展示
transparent	adj.	透明的；清澈的
mechanism	n.	机械装置
artifice	n.	诡计，奸计
elucidation	n.	阐明，说明
concurrence	n.	同意；一致
affinity	n.	密切的关系；类同
whatsoever	adv.	无论怎样；丝毫
symmetry	n.	对称

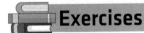

Exercises

Chapter 1 Literature—Literary Giants and Their Masterpieces

Great Authors and Their Novels of the Victorian Period

Literature is a kind of intellectual light which, like the light of the sun, may sometimes enable us to see what we do not like.

—Samuel Johnson

 Test Your Knowledge

I. **Discuss the following questions with your partner.**

1. Could you make a list of the famous authors during the Victorian period, and their masterpieces as well?
2. Among the prominent authors during the Victorian period, who has impressed you the most with his or her masterpiece?

II. **Match the Victorian authors with the corresponding masterpieces.**

1. *Pride and Prejudice*
2. *Tess of the d'Urbervilles*
3. *The Mill on the Floss*
4. *Strange Case of Dr. Jekyll and Mr. Hyde*
5. *A Tale of Two Cities*
6. *Jane Eyre*
7. *The Picture of Dorian Gray*
8. *Wuthering Heights*

A. Charles Dickens
B. Jane Austen
C. Charlotte Brontë
D. Emily Brontë
E. George Eliot
F. Thomas Hardy
G. Robert Louis Stevenson
H. Oscar Wilde

Intensive Reading

Text I Gender Roles in the 19th Century*

From marriage and sexuality to education and rights, Professor Kathryn Hughes

---

* Retrieved from British Library website.

looks at attitudes towards gender in 19th-century Britain.

During the Victorian period men and women's roles became more sharply defined than at any time in history. In earlier centuries it had been usual for women to work alongside husbands and brothers in the family business. Living "over the shop" made it easy for women to help out by serving customers or keeping accounts while also attending to their domestic duties. As the 19th century progressed, men increasingly **commuted** to their place of work—the factory, shop or office. Wives, daughters and sisters were left at home all day to oversee the domestic duties that were increasingly carried out by servants. From the 1830s, women started to adopt the **crinoline**, a huge bell-shaped skirt that made it virtually impossible to clean a grate or sweep the stairs without **tumbling** over.

"Separate Spheres"

The two sexes now inhabited what Victorians thought of as "Separate **Spheres**", only coming together at breakfast and again at dinner.

The ideology of Separate Spheres rested on a definition of the "natural" characteristics of women and men. Women were considered physically weaker yet morally superior to men, which meant that they were best suited to the domestic sphere. Not only was it their job to **counterbalance** the moral taint of the public sphere in which their husbands laboured all day, they were also preparing the next generation to carry on this way of life. The fact that women had such great influence at home was used as an argument against giving them the vote.

Educating Women

Women did, though, require a new kind of education to prepare them for this role of "Angel in the House". Rather than attracting a husband through their domestic abilities, middle-class girls were coached in what were known as "accomplishments". These would be learned either at a **boarding school** or from a **resident** governess. In Jane Austen's *Pride and Prejudice* the snobbish Caroline Bingley lists the skills required by any young lady who considers herself accomplished:

> "A woman must have a thorough knowledge of music, singing, drawing, dancing, and the modern languages... ; and besides all this, she must possess a certain something in her air and manner of walking, the tone of her voice, her address and expressions... (ch. 8)"

Chapter 1 Literature—Literary Giants and Their Masterpieces

As Miss Bingley emphasizes, it was important for a well-educated girl to soften her **erudition** with a graceful and feminine manner. No one wanted to be called a **"blue-stocking"**, the name given to women who had devoted themselves too enthusiastically to intellectual pursuits. Blue-stockings were considered unfeminine and off-putting in the way that they attempted to **usurp** men's "natural" intellectual superiority. Some doctors reported that too much study actually had a damaging effect on the **ovaries**, turning attractive young women into dried-up **prunes**. Later in the century, when Oxford and Cambridge opened their doors to women, many families refused to let their clever daughters attend for fear that they would make themselves unmarriageable.

Marriage and Sexuality

Girls usually married in their early to mid-20s. Typically, the groom would be five years older. Not only did this **reinforce** the "natural" **hierarchy** between the sexes, but it also made sound financial sense. A young man needed to be able to show that he earned enough money to support a wife and any future children before the girl's father would give his permission. Some unfortunate couples were obliged to endure an engagement lasting decades before they could afford to marry.

Young and not-so-young women had no choice but to stay **chaste** until marriage. They were not even allowed to speak to men unless there was a married woman present as a **chaperone**. Higher education or professional work was also out of the question. These emotional frustrations could lead to all sorts of **covert** rebellion. Young Florence Nightingale longed to be able to do something useful in the world, but was expected to stay with her mother and sister, helping supervise the servants. She suffered from **hysterical outbursts** as a teenager, and could not bear to eat with the rest of the family. Elizabeth Barrett, meanwhile, used illness as an excuse to retreat to a room at the top of her father's house and write poetry. In 1847 Charlotte Brontë put strong feelings about women's limited role into the mouth of her heroine Jane Eyre:

> "Women are supposed to be very calm generally: But women feel just as men feel; they need exercise for their faculties and a field for their efforts as much as their brothers do; they suffer from too rigid a **restraint**, too absolute a **stagnation**, precisely as men would suffer; and it is narrow-minded in their more privileged fellow-creatures to say that they ought to confine themselves to making puddings and knitting stockings, to playing on the piano and embroidering bags. (ch. 12)"

英国社会与文化

This passage was considered so shocking that conservative commentators such as Lady (Elizabeth) Eastlake in a famously **scathing** review of *Jane Eyre* likened its tone to **Chartism**, the popular labour movement that advocated universal **suffrage**.

In her review—which also covered William Thackeray's *Vanity Fair*—Lady Eastlake took a strong dislike to the sexual ambition of Jane Eyre and Becky Sharp, both of whom end up marrying into the households by which they are employed. The figure of the governess was **unsettling**, especially in literature, because it drew attention to the fact that not all Victorian women were as sexless as Dr. Acton had suggested.

Vocabulary

commute	*v.*	（搭乘车、船等）通勤
crinoline	*n.*	带衬的裙；四周鼓出的裙
tumble	*v.*	摔倒
sphere	*n.*	领域；空间
counterbalance	*v.*	使平衡；抵消
boarding school		寄宿学校
resident	*adj.*	居住的；常驻的
erudition	*n.*	博学，学识
blue-stocking	*n.*	女学者；才女
usurp	*v.*	篡夺，夺取，侵占
ovary	*n.*	卵巢
prune	*n.*	李子干
reinforce	*v.*	加强，强化
hierarchy	*n.*	层级，等级制度
chaste	*adj.*	纯洁的，贞洁的
chaperone	*n.*	女伴；行为监督人
covert	*adj.*	隐蔽的；秘密的
hysterical	*adj.*	歇斯底里的；异常兴奋的
outburst	*n.*	（火山、情感等的）爆发
restraint	*n.*	抑制，克制；约束
stagnation	*n.*	停滞，滞止
scathing	*adj.*	严厉的；尖刻的
Chartism	*n.*	人民宪章主义；民权运动

Chapter 1 Literature—Literary Giants and Their Masterpieces

suffrage	*n.*	选举权；投票；参政权
unsettling	*adj.*	令人不安（或紧张、担忧）的

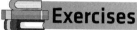

Exercises

I. **Decide whether the following statements are true or false, and mark T or F accordingly.**

_____ 1. During the Victorian period, women would work outside to serve customers or keep accounts without dealing with domestic household.

_____ 2. Since women were considered physically weaker but morally superior to men, they were guaranteed the right to vote.

_____ 3. Middle-class girls could learn how to attract a husband through their domestic abilities at a boarding school or from a resident governess.

_____ 4. During the Victorian period, a well-educated girl wanted to be called a "blue-stocking" to devote herself to intellectual pursuits.

_____ 5. Many families refused to send their clever daughters to Oxford or Cambridge because they were afraid that their daughters could not find ideal husbands after graduation.

_____ 6. Some engagement might last for decades because the groom could not earn enough money to gain the permission of the girl's father.

_____ 7. Young Florence Nightingale used illness as an excuse to retreat to a small room to write poetry.

_____ 8. Chartism was a popular labour movement that advocated the universal suffrage.

II. **Choose the best option to answer each question.**

1. Why did women start to adopt the crinoline from the 1830s?
   A. It was convenient for women to work alongside husbands and brothers to handle family business.
   B. It was easy for women to help out by serving customers or keeping accounts.

C. They were left all day to supervise the domestic duties carried out by servants.

D. It was impossible to clean a grate or sweep the stairs without tumbling over.

2. Which of the following was used as an argument against giving women the vote?

   A. Women were considered physically weaker yet morally superior to men.

   B. Women were supposed to counterbalance the moral taint of the public sphere.

   C. Women needed to prepare the next generation to carry on the normal way of life.

   D. Women were best suited to the domestic sphere and had great influence at home.

3. Which of the following was **NOT** the accomplishment for middle-class girls to learn?

   A. Preparing themselves for the role of "Angle in the House".

   B. Devoting themselves enthusiastically to intellectual pursuits.

   C. Softening their erudition with a graceful and feminine manner.

   D. Having a thorough knowledge of art, languages and skills to perform as an accomplished lady.

4. Which of the following can **NOT** be used to describe a "blue-stocking"?

   A. Unfeminine.

   B. Off-putting.

   C. Unmarriageable.

   D. Attractive.

5. Which of the following was **NOT** Lady Eastlake's opinion in her review?

   A. She showed a strong appreciation to the sexual ambition of Jane Eyre.

   B. She made a harshly abusive criticism of *Jane Eyre*.

   C. She likened the tone of *Jane Eyre* to Chartism.

   D. She covered William Thackeray's *Vanity Fair* to show a strong dislike of Becky Sharp.

Chapter 1 Literature—Literary Giants and Their Masterpieces

III. Match each person with his or her identity or relevant description.

1. Jane Austen
2. Florence Nightingale
3. Elizabeth Barrett
4. Jane Eyre
5. Lady Eastlake
6. Becky Sharp

A. a conservative commentator who disliked *Jane Eyre*
B. pretend to be ill to retreat to a small room to write poetry
C. is expected to help supervise the servants
D. the author of *Pride and Prejudice*
E. the heroine in a novel written by Charlotte Brontë
F. the heroine of *Vanity Fair*

IV. Fill in the blanks with the appropriate forms of the words in the box.

| commute | counterbalance | usurp | reinforce | hysterical |
| outburst | stagnation | scathing | suffrage | unsettling |

1. Mr. Jones was _____ about the report, denouncing it as out of date and biased.
2. The planned increase in public infrastructure spending and lower official interest rates will be insufficient to _____ these negative forces.
3. If jobs require people to _____ a great distance or to move themselves to another state, employers may find they need to sweeten their offers.
4. Police and bodyguards had to form a human shield around him as the _____ crowds struggled to approach him.
5. It feels like anxiety, like a constant _____ sense that something is wrong.
6. No organization or individual may retain, misappropriate or _____ any of the assets of non-governmental institutions.
7. _____ comes because there isn't anything that excites you enough to take action.
8. Susan B. Anthony, the American champion of woman's _____, was also a participant in the movement to end slavery.
9. The visual materials are used to _____ your message, not detract the audience from what you are saying.
10. There was an extraordinary _____ of applause from every corner of the auditorium.

IV. Translate the following sentences into Chinese.

You think I could stay here to become nothing to you? Do you think because I am poor, obscure and plain that I am soulless and heartless? I have as much soul as you and fully as much heart. And if God had gifted me with wealth and beauty, I should have made it as hard for you to leave me as it is now for me to leave you.

Further Reading

Text II Charles Dickens' Gift of Giving*

—How *The Man Who Invented Christmas* Kept Charity in His Heart His Whole Life

Peter Bowen

In Bharat Nalluri's *The Man Who Invented Christmas*, Charles Dickens (Dan Stevens) took on the project writing *A Christmas Carol* to **revive** his career and pump up his bank account. But as he wrestled with the tale of how Ebenezer Scrooge (Christopher Plummer) changed his miserly ways and **embraced** the holiday spirit of charity and merriment, Dickens found his own belief in the power of the season shifting as well. In Les Standiford's book *The Man Who Invented Christmas*, the work that inspired Susan Coyne's inventive screenplay, Dickens' holiday volume helped **usher** in many of the holiday traditions we still love today. But Dickens also brought a new focus to the joy of giving that fuels our **Yuletide** merriment. "Dickens makes us remember that there are bigger things in life than our own selfish interests," notes Coyne. While Dickens had always brought a particular social consciousness to his works, *A Christmas Carol* reignited in him a passion for caring for those in need all year long.

Terrible Times Inspired *A Christmas Carol*

Dickens first **conceived** *A Christmas Carol* after giving a talk on October 5, 1843, at Manchester's Athenaeum, an educational center for the working class. Sharing the stage with the social reformer Richard Cobden and the politician Benjamin Disraeli (who'd become Prime Minister 25 years later), Dickens spoke passionately about society's responsibility for educating and caring for

---

* Retrieved from Bleecker Street website.

Chapter 1 Literature—Literary Giants and Their Masterpieces

its **impoverished** children. Without help, the poor were forced to walk a path "of jagged flints and stones, laid down by brutal ignorance", Dickens told the crowd. After the event, he **rambled** through the streets witnessing firsthand the conditions he'd just **lamented**. Manchester, which had seen unchecked growth from rapid industrialization in recent years, was so **awash** in poverty and abuse that Friedrich Engels called it "Hell upon Earth". But it was here that Dickens first imagined the story that would become *A Christmas Carol*.

Dickens Calls for Change

For the next few months, Dickens poured his creativity into transforming a ghost story into a masterpiece of English literature, into a tale that not only **showcases** the **deplorable** conditions of the poor and working class, but also suggests a way forward. Of course, using his fiction to lay bare social ills was nothing new for Dickens. His 1837 *Oliver Twist* directly addressed the **plight** of children and the criminal gangs in London. In his 1838 *Nicholas Nickleby*, Dickens took aim at abusive educational institutions, especially in the cruel punishments meted out by the headmaster Wackford Squeers. And later he would provide an **unflinching** look at the **collateral** damage **inflicted** by **unfettered** industrialization on the working class in *Hard Times*. But few of his social novels also delivered such a clear and joyous message of hope as *A Christmas Carol* did. "What Dickens wanted was for us take it upon ourselves to be more generous," explains *The Man Who Invented Christmas* producer Susan Mullen. "That we should lend a hand, that we must care for others—it's a beautiful message. And it really did change the way everybody viewed Christmas."

He Took Charity Seriously

Dickens used his celebrity and cash to aid charitable institutions. Over his life he supported in various ways over 43 different charitable organizations, including Poor Man's Guardian Society, the Birmingham and Midland Institute, the **Metropolitan** Sanitary Association, the Orphan Working School, the Royal Hospital for the Incurables, and the Hospital for Sick Children. Sometimes he would give money, other times he would push the more powerful and wealthy to contribute, but more often than not, he would lend his talent in support as well. For the Hospital for Sick Children, Dickens wrote a **stirring** article about the institution in his magazine *Household Works* when it opened. While the writer gave generously, he was no **pushover**. He regularly poked fun at a society of **do-gooders** lining their own pockets. "For a good many years I have suffered a great deal from charities," Dickens wrote in a letter. "**Benevolent** bullies ride up in hansom cabs...and stay long at the door."

Getting Personality Involved

In addition to lending his name and purse to established charities, Dickens was famous for his personal acts of kindness. In 1843, just months before he wrote *A Christmas Carol*, the actor Edward Elton died suddenly, leaving his family **destitute**. Dickens stepped up to form a committee to raise money to care for Elton's orphaned children. Throughout his life, Dickens would quietly give money to friends and associates in need.

When he deeply believed in cause, Dickens would go further than just raising money or public attention. In 1846, he was **instrumental** in the founding of Urania Cottage, an institution that provided housing and support for unwed mothers and, in the terms of the times, "fallen women". In addition to helping find the location and designing the structure, Dickens personally interviewed potential staff. He also threw his support behind the Field Land Ragged School, which provided free education to destitute children, even though he had **reservations** about the school's **evangelic** tenor. In 1853, Dickens had become so well known for his generosity that his friend and sometimes rival William Thackery expressed in a lecture, "I take my share of the feast of love and kindness, which this gentle, and generous, and charitable soul has contributed to the happiness of the world."

Vocabulary

revive	*v.*	使复兴
embrace	*v.*	信奉
usher	*v.*	引导，引领
Yuletide	*adj.*	圣诞节期间的
conceive	*v.*	构思
impoverished	*adj.*	穷困的
ramble	*v.*	漫步，闲逛
lament	*v.*	哀悼，悲叹
awash	*adj.*	充斥的
showcase	*v.*	展现，表现
deplorable	*adj.*	令人震惊的；糟透的
plight	*n.*	困境

Chapter 1 Literature—Literary Giants and Their Masterpieces

unflinching	*adj.*	不畏缩的，不畏惧的
collateral	*adj.*	并行的
inflict	*v.*	造成
unfettered	*adj.*	不受约束的
metropolitan	*adj.*	大都市的
stirring	*adj.*	激动人心的
pushover	*n.*	易于征服或控制的人；容易打败的对手
do-gooder	*n.*	善意但不现实的慈善家（或改革家）
benevolent	*adj.*	仁慈的，慈善的
destitute	*adj.*	穷困的
instrumental	*adj.*	有帮助的
reservation	*n.*	保留
evangelic	*adj.*	福音传道的

Exercises

Unit 3

Notable Poets of Romanticism—Byron, Shelley and Keats

A great poem is a fountain forever overflowing with the waters of wisdom and delight.

—Percy Bysshe Shelley

Test Your Knowledge

I. Write down one or two representative works of each of the following poets.

1. Robert Burns: _____
2. John Keats: _____
3. Lord Byron: _____
4. Percy Bysshe Shelley: _____
5. William Wordsworth: _____
6. Samuel Taylor Coleridge: _____

II. Match the prominent poets with the corresponding masterpieces.

1. *Ode to the West Wind*   A. Robert Burns
2. *Ode to the Nightingale*   B. John Keats
3. *Don Juan*   C. Lord Byron
4. *The Prelude*   D. Percy Bysshe Shelley
5. *A Red Red Rose*   E. William Wordsworth
6. *Kubla Khan*   F. Samuel Taylor Coleridge

Chapter 1 Literature—Literary Giants and Their Masterpieces

Intensive Reading

Text I Famous Last Words*

While poets may not always experience the most poetic of deaths, many mark their final moments with the most lyrical, memorable, funny—and occasionally mysterious—last words. Check out this list of famous last lines from historic poets and the strange, sad and interesting tales that accompany them.

Robert Burns: "Don't let the awkward squad fire over me!"

Though there is much **speculation** and disagreement about the exact cause of Robert Burns' death, what is known is the fact that the poet exhibited good humour and wit, even as he faced the end of his life. When his doctor visited him, Burns said, "**Alas!** What has brought you here? I am but a poor crow and not worth **plucking**." And when Burns saw a fellow member of the Royal Dumfries Volunteers standing teary-eyed at his bedside, Burns **proclaimed**, "John, don't let the **awkward squad** fire over me!" Poet and biographer Allan Cunningham reports that Burns then reassured his friends that he had lived long enough. Over the course of the next few days, Burns' fever worsened, his strength **diminished**, and he was reduced to a state of **delirium**. He died on July 21, 1796.

John Keats: "I can feel the daisies growing over me."

In 1818, John Keats returned home from a tour of Northern England and Scotland to care for his brother, who had **contracted tuberculosis**. Unfortunately, Keats' brother died in December of that year and by that time Keats himself had contracted the disease and knew that his death was **imminent**. Following his doctor's orders to seek a warm climate for the winter, Keats traveled to Rome with his friend, the painter Joseph Severn. Keats recovered briefly for Christmas but on January 10, 1819, his health took a final turn for the worst and Keats was unable to leave his bedroom. Just before Keats' death, Severn asked the poet how he was doing, to which Keats quietly replied, "Better, my friend. I feel the daisies growing over me." Keats died in Severn's arms on February 23, 1821, at the age of 25.

Lord Byron: "Come, come, no weakness! Let's be a man to the last!"/ "Now, I shall go to sleep."

There is some debate over the last words of Lord Byron, but the **circumstances**

---

* Retrieved from Poets.org website.

around his death in both versions remain the same. When he was a boy, a famous fortune-teller in Scotland told Byron he should beware of his 37th year. That year the poet found himself in Greece, where he fell ill. Unfortunately, he was attended to by two young, inexperienced doctors who repeatedly drew his blood in an attempt to heal his illness—a common practice in that day. Byron clearly had **forebodings** of death and initially resisted the treatments, calling the doctors a "damned set of butchers", but he **allegedly** rallied at the last moment, declaring, "Come, come, no weakness! Let's be a man to the last!" In *The Life, Letters and Journals* of Lord Byron, Thomas Moore writes the following account of Byron's death: "It was about six o'clock in the evening of this day when he said, 'Now I shall go to sleep'; and then turning round fell into that **slumber** from which he never awoke. For the next 24 hours he lay incapable of either sense or motion—with the exception of, now and then, slight symptoms of **suffocation**, during which his servant raised his head—and at a quarter past six o'clock on the following day, the 19th, he was seen to open his eyes and immediately shut them again. The physicians felt his pulse—he was no more!" Byron died on April 19, 1824.

Charlotte Brontë: "Oh, I am not going to die, am I? He will not separate us. We have been so happy."

On June 29, 1854, Charlotte Brontë wed Arthur Bell Nicholls in Haworth, England, and enjoyed a month-long honeymoon in Ireland. Once the couple returned home in August, Brontë was in high spirits and good health, writing to a friend, "It is long since I have known such comparative **immunity** from headache, sickness and indigestion as during the past three months." However, that soon changed in January 1855, when she wrote that her "stomach seemed quite suddenly to lose its tone, indigestion and continual faint sickness has been my portion ever since". Soon Brontë was suffering from constant **nausea**, vomiting and faintness, which her physician **attributed to** a "natural cause" that would pass, such as morning sickness. But Brontë's symptoms only became worse; she became **emaciated** and spent more and more time in bed. In mid-February, Brontë made her will, and most of her remaining time was spent in a state of delirium. In one **lucid** moment, however, in the early morning of March 31, 1855, while her husband was praying for her life, she declared, "Oh, I am not going to die, am I? He will not separate us. We have been so happy." But Brontë died that day, just nine months after her wedding and three weeks before her 39th birthday.

Chapter 1 Literature—Literary Giants and Their Masterpieces

📖 Vocabulary

awkward squad		乌合之众
speculation	*n.*	推测；思索
alas	*int.*	唉（表悲伤、遗憾、恐惧、关切等）
pluck	*v.*	拔掉（死禽的毛）
proclaim	*v.*	宣告，声明
diminish	*v.*	减少；缩小
delirium	*n.*	精神错乱
daisy	*n.*	雏菊，菊科植物
contract	*v.*	感染
tuberculosis	*n.*	肺结核，结核病
imminent	*adj.*	即将来临的，迫近的
circumstance	*n.*	情况，情形
foreboding	*n.*	预感；先兆
allegedly	*adv.*	据说
slumber	*n.*	睡眠
suffocation	*n.*	窒息
immunity	*n.*	免疫力；免除
nausea	*n.*	恶心
attribute...to		把……归因于
emaciated	*adj.*	瘦弱的；憔悴的
lucid	*adj.*	清醒的

📖 Exercises

I. **Decide whether the following statements are true or false, and mark T or F accordingly.**

_____ 1. When Robert Burns was confronted with death, he was extremely scared and wanted to live longer.

_____ 2. Thomas Moore was a poet and biographer, a close friend of Robert Burns.

_____ 3. John Keats contracted tuberculosis from his brother and died at the age of 25.

_____ 4. When Lord Byron was a boy, he was warned by a fortune-teller to beware of his safety at the age of 37.

_____ 5. Lord Byron lost his consciousness and was unable to move

_____ 6. Only three weeks after her wedding, Charlotte Brontë suffered from constant nausea, vomiting and faintness, and died nine months before her 39th birthday.

after he fell into the slumber for 24 hours, and never opened his eyes again.

II. Match each person with his or her description.

1. Arthur Bell Nicholls   A. a poet and biographer
2. Robert Burns   B. a poet who had clear forebodings of death and showed distrust to his doctors
3. Lord Byron
4. Allan Cunningham   C. a painter
5. Thomas Moore   D. the husband of Charlotte Brontë
6. Joseph Severn   E. a famous poet who died in 1796
7. John Keats   F. a man who wrote the account of Byron's death
   G. a young poet who died at the age of 25

III. Fill in the blanks with the appropriate forms of the words in the box.

| speculation | proclaim | diminish | delirium | contract | imminent |
| circumstance | foreboding | allegedly | immunity | emaciated | lucid |

1. So weak does the body's _____ system become that the person often becomes very ill from usually mild sicknesses.
2. Under these _____, child education is for many families more luxury than priority.
3. It begins with the symptoms of headache, aching and restlessness, and later develops with high fever and _____.
4. On January 1, 1863, during the war, Lincoln issued his famous Emancipation _____, which abolished slavery in the United States.
5. He _____ AIDS from a blood transfusion, which made him desperate.
6. Police were hunting for a gang that had _____ stolen 55 cars.
7. Every one feels that a disaster is _____, as if a catastrophe is about to come.
8. Some scientists _____ that Mars may have enjoyed an extended early period during which rivers, lakes, and perhaps even oceans adorned its surface.

Chapter 1 Literature—Literary Giants and Their Masterpieces

9. Toward the end of his life while he was still 100% _____, it was more difficult for him to be mobile and to go into organizations.
10. Conversely, teachers who have a tendency to "overdirect" can _____ their gifted pupils' learning autonomy.
11. At the same time many people over-exercise, leaving themselves weak or even _____.
12. His triumph was overshadowed by an uneasy sense of _____.

IV. Match the following phrases with their explanations.

A. check out
B. over the course of
C. to the last
D. beware of
E. attend to
F. in an attempt to
G. be incapable of
H. with the exception of
I. now and then
J. attribute to
K. make a will

1. try hard to; strive for
2. be careful; be cautious
3. except for; apart from
4. take care of; care for
5. be unable to
6. now and again; from time to time
7. examine so as to determine accuracy, quality, or condition
8. in the process of
9. put down to; ascribe
10. make one's testament
11. to the bitter end

V. Try to figure out the title and poet of each of the following excerpts, and then translate them into Chinese.

1. The trumpet of a prophecy! O Wind,
   If Winter comes, can Spring be far behind?

2. In secret we met—
   In silence I grieve,
   That thy heart could forget,
   Thy spirit deceive.
   If I should meet thee
   After long years,
   How should I greet thee?—
   With silence and tears.

3. When old age shall this generation waste,
   Thou shalt remain, in midst of other woe
   Than ours, a friend to man, to whom thou say'st,
   "Beauty is truth, truth beauty,"—that is all
   Ye know on earth, and all ye need to know.

Further Reading

Text II The Later Romantics: Shelley, Keats and Byron*

The poets of the next generation shared their **predecessors'** passion for liberty (now set in a new perspective by the Napoleonic Wars) and were in a position to learn from their experiments. Percy Bysshe Shelley in particular was deeply interested in politics, coming early under the spell of the **anarchist** views of William Godwin, whose *Enquiry Concerning Political Justice* had appeared in 1793. Shelley's revolutionary **ardour** caused him to claim in his critical essay "A Defence of Poetry" (1821, published 1840) that "the most unfailing **herald**, companion, and follower of the awakening of a great people to work a beneficial change in opinion or institution, is poetry", and that poets are "the **unacknowledged** legislators of the world". This fervour burns throughout the early *Queen Mab* (1813), the long *Laon and Cythna* (retitled *The Revolt of Islam*, 1818), and the lyrical drama *Prometheus Unbound* (1820). Shelley saw himself at once as a poet and prophet, as the fine "Ode to the West Wind" (1819) makes clear. Despite his grasp of practical politics, however, it is a mistake to look for concreteness in his poetry, where his concern is with **subtleties** of perception and with the **underlying** forces of Nature: His most characteristic images are of sky and weather, of lights and fires. His poetic stance invites the reader to respond with similar outgoing aspiration. It adheres to the **Rousseauistic** belief in an underlying spirit in individuals, one truer to human nature itself than the behaviour **evinced** and approved by society. In that sense his material is **transcendental** and cosmic and his expression thoroughly appropriate. Possessed of great technical brilliance, he is, at his best, a poet of excitement and power.

---

* Retrieved from Britannica website.

Chapter 1 Literature—Literary Giants and Their Masterpieces

John Keats, by contrast, was a poet so sensuous and physically specific that his early works, such as *Endymion* (1818), could produce an over-luxuriant, cloying effect. As the program set out in his early poem "Sleep and Poetry" shows, however, Keats was determined to discipline himself: Even before February 1820, when he first began to cough blood, he may have known that he had not long to live, and he devoted himself to the expression of his vision with **feverish** intensity. He experimented with many kinds of poems: "Isabella" (published 1820), an adaptation of a tale by Giovanni Boccaccio, is a **tour de force** of craftsmanship in its attempt to reproduce a medieval atmosphere and at the same time a poem involved in contemporary politics. His epic fragment *Hyperion* (begun in 1818 and abandoned, published 1820; later begun again and published **posthumously** as *The Fall of Hyperion* in 1856) has a new **spareness** of imagery, but Keats soon found the style too **Miltonic** and decided to give himself up to what he called "other sensations". Some of these "other sensations" are found in the poems of 1819, Keats' **annus mirabilis**: "The Eve of St. Agnes" and the great odes "To a Nightingale", "On a Grecian Urn", and "To Autumn". These, with the Hyperion poems, represent the summit of Keats' achievement, showing what has been called "the disciplining of sensation into symbolic meaning", the complex themes being handled with a concrete richness of detail. His superb letters show the full range of the intelligence at work in his poetry.

George Gordon, Lord Byron, who differed from Shelley and Keats in themes and manner, was at one with them in reflecting their shift toward **"Mediterranean"** topics. Having thrown down the gauntlet in his early poem "English Bards and Scotch Reviewers" (1809), in which he directed particular scorn at poets of sensibility and declared his own **allegiance** to Milton, Dryden, and Pope, he developed a poetry of dash and flair, in many cases with a striking hero. His two longest poems, *Childe Harold's Pilgrimage* (1812—1818) and *Don Juan* (1819—1824), provided alternative personae for himself, the one a bitter and **melancholy** exile among the historic sites of Europe, the other a **picaresque** adventurer enjoying a series of amorous adventures. The gloomy and **misanthropic** vein was further mined in dramatic poems such as *Manfred* (1817) and *Cain* (1821), which helped to secure his reputation in Europe, but he is now remembered best for witty, ironic, and less **portentous** writings, such as *Beppo* (1818), in which he first used the **ottava rima** form. The easy, **nonchalant**, biting style developed there became a **formidable** device in *Don Juan* and in his satire on Southey, *The Vision of Judgment* (1822).

英国社会与文化

Vocabulary

predecessor	n.	前任，前辈
anarchist	n.	无政府主义者
ardour	n.	激情，热情
herald	n.	先驱
unacknowledged	adj.	未公开承认的；未确认的
subtlety	n.	微妙；敏锐
underlying	adj.	根本的
Rousseauistic	adj.	卢梭主义的；回归自然论的
evince	v.	表明
transcendental	adj.	先验的；卓越的
feverish	adj.	极度兴奋的
tour de force	n.	杰作
posthumously	adv.	于著作者死后出版地
spareness	n.	缺乏
Miltonic	adj.	庄严的；弥尔顿风格的
annus mirabilis		奇迹迭出的一年
Mediterranean	adj.	地中海的
allegiance	n.	忠诚
melancholy	adj.	忧郁的，使人悲伤的
picaresque	adj.	以流浪汉和无赖为题材的；传奇式流浪冒险的
misanthropic	adj.	厌恶人类的；不愿与人来往的
portentous	adj.	令人惊讶的
ottava rima		八行体（一种诗体，每行十个或十一个音节，前六行交替押韵，后两行另成一组同脚韵）
nonchalant	adj.	冷淡的，漠不关心的
formidable	adj.	强大的

Exercises

Chapter 2　History—Figures and Events of Significance

Introduction

  The chapter focuses on three themes which to some extent represent three typical phases in English history: The early history was marked by constant foreign invasions till the Norman Conquest when the feudalism was established; the period from King John's Magna Carta down to the turbulent 17th century when two civil wars, regicide, a republic, a restoration, and a revolution followed each other in bewildering succession witnessed the evolution of parliamentary institution; the sun-never-set-on-the-empire was the phase when Britain colonized the world.

  There are certain figures and events of significance during this course. The chapter portrays not only the king who embodied the very idea and ideal of kingship but also the kings whose belief in the divine right to rule doomed them. It expounds on the French influence on Britain in its early days and British "spheres of influence" around the world in the 20th century.

Unit 1

King Arthur and William of Normandy: Early History of Britain and the French Influence

A people without the knowledge of their past history, origin and culture is like a tree without roots.

—Marcus Garvey

 Test Your Knowledge

I. **Search for relevant information to answer the following questions.**

   1. Who arrived in Britain from northwestern Europe and brought with them the skill of iron-working around 700 BC?
   2. Where did the earliest written records of Britain's inhabitants come from?
   3. Which group of people is the name England related to?
   4. When did the legendary King Arthur live?
   5. Whose invasion did King Arthur defend against?

II. **Match the pictures with the descriptions related to them.**

   1.

      A. The pagan Angles, Saxons and Jutes came from what is now Denmark and northern Germany from AD 450 on.

   2.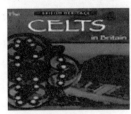

      B. The French-speaking Normans under William the Conqueror invaded England from France and defeated the Saxon king Harold at the battle of Hastings.

   3.

      C. Stonehenge was built 3,500 years ago.

Chapter 2 History—Figures and Events of Significance

4.    **D.** Arthur pulled the sword out of the stone.

5.    **E.** Arthur's castle and his round table showed his inclusionary mode of ruling.

6.    **F.** Around 700 BC, Celtic peoples had arrived from northwestern Europe.

Intensive Reading

Text I King Arthur*

The phrase "Arthurian Legend" **encompasses** a number of different versions of the tale but, in the present day, mainly refers to the English works of Sir Thomas Malory, *Le Morte D'Arthur* (*Death of Arthur*) published by William Caxton in 1485. The legend developed from *History of The Kings of Britain*, passing over to France, to Germany, to Spain and Portugal, and back to England with numerous additions and versions **proliferating**, until Malory **compiled**, edited, revised, and rewrote a prose version in 1469 while he was in prison.

The basic story goes that, once upon a time, there was a **wizard** named Merlin who arranged for a mighty king named Uther Pendragon to sleep with a queen named Igrayne who was another king's wife. Merlin's **stipulation** was that, when the child of their union was born, it would be given to him. All of this happens as it should. The child is named Arthur, and he is given to another lord, Sir Hector, to raise with his own son Kay. Many years later, when Arthur is grown, he accompanies Kay and Hector to a **tournament** in which Kay is to compete, and finds that he forgot Kay's sword at home. So he takes one he finds

---

* Retrieved from World History Encyclopedia website.

in the forest stuck in a stone. This is the Sword in the Stone which can only be drawn from the rock by the true king of Britain.

Merlin returns at this point to explain the situation to Arthur, who had no idea he was adopted, and helps him fight the other lords who **contest** his claim to the throne. Although the Sword in the Stone is frequently associated with the famous weapon Excalibur, they are two different swords. The sword Arthur draws from the stone is broken in a fight with Sir Pellinore and Merlin brings Arthur to a mystical body of water where the Lady of the Lake gives him Excalibur.

Excalibur is more than just a sword; it is a symbol of Arthur's greatness. In some versions of the legend Arthur gives the sword to Sir Gawain but, in most, it is **exclusively** Arthur's. This is in keeping with many ancient tales and legends in which a great hero has some kind of magical weapon. Once Arthur has forced the other lords to recognize his **legitimacy**, he marries the beautiful queen Guinevere and sets up his court at Camelot.

He invites the greatest knights of the **realm** to come and dine in his **banquet** hall but, when they do, they begin fighting over who will get the best seat. Arthur severely punishes the knight who began the trouble and, to **avert** any repeat in the future, accepts a round table from his father-in-law. From this time on, he explains, everyone sitting at the table will be equal, including himself, and everyone's opinions will be weighed seriously regardless of their social standing. Further, anyone requiring assistance will be welcomed in the hall to request it and every wrong shall be righted by Arthur and his knights.

The **motif** of the Round Table, along with the magical weapon, sets Arthur above the kings who have preceded him who believed that their position of power **dictated** what was right or wrong; Arthur believes that everyone's opinion is **valid** and that might should be used to support right, not define it. Arthur again sends out invitations to noble knights to join him but this time his messengers are to go even farther, beyond the boundaries of Britain.

Among the knights who answer his call is Lancelot of the Lake, a French knight who is **unrivaled** in combat. He and Arthur become friends at the same time that he falls in love with Guinevere and she with him. While this affair is going on behind the scenes, the Knights of the Round Table are engaging in all kinds of fantastic adventures. If there is no apparent adventure, Arthur will go off and find one. In the famous story of Gawain and the Green Knight, a challenger comes to court to start the adventure. In the story of Jaufre (also known as Girflet) he arrives at the court to be knighted and then proceeds on his

Chapter 2 History—Figures and Events of Significance

own adventures before returning and involving the others.

The greatest adventure the knights undertake is the quest for the Holy **Grail**. The grail is originally a **platter** in the French version of the legend or **cauldron** in the Welsh. It is transformed, however, into the cup of Christ used at the Last Supper by the time Malory revises the story and this is how it is generally understood. The grail **quest** can only be completed by a knight pure of heart and this is finally accomplished by Galahad, son of Lancelot.

Arthur remains a good and noble king until the affair of his queen and best friend is revealed by Arthur's **illegitimate** son Mordred who then challenges Arthur's right to rule.

In the final battle between Mordred and Arthur, Mordred is killed and Arthur mortally wounded. Guinevere retires to a **convent** and Lancelot to a **hermitage**. All of the other great knights of the court are killed. Sir Bedevere helps Arthur from the field and returns Excalibur to the Lady of the Lake. Once the sword has been returned, Arthur dies and is carried away on a ship to the isle of Avalon.

Vocabulary

encompass	*v.*	包含；围住
proliferate	*v.*	迅速繁殖（或增殖）；猛增
compile	*v.*	编写（书、列表、报告等）；编纂
wizard	*n.*	（传说中的）男巫；术士
stipulation	*n.*	约定，规定
tournament	*n.*	联赛，比赛
contest	*v.*	争辩，提出异议；争取赢得，角逐
exclusively	*adv.*	排他地；独占地
legitimacy	*n.*	合法，合理
realm	*n.*	王国，领域
banquet	*n.*	正式宴会
avert	*v.*	防止；转移（视线）
motif	*n.*	主题；主旨
dictate	*v.*	指示；命令
valid	*adj.*	合理的；（法律上）有效的
unrivaled	*adj.*	无敌的，至高无上的
grail	*n.*	杯；圣杯（传说中耶稣最后晚餐所用之杯）

platter	n.	大浅盘
cauldron	n.	大汽锅；大锅
quest	n.	探索，寻找
illegitimate	adj.	私生的，非婚生的
convent	n.	女隐修院，女修道院
hermitage	n.	（隐士）隐居处

Exercises

I. Decide whether the following statements are true or false, and mark T or F accordingly.

_____ 1. In the present day, the phrase "Arthurian Legend" mainly refers to the French works of Sir Thomas Malory, *Le Morte D'Arthur* (*Death of Arthur*).

_____ 2. Arthur is adopted by Uther Pendragon and Uther raised him with his own son Kay.

_____ 3. When Arthur accompanies Kay to a tournament in which Kay is to compete and finds that he forgot Kay's sword at home, he takes one he finds in the forest stuck in a stone—Excalibur.

_____ 4. The kings who have preceded Arthur believed that their position of power endowed them with the might to define what was right or wrong.

_____ 5. In the final battle between Mordred and Arthur, both Mordred and Arthur are killed. It is Sir Bedevere that returns Excalibur to the Lady of the Lake.

II. Put the following events in the right order according to the accounts in the passage.

1. Arthur accompanies Kay and Hector to a tournament in which Kay is to compete.

2. Arthur finds a sword stuck in a stone. This is the Sword in the Stone which can only be drawn from the rock by the true king of Britain.

3. Arthur was given to another lord, Sir Hector, and Hector raised Arthur with his own son Kay.

4. Once Arthur has forced the other lords to recognize his legitimacy, he marries the beautiful queen Guinevere and sets up his court at Camelot.

Chapter 2 History—Figures and Events of Significance

5. In the final battle between Mordred and Arthur, Mordred is killed and Arthur mortally wounded.

6. Merlin arranged for a mighty king named Uther Pendragon to sleep with a queen named Igrayne who was another king's wife.

7. Merlin returns to explain the situation to Arthur, who had no idea he was adopted, and helps him fight the other lords who contest his claim to the throne.

8. Arthur invites the greatest knights of the realm to come and dine in his banquet hall and, to avert fighting over who will get the best seat and any repeat in the future, Arthur accepts a round table from his father-in-law.

9. Arthur is helped from the field and Excalibur is returned to the Lady of the Lake. Once the sword has been returned, Arthur dies and is carried away on a ship to the isle of Avalon.

10. The Knights of the Round Table are engaging in all kinds of fantastic adventures. The greatest adventure the knights undertake is the quest for the Holy Grail.

_____ → _____ → _____ → _____ → _____ → _____ → _____ → _____ → _____ → _____

III. Fill in the blanks with the appropriate forms of the words in the box.

avert	dictate	compile	encompass	exclusively
motif	proliferate	valid	stipulation	illegitimate

1. The job _____ a wide range of responsibilities.

2. They put forward many _____ reasons for not exporting.

3. What gives them the right to _____ to us what we should eat?

4. We are trying to _____ a list of suitable people for the job.

5. The election was dismissed as _____ by the international community.

6. The aim of the current round of talks is to promote free trade and to _____ the threat of increasing protectionism.

7. Alienation is a central _____ in her novels.

8. The only _____ is that the topic you choose must be related to your studies.

9. Books and articles on the subject have _____ over the last year.

10. Today he is able to focus his message _____ on the economy.

IV. Complete the following sentences by translating the Chinese in the brackets into English using words in the passage.

1. The phrase "Arthurian Legend" _____ （包括）a number of different versions of the tale.

2. He _____ （陪伴）Kay and Hector to a tournament in which Kay is to compete.

3. Merlin helps him fight the other lords who _____ （争夺）his claim to the throne.

4. Once Arthur has forced the other lords to recognize his _____ （合法性）, he marries the beautiful queen Guinevere and sets up his court at Camelot.

5. He invites the greatest knights of the _____ （领域，王国）to come and dine in his banquet hall.

6. He explains that everyone sitting at the table will be equal, including himself, and everyone's opinion will be _____ （权衡，考虑）seriously regardless of their social standing.

7. The motif of the Round Table, along with the magical weapon, sets Arthur above the kings who have _____ （处在……之前）him who believed that their position of power dictated what was right or wrong.

8. Arthur believes that everyone's opinion is _____ （有效的）and that might should be used to support right, not define it.

9. The Knights of the Round Table are _____ （从事，参加）in all kinds of fantastic adventures.

10. The greatest adventure the knights undertake is the _____ （设法找到，追求）for the Holy Grail.

V. Surf the Internet and find out another version of the story of Arthur and compare it with the one in the passage. Retell the story you find to your partner and point out the differences in the two versions of Arthur's story.

Chapter 2 **History—Figures and Events of Significance**

> **Further Reading**

Text II The Emergence of the British State*

When the Romans under Julius Caesar first arrived in Britain in 55–54 BC, they found it peopled by Celts who had arrived there between 800 and 200 BC, the latest in a long line of immigrants from Northern Europe and the **Iberian peninsula**. The Celts—ancestors of the Irish, Scots and Welsh of today—were less a race than a **disparate** group of peoples who shared a language, religious patterns, and social norms. When the Romans came again in AD 43 (this time to stay), they occupied most of what is now England, Wales and southern Scotland, pushing the Celts west and north. England developed a distinctive social and political system—it had roads, planned towns, a centralized economy, a **thriving** commercial system, and for 300 years was mainly at peace. Signs of the Roman occupation are still evident, from the **stretches** of straight road that can be found in parts of England, to many place names, including London (Londinium during Roman times) and any of the cities with the Latin **termination** for camp (castra), such as Winchester, Lancaster and Worcester.

The departure of the Romans at the beginning of the fifth century left behind a political **vacuum** into which later moved several more waves of invaders, notably Germanic tribes such as the Angles and the Saxons, who arrived in about 500–700. While the Irish Celts were **converted** to Christianity in the early fifth century by St. Patrick, the arrival in 597 of the monk Augustine— on a mission from the Pope in Rome—brought a different form of Christianity to England: At a conference of bishops in 664 (the Synod of Whitby), it was decided to adopt the Roman rather than the Celtic form.

In the eighth century the first Viking and Danish raids took place, turning into a **full-blown** invasion by the mid-ninth century, an attempt to drive out the native population and to settle permanently, a goal that was only prevented by the resistance of King Alfred of Wessex. By the time of the last successful invasion of Britain—by William, Duke of Normandy, in 1066—the British Isles had become divided into two zones, one predominantly Celtic and the other predominantly Anglo-Saxon. Although England was now united under the Normans, the cultural and religious divisions persisted, England being

---

* Excerpted from John McCormick. *Contemporary Britain*. Beijing: China Renmin University Press, 2009: 7–10.

distinguished from the Celtic regions by the development of a more stable and centralized system of government. At the same time, England and France were bound together under the Angevins, whose rule peaked between 1150 and 1220, and whose lands stretched from the Scottish border to the Pyrenees.

Like the rest of Europe, England was a feudal society. Sovereign power lay in the hands of the monarch, who owned the land managed by **aristocrats**, who in turn bought access to that land with military service and used landless peasants to do the work. Monarchs also claimed to rule by divine right, arguing that they were answerable only to God, exercised religious power on earth, and might even have been gods themselves. But the powers of the monarch began their long decline in 1215 when the **despotic** King John was forced by his **barons**—with the support of the Church—to sign the contract known as Magna Carta. Under its terms he was obliged to consult with his aristocrats before **levying** taxes, and to agree that he could not **arbitrarily** arrest or seize property from his subjects. Magna Carta did little more than confirm the privileges of the Church and the barons, but it was the first critical step in the redistribution of political power in Britain.

A second step was taken in 1265 when the Norman baron Simon de Montfort—exploiting the political weaknesses of King Henry III (1216–1272)—**convened** the first British Parliament. It was unelected and met only **sporadically**, but it included both commoners and aristocrats. Monarchs came to rely on it for political support, and it provided an alternative focus of political power. Magna Carta and the creation of Parliament by no means moved power into the hands of the ordinary person, but they marked the beginning of the long and complex process by which democracy came to Britain.

Meanwhile, the supremacy of England over the British Isles was established as wars and **attrition** led to the **incorporation** of its Celtic neighbours, and as nationalism **superseded feudalism** as the driving force in politics. The Normans conquered Wales in 1285 but did not fare so well in Scotland—they invaded in 1296, meeting resistance first from William Wallace, and then from Robert Bruce who **routed** the invaders at the Battle of Bannockburn in 1314. The Normans now looked to expand outside the British Isles, setting off the Hundred Years' War against France in 1337. **Revenue** from estates was not enough to pay for the war so the king—Edward III—looked to Parliament for help. It began meeting more regularly and the house of Commons began sitting separately from the barons. The war started well, with notable victories at Crecy and Poitiers, but then the Black Death in 1348–1349 halved the population of England. Another victory over the French at Agincourt in 1415 marked the end of the war for the

Chapter 2 History—Figures and Events of Significance

English, who now became **diverted** by their own Wars of the Roses (1455–1485), in which two **factions**—the Lancastrians and the Yorkists—fought for control of the throne. The Lancastrians **prevailed** at the Battle of Bosworth in 1485, the King Henry VII became the first member of the Tudor dynasty.

Vocabulary

Iberian	adj.	伊比利亚的；西班牙和葡萄牙的
peninsula	n.	半岛
disparate	adj.	由不同的人（或事物）组成的
thriving	adj.	欣欣向荣的，兴旺发达的
stretch	n.	一段；延伸
termination	n.	结束；末端
vacuum	n.	空缺；真空
convert	v.	改变信仰；转变
full-blown	adj.	完全成熟的
aristocrat	n.	贵族
despotic	adj.	专治的
baron	n.	男爵（英国贵族的最低爵位）
levy	v.	征税
arbitrarily	adv.	随意地
convene	v.	召集（会议）；召开
sporadically	adv.	零星地；偶发地
attrition	n.	摩擦；磨损
incorporation	n.	合并
supersede	v.	取代
feudalism	n.	封建制度
rout	v.	一举击败
revenue	n.	（公司、组织或政府的）收入
diverted	adj.	转移注意力的
faction	n.	派系
prevail	v.	获胜；占上风

Exercises

Unit 2

King John and King Charles I: Is King's Right Divine?

Britain is probably the most sophisticated combination of a monarchy and a democracy.

—John Lithgow

 Test Your Knowledge

I. Search for relevant information to answer the following questions.

1. What is regarded as the foundation of the British constitutionalism?
2. Which king was forced to sign the Magna Carta?
3. When was the Magna Carta signed?
4. Did the Magna Carta establish the idea that the king could be limited by some form of agreement with his subjects?
5. What do you know about King John's brother?

II. Match the persons with the descriptions of them.

1. Richard I   A. He quarreled with Parliament, which provoked a civil war that led to his execution.
2. William III   B. Glorious Revolution resulted in joint sovereign of Mary II and him.
3. Oliver Cromwell   C. He earned the title "Lion Heart" as he was a brave soldier and great crusader.
4. Charles I   D. He returned as king following the period of Oliver Cromwell's Commonwealth.
5. Charles II   E. He led parliamentary forces in the English Civil Wars and was the lord protector during the republican period.

Chapter 2 History—Figures and Events of Significance

Intensive Reading

Text I King John*

Richard I left no legitimate children, and when he died, the different parts of the Angevin Empire chose different **successors**. The barons of England and Normandy **opted** for John; Anjou, Maine, and Touraine preferred Arthur of Brittany, now twelve years old; Aquitaine continued to be held—on John's behalf—by his mother, Eleanor. By May 1200 John had **ousted** Arthur and had established himself as lord of all the Angevin **dominions**. Later that year his first marriage was **annulled** and he married Isabella of Angouleme. There were great strategic advantages to be gained from marrying the heiress to Angouleme and had John given her **fiancé**, Hugh of Lusignan, adequate compensation, all might yet have been well. As it was, this marriage set in motion a train of events which led to Hugh appealing to the court of France and, in 1202, to Philip's declaration that all John's Continental dominions—the lands which he held as **fiefs** of the king of France—were **forfeit**. The sentence still had to be enforced. By John's tactless treatment of the leading barons of Anjou and Poitou, he threw away all the advantages he won when he captured Arthur; the well-founded rumour that he was responsible for his nephew's murder (April 1203) further undermined an already shaky reputation. In an atmosphere of suspicion and fear John found it impossible to organize an effective defence. In December 1203 he withdrew to England. Philip **overran** Normandy, Anjou, Maine, Touraine, and all of Poitou except La Rochelle. These humiliating military reverses earned for John a new nickname. "Lackland" now became "Softsword".

Until December 1203 John, like his father and brother, spent most of his reign in his Continental possessions. After that date he became, by force of circumstances, an English king. The country saw more of its ruler, but there was little pleasure or profit to be got from a king who constantly suspected that men were plotting against him. The weight of John's presence was even felt in the north where men were not accustomed to visits from kings of England. The extent of their resentment can be measured by the number of northerners who opposed John in 1215–1216. Undoubtedly he faced genuine problems. He was duty-bound to try to recover his lost inheritance, but the conquests of 1203–1204 meant that the French king was now a much more **formidable** opponent. An unusually high

---

* Excerpted from Kenneth O. Morgan (Ed.). *The Oxford History of Britain.* Oxford: Oxford University Press, 1993: 148–151.

rate of inflation meant that many families and religious houses were in financial difficulties and they found it easier to blame the king than to understand the underlying economic forces. Inflation tended to **erode** the real value of royal revenues. As a result, John levied frequent taxes and tightened up the laws governing the forest (a profitable but highly unpopular source of income).

John also quarrelled with the Church. A **disputed** election in 1205 led to a clash with Innocent III. In 1208 Innocent laid an **interdict** on England and Wales; all church services were suspended and remained so for six years. In 1209 John himself was **excommunicated**. Neither John nor lay society in general seemed to have been very worried by this state of affairs; indeed since John's response to the interdict was to confiscate the estates of the Church, it even helped to ease his financial problem. But in 1212 a baronial plot and Philip's plans to cross the Channel served to remind John that an excommunicated king was particularly **vulnerable** to rebellion and invasion, so he decided to make peace with the Church in order to have a free hand to deal with his more dangerous enemies. By agreeing to hold England as a fief of the **papacy** in May 1213 he completely won over Innocent and assured himself of the pope's support in the coming struggles.

All now led to the outcome of John's attempt to recover his lost lands. In 1214 he led an expedition to Poitou but the defeat of his allies at the battle of Bouvines (July 1214) **entailed** both the failure of his Continental strategy and the **onset** of rebellion in England. Rebels had genuine problems too. Leadership was normally provided by a discontented member of the Royal Family. After the elimination of Arthur, John faced no such rivals. His own sons were too young. The only possible candidate was Louis, son of Philip Augustus, but a Capetian prince was hardly an attractive anti-king. So the rebels devised a new kind of focus for revolt: a programme of reform. In June 1215, after they had captured London, the rebels forced John to accept the terms laid out in a document later to be known as Magna Carta. In essence it was a hostile commentary on some of the more objectionable features of the last sixty years of Angevin rule. As such it was clearly unacceptable to John who regarded the agreement made at Runnymede merely as a means of buying time. Attempts to implement Magna Carta only led to further quarrels. In the end the rebels had to invite Louis to take the throne. In May 1216 he entered London. When John died in October 1216, the country was torn in two by a civil war which was going badly for the Angevins.

John possessed qualities which have **endeared** him to some modern historians. He took a close interest in the details of governmental and legal

Chapter 2 History—Figures and Events of Significance

business, but in his own day this counted for little. It is a mistake to see him as a busier king than his **predecessors**. The survival of **chancery** records from 1199 onwards permits historians to look, for the first time, into the daily routine of the king's government at work. As a result they have sometimes given the impression that John was unusually competent. In fact he was a very poor king, incompetent where it really mattered, in the management of his more powerful subjects.

Vocabulary

successor	n.	继任者
opt	v.	选择
oust	v.	驱逐；把……撤职
dominion	n.	英联邦自治领地；统治（权）
annul	v.	宣布……无效
fiancé	n.	未婚夫
fief	n.	（尤指）采邑，封地
forfeit	adj.	（因犯错）丧失的，被没收的
overrun	v.	迅速占领；泛滥
formidable	adj.	可怕的；令人敬畏的
erode	v.	侵蚀
disputed	adj.	有争议的
interdict	v.	阻断；封锁
excommunicate	v.	将……革出教门
vulnerable	adj.	易受伤害的
papacy	n.	教皇权力；教皇职务
entail	v.	牵连，导致
onset	n.	发生；开端
endear	v.	使受欢迎；使人喜爱
predecessor	n.	前任
chancery	n.	（英格兰）大法官法庭

Exercises

I. Decide whether the following statements are true or false, and mark T or F accordingly.

_____ 1. England, Normandy, Anjou, Maine, Touraine and Aquitaine were all part of the Angevin Empire.

_____ 2. John married the heiress to Angouleme by giving her **fiancé**, Hugh of Lusignan, adequate compensation.

_____ 3. The rumour that John was responsible for his nephew's murder undermined his good reputation he had previously enjoyed.

_____ 4. Both the failure of his Continental strategy and the onset of rebellion in England were contributive to the defeat of John's allies at the battle of Bouvines.

_____ 5. John was unusually competent and the rebels were not John's rivals.

II. Match the causes with the effects they bring about according to the passage.

1. John married Isabella of Angouleme and didn't give her fiancé, Hugh of Lusignan, adequate compensation.
2. John treated barons of Anjou and Poitou tactlessly.
3. John withdrew to England and Normandy, Anjou, Maine, Touraine, and all of Poitou except La Rochelle were lost.
4. After December 1203 John became an English king and didn't spend most of his reign in his Continental possessions.
5. Inflation tended to erode the real value of royal revenues.
6. John also quarrelled with the Church. A disputed election in 1205 led to a clash with Innocent III.
7. In 1212 a baronial plot and Philip's plans to cross the Channel served to remind John that an excommunicated king was particularly vulnerable to rebellion and invasion.
8. John took a close interest in the details of governmental and legal business.

A. The country saw more of its ruler, but there was little pleasure or profit.
B. John threw away all the advantages he won when he captured Arthur.
C. John earned a new nickname "Softsword".
D. In 1208 Innocent laid an interdict on England and Wales; all church services were suspended and remained so for six years. In 1209 John himself was excommunicated.
E. John levied frequent taxes and tightened up the laws governing the forest (a profitable but highly unpopular source of income).
F. Hugh appealed to the court of France and, in 1202, Philip declared that all John's Continental dominions—the lands which he held as fiefs of the king of France—were forfeit.
G. John made himself loved by some modern historians.
H. John decided to make peace with the Church in order to have a free hand to deal with his more dangerous enemies.

Chapter 2 History—Figures and Events of Significance

III. Fill in the blanks with the appropriate forms of the words in the box.

> dispute annul formidable erode entail
> legitimate opt predecessor revenue levy

1. The two players together make a(n) _____ combination.
2. Is his business strictly _____?
3. Then over many more years, the rocks of the new land began to _____ and the cycle continues.
4. Depending on your circumstances you can _____ for one method or the other.
5. It should not be beyond the wit of man to resolve this _____.
6. Opposition party leaders are now pressing for the entire election to be _____.
7. Such a decision would _____ a huge political risk in the midst of the presidential campaign.
8. Although the car is some two inches shorter than its _____, its boot is 20% larger.
9. The company's annual _____ rose by 30%.
10. Many countries _____ special taxes and fees on tourists.

IV. Complete the following sentences with the appropriate forms of the words or phrases in the box.

> throw away enforce earn establish erode recover
> tighten up suspend set undermine lay out ease

1. By May 1200 John had ousted Arthur and had _____ himself as lord of all the Angevin dominions.
2. As it was, this marriage _____ in motion a train of events which led to Hugh appealing to the court of France.
3. The sentence still had to be _____.
4. By John's tactless treatment of the leading barons of Anjou and Poitou he _____ all the advantages he won when he captured Arthur.
5. The well-founded rumour that he was responsible for his nephew's murder (April 1203) further _____ an already shaky reputation.

6. These humiliating military reverses _____ for John a new nickname. "Lackland" now became "Softsword".

7. He was duty-bound to try to _____ his lost inheritance.

8. Inflation tended to _____ the real value of royal revenues.

9. As a result, John levied frequent taxes and _____ the laws governing the forest (a profitable but highly unpopular source of income).

10. All church services were _____ and remained so for six years.

11. The confiscation of the estates of the Church even helped to _____ his financial problem.

12. In June 1215, after they had captured London, the rebels forced John to accept the terms _____ in a document later to be known as Magna Carta.

V. Retell what you know about King John. Discuss his personalities and governing policies that led to the revolt from people.

Further Reading

Text II Charles I*

Charles was brought up in the shadow of an accomplished elder brother who died of smallpox when Charles was twelve. Charles was short, a stammerer, a man of deep indecision who tried to simplify the world around him by persuading himself that where the king led by example and where order and uniformity were set forth, obedience and peace would follow. Charles I was one of those politicians so confident of the purity of his own motives and actions that he saw no need to explain his actions or justify his conduct to his people. Government was very differently run. In the years of peace after 1629 the budgets were balanced, the administration **streamlined**, and the Privy Council reorganized. In many respects, government was made more efficient and effective. But a heavy price was paid. In part this was due to misunderstandings, to failures of communication. The years 1625–1630 saw England at war with Spain (to regain the territories seized from Charles' brother-in-law the elector

---

* Excerpted from Kenneth O. Morgan (Ed.). *The Oxford History of Britain*. Oxford: Oxford University Press, 1993: 354–357.

Chapter 2 **History—Figures and Events of Significance**

Palatine and generally to support the Protestant cause) and with France (to make Louis XIII honour the terms of the marriage treaty uniting his sister Henrietta Maria to Charles I). Parliament **brayed** for war but failed to provide the supply to make the campaigns a success. A **mercenary** army was sent in vain into Germany; naval expeditions were mounted against French and Spanish. Nothing was achieved.

The administrative and military preparations themselves, together with financial devices to make good the **deficiencies** of parliamentary supply, were seen as oppressive and burdensome by many. Throughout his reign, however, Charles **blithely** ruled as he thought right and did little to explain himself. By 1629, king and Parliament had had a series of confrontations over the failure of his foreign policy, over the fiscal **expedients** needed to finance that policy, over the use of imprisonment to enforce those expedients, and over the king's sponsorship of a new minority group within the Church, whose beliefs and practices sharply **diverged** from the developing practice and teachings of the Anglican mainstream. In 1629, passions and frustrations reached such a peak that Charles decided that for the foreseeable future he would govern without calling Parliament. The three Parliaments of 1625–1629 had been bitter and **vindictive**. But they represented a range of frustrations rather than an organized resistance. They also demonstrated the institutional **impotence** of Parliament. There was much **outspoken** criticism of royal policies, but no unity of criticism. No change of political institutions and no change in the constitution was available. They lacked the unity of purpose even to stand forth as an alternative government team.

So in the 1630s the king ruled without Parliament and in the absence of any **concerted** action to bring back Parliament. The king raised substantial revenues, adequate for peacetime purposes, and he faced **obstruction**, and that largely ineffective obstruction. By 1637 Charles had a balanced budget, effective social and economic policies, an efficient council, and a secure title. There was a greater degree of political **acquiescence** than there had been for centuries.

He was, however, alienating a huge majority of his people by his religious policies, for his support for Archbishop William Laud was re-creating some of the religious passions of the 1570s and 1580s. But it was not leading to the development of an underground church or of **subversive** religious activity. Indeed, those who found the religious demands of Laud unacceptable now had an option not available to previous generations: They could and did emigrate to the New World. There were, however, two things about Laud which dangerously weakened loyalty to the Crown. One was that the teachings of many of those **sponsored** by the archbishop, and many of the practices encouraged by Laud himself and his colleagues, were **reminiscent** of Roman Catholic beliefs and ritual. Just as bad was Laud's attempt to restore the power and authority of the bishops, of the Church courts, of the **parish** clergy by attacking **encroachments** on the wealth and **jurisdiction** of the Church.

Despite this, in 1637 Charles stood at the height of his power. Yet five years later civil war broke out. The most obvious lesson the king should have learned from the 1610s (if not the 1590s) was that the Tudor-Stuart system of government was ill-equipped to fight successful wars, with or without parliamentary help. What Charles had to avoid was **blundering** into an unnecessary war. In 1637, however, he blundered into civil war with his Scots subjects. Poor co-ordination, poor **morale**, and a general lack of urgency both forced Charles to abandon the campaign of 1639 and allowed the Scots to invade England. A unique opportunity thus arose for all those unhappy with royal policies to put things right.

Vocabulary

streamline	v.	提高……的效率
bray	v.	以刺耳的高声讲话
mercenary	n.	雇佣兵
deficiency	n.	缺乏；缺点
blithely	adv.	快活地；无忧无虑地
expedient	n.	权宜之举
diverge	v.	相异，有分歧
vindictive	adj.	想复仇的
impotence	n.	无能为力
outspoken	adj.	直言不讳的
concerted	adj.	共同筹划决定的
obstruction	n.	阻挡，阻碍
acquiescence	n.	默然接受，默认
subversive	adj.	颠覆性的；暗中起破坏作用的
sponsor	v.	主办，举办；赞助
reminiscent	adj.	使人联想的
parish	n.	教区

Chapter 2 **History—Figures and Events of Significance**

encroachment	*n.*	侵入，侵犯
jurisdiction	*n.*	司法权，管辖权
blunder	*v.*	犯愚蠢的错误；误入（危险境地或困境）
morale	*n.*	士气

Exercises

Unit 3

Spanish Armada and the Two World Wars: The Empire on Which the Sun Never Sets

The empire on which the sun never set was also the empire on which the gore never dried.

—Christopher Hitchens

 Test Your Knowledge

I. Search for relevant information to answer the following questions.

1. What marked the beginning of the British Empire according to some historians?
2. Which country was the greatest colonial power in the 16th century?
3. When did England defeat the Spanish Armada?
4. What was the sparkle that set off World War I?
5. What happened to the colonies of the old British Empire after World War II?

II. What do you know about the following figures? Fill in the blanks in the table below.

Portrait					
Name	(1) _____	King Philip II of (2) _____	(3) _____ Bonaparte	(4) _____	Adolf (5) _____

Chapter 2 History—Figures and Events of Significance

(Continued)

Event	She saw the defeat of the Spanish Armada.	He gathered and fit out a great fleet—the Armada—for the conquest of England.	As a French military leader and emperor, he conquered much of Europe in the early 19th century.	He rallied the British people during World War II and led his country from the brink of defeat to victory.	As the leader of the Nazi Party (from 1920/1921) and chancellor (*Kanzler*) and Führer of Germany (1933–1945), he was principally, responsible for starting World War II.

Intensive Reading

Text I Rivalry Between Britain and France*

The **duel** between British and French empires during the 17th and 18th centuries ended in an overwhelming British triumph. One reason was that France was less interested in overseas possessions than in European **hegemony**. Since the 16th century, the French Bourbons had concentrated primarily on gaining ground in Italy and on combating the Hapsburgs in Austria and Spain.

Another reason for Britain's triumph was that many more Englishmen than Frenchmen emigrated to the colonies. By 1688 there were 300,000 English settlers concentrated in the narrow region along the Atlantic coast compared to a mere 20,000 French scattered over the vast areas of Canada and the Mississippi Valley. At the time of the American Revolution the population of the English colonies amounted to no fewer than 2 million. The mass transplantation explains in large part why Britain was victorious over France in 1763 and why the American Republic defeated Britain two decades later.

---

* Excerpted from Leften Stavrianos. *A Global History from Prehistory to the 21st Century*. Beijing: Peking University Press, 2004: 364–376.

英国社会与文化

The colonial and commercial rivalry between Britain and France was fought out in a series of four wars that dragged on for almost a century until England's great victory in 1763. All these wars had two phases: one European and the other overseas. The European revolved about dynastic ambitions, especially those of Louis XIV of France and Frederick the Great of Prussia. The overseas operations were fought over diverse issues—the balance of power in India, conflicting territorial claims in America, terms of trade in the Spanish colonies, and control of the world trade routes. The **dichotomy** between the European and overseas aspects of these wars was **sufficiently** marked so that each one was known by one name in Europe and another in America. Hence the wars have come down in history as the War of the **League** of Augsburg, or King William's War (1689–1697); the War of the Spanish **Succession**, or Queen Anne's War (1701–1713); the War of the Austrian Succession, or King George's War (1740–1748); and the Seven Years' War, or the French and Indian War (1756–1763).

The net result of the first three of these wars was that the British acquired Nova Scotia, Newfoundland, and the Hudson Bay territories. But these conquests did not settle the basic question of whether the French would retain Canada and the Mississippi Valley, and thereby restrict the English to the Atlantic seaboard. This question was finally answered conclusively by the fourth war, which also settled the future of India.

This fateful struggle is known as the Seven Years' War because it was waged for seven years—between 1756 and 1763. The turning point of the war came in 1757, largely because of William Pitt (the Elder), who then entered the British cabinet. Pitt concentrated his resources on the navy and the colonies, while **subsidizing** his ally, Frederic of Prussia, to fight on in Europe. His strategy was, as he put it, to win an empire on the plains of Germany, and he succeeded brilliantly. His reinforced navies swept the French off the seas, and the American colonists, stirred by his leadership, joined the British regulars to form a force of about 50,000 men. This huge army overwhelmed one French fort after another. The climax came with the siege of Quebec, the heart of French Canada and a great natural **stronghold** on the banks of the St. Lawrence. In the **ensuing** battle, the British and the French commanders, General James Wolfe and the Marquis de Montcalm, were killed. But the British **veterans** prevailed, and Quebec surrendered in September 1759. The fall of Montreal the following year spelled the end of the French colonial empire in America.

In India the success of the English was no less complete. Again naval

Chapter 2 History—Figures and Events of Significance

superiority was the deciding factor. Britain was able to transport troops, money and supplies from Europe while preventing France from doing likewise. The British, too, had the inspired leadership of Robert Clive, a company official who had come out years before as a clerk. Clive possessed both outstanding military talents and an ability to understand Indian politics. In 1756, on hearing of the war in Europe, he marched on **Bengal**. With the support of Indian merchants who had become wealthy in the trade with Europe, Clive defeated the pro-French Moslem ruler at the battle of Plassey in 1757. He put his own **puppet** on the throne and **extorted** huge **reparations** both for himself and for his company. During the rest of the war thanks to the strong British navy, Clive was able to shift his forces at will from one part of India to another. At the same time he **severed** the communications of the French posts with each other and with France. The end came with the surrender in 1761 of the main French base at Pondichery.

The overseas phase of the Seven Years' War was decided by the fall of Quebec in America and of Pondichery in India. But the war dragged on in Europe until 1763, when the **belligerents** concluded the Peace of Paris. Of its American possessions, France retained only Guiana in South America; the insignificant islands of St. Pierre and Miquelon on the Newfoundland coast; and a few islands in the West Indies, including Guadeloupe and Martinique. Britain therefore received from France the whole of the St. Lawrence Valley and all the territory east of the Mississippi. Spain had entered the war late on the side of France and was, therefore, **compelled** to **cede** Florida to Britain. As compensation, France gave Spain western Louisiana; that is, the territory west of the Mississippi River. In India the French retained possession of their commercial installations—offices, warehouses, and docks—at Pondichery and other towns. But they were forbidden to build **fortifications** or make political alliances with the Indian princes. In other words, the French returned to India as traders and not as empire builders.

France's loss of north America and India meant America north of the Rio Grande was to develop in the future as a part of the English-speaking world. France's **expulsion** from India was a historical event of global significance, for it meant that the British were to take the place of the **Moguls** there. Once installed in Delhi, the British were well on their way to world empire and world **primacy**.

Vocabulary

duel	n.	双人决斗
hegemony	n.	霸权
dichotomy	n.	天壤之别；二分法
sufficiently	adv.	足够地
league	n.	联盟；协会
succession	n.	继任；继任权
subsidize	v.	补贴
stronghold	n.	（大多数人有共同态度或信仰的）大本营
ensuing	adj.	随后发生的
veteran	n.	经验丰富的人；退伍军人
Bengal	n.	孟加拉（位于亚洲）
puppet	n.	傀儡
extort	v.	勒索
reparation	n.	补偿，赔偿
sever	v.	切断，切掉
belligerent	n.	交战国
compel	v.	迫使
cede	v.	（迫于军事、政治压力）割让，让出（领土、主权）
fortification	n.	防御工事
expulsion	n.	被逐出
Mogul	n.	莫卧儿人（16—18世纪印度的穆斯林统治者）
primacy	n.	首要；首位

Exercises

I. Decide whether the following statements are true or false, and mark T or F accordingly.

_____ 1. Many more Frenchmen than Englishmen emigrated to the colonies and they scattered along the Atlantic coast during the 16th and the 17th century.

_____ 2. The rivalry between Britain and France was fought out in a series of four wars: the War of the League of Augsburg, King William's War, the War of the Spanish Succession, and the War of the Austrian Succession.

_____ 3. In the Seven Years' War, the British acquired Nova Scotia, Newfoundland, and the Hudson Bay territories.

Chapter 2 **History—Figures and Events of Significance**

_____ 4. William Pitt's strategy was to concentrate his resources on the navy and the colonies to help Frederic of Prussia fight on in Europe.

_____ 5. Britain's installment in Delhi signified that the British were well on their way to world empire and world primacy.

II. Match the causes with their corresponding effects according to the passage.

1. Clive defeated the pro-French Moslem ruler at the battle of Plassey in 1757.

2. The colonial and commercial rivalry between Britain and France was fought out in the War of the League of Augsburg, the War of the Spanish Succession, and the War of the Austrian Succession.

3. Spain had entered the Seven Years' War on the side of France.

4. France lost North America and India.

5. France was less interested in overseas possessions than in European hegemony and many more Englishmen than Frenchmen emigrated to the colonies.

6. William Pitt concentrated his resources on the navy and the colonies, while subsidizing his ally, Frederic of Prussia, to fight on in Europe.

7. The Seven Years' War was waged for seven years—between 1756 and 1763.

A. The duel between British and French empires during the 17th and 18th centuries ended in an overwhelming British triumph.

B. The net result was that the British acquired Nova Scotia, Newfoundland, and the Hudson Bay territories.

C. It not only answered the question whether the French would retain Canada and Mississippi Valley but also settled the future of India.

D. British navies were reinforced and naval superiority became one of the deciding factors for France's loss of North America and India.

E. Clive put his own puppet on the throne and extorted huge reparations both for himself and for his company.

F. Spain was compelled to cede Florida to Britain. As compensation, France gave Spain western Louisiana; that is, the territory west of the Mississippi River.

G. America north of the Rio Grande was to develop as a part of the English-speaking world and India as an incomparable base enabled the British to expand into the rest of South Asia and then beyond to East Asia.

III. Fill in the blanks with the appropriate forms of the words in the box.

| compel | ensuing | expulsion | sufficiently | duel |
| primacy | retain | amount | succession | sever |

1. They gave me some help in the beginning but it did not _____ to much.
2. However, I think you are right that it will change if the market changes _____.
3. He killed a man in one _____ and was wounded in another.
4. She's third in order of _____ to the throne.
5. But as to what happened thereafter, that will be disclosed in the _____ chapter.
6. The interior of the shop still _____ a 19th-century atmosphere.
7. The _____ of politics is clear from the prime minister's decisions on wages and petrol prices.
8. The two countries have _____ all diplomatic links.
9. The law can _____ fathers to make regular payments for their children.
10. These events led to the _____ of senior diplomats from the country.

IV. Complete the following sentences with the appropriate forms of the words in the box.

| acquire | balance | decide | drag | concentrate |
| rivalry | settle | sever | wage | gain |

1. Even as other nations _____ ground, the US remains the world leader in science.
2. So Benjamin Franklin, John Jay and John Adams were able to exploit the rivalry of the European powers to _____ this huge territory without either conquest or migration.
3. There is a certain amount of friendly _____ between the teams.
4. This case has _____ on for months. When will it finally end?
5. The stability pact, policed by the European Commission, was supposed to _____ that question.

6. He can now _____ on a project he'd originally put to one side.

7. "The _____ factor is whether the employer will find out about it," MacDougall says.

8. A team of neuroscientists has identified a crucial part of the nervous system whose malfunction could _____ communication between brain and heart.

9. The new resolution gives the Security Council a role in the decision to _____ war.

10. How do you _____ power between 13 states and the new federal government for the effective administration?

V. Read the following sentences and find out the expressions the author uses to show cause and effect.

1. One reason was that France was less interested in overseas possessions than in European hegemony.

2. Another reason for Britain's triumph was that many more Englishmen than Frenchmen emigrated to the colonies.

3. The mass transplantation explains in large part why Britain was victorious over France in 1763 and why the American Republic defeated Britain two decades later.

4. The dichotomy between the European and overseas aspects of these wars was sufficiently marked so that each one was known by one name in Europe and another in America.

5. Hence the wars have come down in history as the War of the League of Augsburg, or King William's War (1689–1697); … ; and the Seven Years' War, or the French and Indian War (1756–1763).

6. The net result of the first three of these wars was that the British acquired Nova Scotia, Newfoundland, and the Hudson Bay territories.

7. But these conquests did not settle the basic question of whether the French would retain Canada and the Mississippi Valley, and thereby restrict the English to the Atlantic seaboard.

8. Again naval superiority was the deciding factor.

9. With the support of Indian merchants who had become wealthy in the trade with Europe, Clive defeated the pro-French Moslem ruler at the battle of Plassey in 1757.

10. During the rest of the war thanks to the strong British navy, Clive was able to shift his forces at will from one part of India to another.

11. Britain therefore received from France the whole of the St. Lawrence Valley and all the territory east of the Mississippi.

Further Reading

Text II   The Battle of Britain*

With Poland easily defeated in less than a month, the Germans in a strong position to invade France, the Soviet Union a partner of Germany in the division of Eastern Europe, and the United States neutral, the situation for Britain looked **grim** indeed. It looked even grimmer for the government of Neville Chamberlain, ill-prepared for war and embarrassed by the failure of appeasement. Winston Churchill, identified as the **premier** supporter of an aggressive policy that had been **vindicated** by events, was brought into the government...and then became Prime Minister on May 9, 1940. The new Churchill government soon faced another disaster: the fall of France. One of the most heavily mythologized actions of the war was the **evacuation** of Dunkirk from May 26 to June 4, 1940. About two weeks after Churchill came to power, the **bulk** of the British troops in France had their backs to the English Channel, surrounded by the Germans. Most of them (along with many French and other Allied soldiers) were successfully evacuated by the Royal Navy, with the help of many civilian sailors in small boats. The "Dunkirk spirit" became a **byword** for **persistence** in the face of disaster. However, despite giving British morale a badly needed shot in the arm, Dunkirk was a **catastrophe** from a purely military point of view, as the British **Expeditionary** Force had to abandon nearly all of its equipment to the Germans. Shortly thereafter, Churchill, who was prepared to continue the war regardless of what happened at Dunkirk, rejected a peace offer from Hitler without discussion and announced his war aim: total victory. Given the nearly uninterrupted stream of German victories that had made Hitler the master of the European continent, this seemed objectively **insane**.

The next challenge was to Britain itself. The German plan for the invasion of Britain was code-named Operation Sea Lion, and its prospects for success remain a topic of controversy. In any event, invasion was never attempted,

---

* Excerpted from William E. Burns. *A Brief History of Great Britain.* New York: Maple-Vail Book Manufacturing Group, 2010: 197–201.

and the actual Battle of Britain was fought in the air. The Battle of Britain, which lasted from July to October 1940, became another heavily mythologized wartime period. (The parts of World War II that resonate most loudly in the British memory were often from its early stages, before the British contribution was **overshadowed** by that of the United States and the Soviet Union.) In the first major military campaign to be fought entirely from the air, heavily **outnumbered** British fighter pilots defeated the attempt of the German Luftwaffe to establish **dominance** of the skies. In large part this was a matter of poor German leadership as the Germans could not settle on a consistent strategy concentrating on airfields, aircraft production, or radar stations. Superior British technology, including radar and the control of fighters from the ground, was also an important factor.

Although the Germans initially focused their attacks on British military targets, by late August they were attacking British cities (as the Royal Air Force [RAF] was attacking German cities). The attack on British cities, which intensified in December, is referred to as the **Blitz**. Although the Germans killed more than 20,000 British civilians and wounded more than 30,000, their bombing of cities did not bring them closer to the objective of destroying the RAF's capacity to fight, nor did it have the destructive effects on British morale that some German leaders, including Hitler, expected. By October, RAF air supremacy over British skies had been established, and the Germans had abandoned plans for an invasion. Despite being a defensive win, the Battle of Britain was the first victory of the war on the Allied side (although Britain at the time was actually without allies, other than the Commonwealth).

British victory did not end the air war, which continued for the remainder of the conflict, as both Germans and British dropped bombs on each other's cities, killing uncounted thousands of civilians in a way that made little contribution to ultimate victory. Dealing with air **raids** became an important part of the wartime experience, particularly for Londoners. The experience of the ordinary Londoner was shared by King George and his **consort**, Queen Elizabeth, who refused to leave the city. Ordinary civilians were much less isolated from World War II than they had been from World War I, which had a relatively **static** front line and little in the way of attacks on the civilian population. With bombing, and also with the overwhelming presence of the state in **allocating** work and food, the ordinary British person felt the war as something in which he or she was personally involved. The extensive temporary **relocation** of children away from cities where they would have been the targets of bombers also contributed to class and regional mixing.

Once it had become clear that Operation Sea Lion could not work due to German failure to establish air and sea dominance, it was a question of how long the British could hold out until the Americans or possibly the Soviet Union would enter the war against Germany. Even aided by its dominions, Britain lacked the military might to challenge the German grip on Europe, although British and British Commonwealth forces remained active in the Mediterranean. What brought about Germany's defeat was the entrance of the two other world powers into the war. Once the Germans invaded the Soviet Union in 1941, the bulk of the German military effort was devoted to the massive war on the eastern front; the war with Britain became a secondary concern. By that time the United States had unmatched economic power and a large population that could be **mobilized**, and German defeat became virtually certain after Hitler's catastrophic decision to declare war on the United States on December 11, 1941, four days after the Japanese attack on Pearl Harbor.

Vocabulary

grim	*adj.*	严酷的；令人沮丧的
premier	*adj.*	最好的；首要的
vindicate	*v.*	证明……正确
evacuation	*n.*	疏散，撤离
bulk	*n.*	大多数；大部分
byword	*n.*	俗语；格言
persistence	*n.*	坚持不懈；执着
catastrophe	*n.*	灾难
expeditionary	*adj.*	远征的，探险的
insane	*adj.*	疯狂的；愚蠢的
overshadow	*v.*	给……蒙上阴影；使……黯然失色
outnumber	*v.*	在数量上超过
dominance	*n.*	统治地位；优势
Blitz	*n.*	闪电战
raid	*n.*	突袭
consort	*n.*	在位君主的配偶
static	*adj.*	静止的；不变的
allocate	*v.*	分配

Chapter 2 **History—Figures and Events of Significance**

relocation	*n.*	重新安置，再布置
mobilize	*v.*	动员

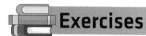

Chapter 3

Communication—Etiquette Here and There

Introduction

A study suggests that the average British people spend the equivalent of four and a half months of their life talking about the weather. Is it because the British weather is unique in the world? When the British talk about the weather, do they automatically follow any rules?

The British are well-mannered. What is their common form of greeting? What are the situations when you are obliged to be on time? A primer on British social etiquette will help you demonstrate decent manners when you are in the UK.

The pub culture is an intrinsic part of British culture. America has its fair share of quality bars. Are there any differences between American bars and British pubs? Some people believe that the closure of pubs has devastated the pub culture in Britain during the COVID-19 pandemic. What is Britain without pubs?

英国社会与文化

Unit 1

English Weather-Speak: How to Talk About the Weather with the English

To an outsider, the most striking thing about the English weather is that there is not very much of it. All those phenomena that elsewhere give nature an edge of excitement, unpredictability and danger—tornadoes, monsoons, raging blizzards, run-for-your-life hailstorms—are almost wholly unknown in the British Isles.

—Bill Bryson

 Test Your Knowledge

Conduct a poll among your classmates asking the following questions. You could add your own questions to the list.

1. Which type of weather do you like the most and least?
2. How would you react to a sudden change in the weather?
3. What is the most distinguishing feature of the British weather?
4. How do the British respond to a sudden change in the weather?

Intensive Reading

Text I Is the British Weather Unique in the World?*

It's often said by **laymen** that the UK's weather is unique. But what makes it so different from anywhere else?

Whatever you think of the British weather, if you don't like it one day, there's always a good chance you might like it the next.

Weather, in **meteorological** terms, refers to the daily elements like

---

* Retrieved from BBC website.

Chapter 3 Communication—Etiquette Here and There

temperature, wind and rain. And in Britain they can all change hour by hour and day by day.

It's the diversity and changeability that make British weather so distinct, say meteorologists. While temperatures are fairly mild and there are four distinct seasons, you can also get warm weather in the middle of February and freezing rain in the middle of August—or both in one day.

"Other countries might have more dramatic weather," says Dr. Liz Bentley, head of the Weather Club at the Royal Meteorological Society. "In India and Pakistan you get **monsoon** season, but you can usually predict the day it will start and the day it will finish."

"In the UK you sometimes have to look at the weather forecast several times in one morning just to plan a trip out that afternoon. Things can change that quickly."

Many meteorologists call the British weather unique, although some say you could argue that the weather in all countries is unique because no two are the same geographically and **geologically**. But they agree that it is hard to find another country in the world with weather that compares to the UK.

So what makes it so distinctly variable?

"Britain's unique weather is all down to the fact that it is an island and it's positioned between the Atlantic Ocean and a large land mass, continental Europe," says Helen Chivers from the Met Office. "There is a lot going on meteorologically where we are."

Britain is under an area where five main air masses meet. An air mass is a large body of air that has similar temperature and moisture properties throughout.

In the UK they are either polar or **tropical**, depending on where the air mass originated; they are also divided into **maritime** or continental, depending on whether the air has passed over land or sea.

They come from all directions and can bring all types of weather.

When they meet it creates a weather **front**. The air masses fight it out and the one that wins **dictates** the weather. The bigger the difference the worse the weather can be. There is a sixth air mass, the returning Polar Maritime, which is a variation of the Polar Maritime.

One more important thing to throw into the mix is the **jet stream**. It is a

high-altitude ribbon of fast-moving air that is associated with weather systems in the UK. The position of the jet stream can make a huge difference to the type of weather we experience.

All in all, it's quite an extraordinary mix of atmospheric conditions battling it out.

"It's what makes the British weather so fascinating," says Bentley. "Experiencing such big changes so quickly is unique."

Fascinating or frustrating, the layman might argue, but no other country in the world gets the same weather, say experts.

"Japan is probably the only other place that has similarities to the UK when it comes to weather," says Chivers.

"It is similar to us but in reverse. It is an island and has the Pacific Ocean to the east and Eurasian continent to the west. Britain's variations in weather really are that rare."

These variations pose problems, from when to have a barbecue to effective planning for businesses. Companies spend millions trying not to be caught out by the British weather.

"From energy companies, supermarkets and insurance firms to banks, technology companies and local authorities, they all need to plan for the weather," says Richard Tipper, director of Ecometrica, which works with companies to get the climate and weather data they need to plan efficiently.

"It's the amazing changeability in British weather that is unique. It also means planning for it isn't always easy."

Subtle changes in the weather are happening and will continue, says Bentley.

"We are starting to see more record-breaking weather, record droughts and record rainfall," she says.

Last year is a good example. The dramatic switch from drought in early 2012 to the wettest April to June on record was of a **magnitude** never seen before, according to the Centre for Ecology & **Hydrology** (CEH).

Hosepipe bans were brought in early in the year but by early autumn levels of groundwater were "well above" average.

But the country's fascination with the weather probably won't change. Nor will some people's love for it.

Chapter 3 **Communication—Etiquette Here and There**

"There is a real beauty about the weather in the UK," says Bentley.

"You might be guaranteed sun in other countries but constant sunshine can get dull. People move to other countries but often they end up missing the British weather and the seasons."

"There are also some real **upsides**. When we get unexpected sunshine in the UK everyone's day is better. It just feels like we are getting a special treat and we are so much happier."

Vocabulary

layman	*n.*	外行；门外汉
meteorological	*adj.*	气象学的
monsoon	*n.*	（南亚地区的）雨季
geologically	*adv.*	从地质角度
tropical	*adj.*	热带的
maritime	*adj.*	海上的
front	*n.*	（冷暖空气交汇的）锋面
dictate	*v.*	决定
jet stream		急流
high-altitude	*adj.*	高空的，高海拔的
magnitude	*n.*	（变化的）剧烈程度
hydrology	*n.*	水文学
upside	*n.*	好的方面

Exercises

I. Decide whether the following statements are true or false, and mark T or F accordingly.

_____ 1. In Britain the daily elements like temperature, wind and rain can all change hour by hour and day by day.

_____ 2. Temperatures are fairly mild and there are four distinct seasons in Britain.

_____ 3. Just like India and Pakistan, Britain has very dramatic weather throughout the year.

_____ 4. The position of the jet stream makes little difference to the type of weather British people experience.

_____ 5. With the data provided by Ecometrica, planning for the weather is always easy.

II. **Match the word partners to form collocations.**

1. distinct   A. change
2. freezing   B. planning
3. effective   C. upside
4. subtle   D. season
5. real   E. rain

III. **Fill in the blanks with the appropriate forms of the words in the box.**

> layman   meteorological   geologically   maritime
> dictate   altitude   magnitude   upside

1. Bill Ford's willingness to seek help starkly shows the _____ of the challenge facing Ford.
2. Residents said the only _____ would be a boost to the island's economy.
3. The mere mention of the words "heart failure" can conjure up, to the _____, the prospect of imminent death.
4. First, _____ speaking, not all countries will benefit from the application of these potentially revolutionary techniques.
5. Of course, a number of factors will _____ how long an apple tree can survive.
6. But many more would have died if not for a tsunami warning from the Japanese _____ Agency.
7. We were more than 4,000 metres above sea level, and the _____ rendered me useless.
8. Japan, anxious to secure its _____ lifeline, has also been pushing for more active collaboration.

IV. **Do research on the Internet and then write a report about the climate in England for about 200 words. You could focus on the following three aspects: temperature, rainfall and sunshine.**

Further Reading

Text II Rules of English Weather-Speak*

The Weather Hierarchy Rule

There is an unofficial English weather hierarchy to which almost everyone **subscribes**. In descending order, from best to worst, the hierarchy is as follows:

- sunny and warm/mild
- sunny and cool/cold
- cloudy and warm/mild
- cloudy and cool/cold
- rainy and warm/mild
- rainy and cool/cold

I am not saying that everyone in England prefers sun to cloud, or warmth to cold, just that other preferences are regarded as deviations from the norm. Even our television weather forecasters clearly subscribe to this hierarchy: They adopt apologetic tones when forecasting rain, but often try to add a note of cheerfulness by pointing out that at least it will be a bit warmer, as they know that rainy/warm is preferable to rainy/cold. Similarly **rueful** tones are used to predict cold weather, brightened by the prospect of accompanying sunshine, because we all know that sunny/cold is better than cloudy/cold. So, unless the weather is both rainy and cold, you always have the option of a "But at least it's not..." response.

If it is both wet and cold, or if you are just feeling **grumpy**, you can indulge what Jeremy Paxman calls our "phenomenal capacity for quiet moaning". This is a nice observation, and I would only add that these English "moaning rituals" about the weather have an important social purpose, in that they provide further opportunities for friendly agreement, in this case with the added advantage of a "them and us" factor—"them" being either the weather itself or the forecasters. Moaning rituals involve displays of shared opinions (as well as wit and humour) and generate a sense of **solidarity** against a common enemy—both valuable aids to social bonding.

---

* Excerpted from Kate Fox. *Watching the English: The Hidden Rules of English Behaviour* (2nd ed.). Boston, Nicholas Brealey, 2014: 42–44.

We now have yet another option for ritual humorous weather-moaning: In recent years, moans about global warming have become commonplace. The most popular form of this new moan is to say "Huh, so much for global warming!" or "So where's all this global warming they keep promising us?" on a cold, grey day.

An equally acceptable, and more positive, response to weather at the lower end of the hierarchy is to predict imminent improvement. In response to "Awful weather, isn't it?", you can say, "Yes, but they say it's going to clear up this afternoon." If your companion is feeling Eeyorish, however, the **rejoinder** may be "Yes, well, they said that yesterday and it poured all day, didn't it?", at which point you may as well give up the Pollyanna approach and enjoy a spot of quiet moaning. It doesn't really matter: The point is to communicate, to agree, to have something in common; and shared moaning is just as effective in promoting sociable interaction and social bonding as shared optimism, shared speculation or shared **stoicism**.

For those whose personal tastes are at variance with the unofficial weather hierarchy, it is important to remember that the further down the hierarchy your preferences lie, the more you will have to qualify your remarks in accordance with the personal taste/sensitivity clause. A preference for cold over warmth, for example, is more acceptable than a dislike of sunshine, which in turn is more acceptable than an active enjoyment of rain. Even the most **bizarre** tastes, however, can be accepted as harmless **eccentricities**, providing one observes the rules of weather-speak.

Snow and the Moderation Rule

Snow is not mentioned in the hierarchy partly because it is relatively rare, compared to the other types of weather included, which occur all the time, often all in the same day. Snow is also socially and conversationally a special and awkward case, as it is **aesthetically** pleasing, but practically inconvenient. It is always simultaneously exciting and worrying. Snow is thus always excellent conversation-**fodder**, but it is only universally welcomed if it falls at Christmas, which it almost never does. We continue to hope that it will, however, and every year the high-street **bookmakers** relieve us of thousands of pounds in "white Christmas" bets.

The only conversational rule that can be applied with confidence to snow is a generic, and distinctively English, "moderation rule": Too much snow, like too much of anything, is to be deplored. Even warmth and sunshine are only

Chapter 3 Communication—Etiquette Here and There

acceptable in moderation: too many **consecutive** hot, sunny days, and it is customary to start **fretting** about drought, muttering about hose-pipe bans and reminding each other, in doom-laden tones, of the summer of 1976, or moaning about global warming.

The English may, as Paxman says, have a "capacity for infinite surprise at the weather", and he is also right in observing that we like to be surprised by it. But we also expect to be surprised: We are accustomed to the variability of our weather, and we expect it to change quite frequently. If we get the same weather for more than a few days, we become uneasy; more than three days of rain, and we start worrying about floods; more than a day or two of snow, and disaster is declared, and the whole country **slithers** and **skids** to a halt.

Vocabulary

subscribe	*v.*	同意，赞成
rueful	*adj.*	悲伤的
grumpy	*adj.*	脾气坏的
solidarity	*n.*	团结一致
rejoinder	*n.*	（机智的）应答
stoicism	*n.*	坚忍刚毅
bizarre	*adj.*	怪异的
eccentricity	*n.*	古怪
aesthetically	*adv.*	从审美的角度
fodder	*n.*	素材
bookmaker	*n.*	赌注经纪人
consecutive	*adj.*	连续的
fret	*v.*	担心
slither	*v.*	滑动
skid	*v.*	打滑

Exercises

英国社会与文化

Greetings and Goodbyes: How to Greet and Say Goodbye

Life is short, but there is always time enough for courtesy.

—Ralph Waldo Emerson

 Test Your Knowledge

Discuss the following questions with your partner.

1. What examples of good manners do you often see on English gentlemen?
2. What social rules does Britain have that a foreigner might not know?

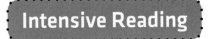

Text I　A Short Primer on British Social Etiquette*

There are no strict etiquette rules that you have to stick to when in the UK. It is advisable, however, to demonstrate decent manners and respect to the local culture and traditions.

The first, and most important, step to British etiquette is to be aware of the clearly distinct nations which form the UK. The United Kingdom of Great Britain and Northern Ireland consists of England, Scotland, Wales and Northern Ireland. The citizens of any of these countries are British. This term is also the safest to use when not certain of a person's heritage. When certain of heritage, you are free to call the different residents as follows: English, Scot, Welsh or Irish. While the four countries share many customs, each has its own set of traditions and history.

Greetings and Meetings

When first meeting a **Brit**, he or she may seem **reserved** and cold, but that is just an impression. In reality, he or she is very friendly and helpful to foreigners. A handshake is the common form of greeting, but try to avoid **prolonged** eye

---

*　Retrieved from Expatica website.

Chapter 3 Communication—Etiquette Here and There

contact, as it may make people feel ill at ease. Use last names and appropriate titles until specifically invited to use first names. It is proper to shake hands with everyone you know, regardless of gender; the appropriate response to an introduction is "pleased to meet you".

Time and Punctuality in British Etiquette

British people are very strict when it comes to **punctuality**. In Britain, people make a great effort to arrive on time, so it is impolite to be late, even by a few minutes. If you are late, be sure to inform the person you are meeting. Here are some situations when you are obliged to be on time, as well as some situations when it is advisable:

- For formal dinners, lunches, or appointments you always come at the exact time appointed.
- For public meetings, plays, concerts, movies, sporting events, classes, church services, and weddings, it's best to arrive a few minutes early.
- You can arrive any time during the hours specified for teas, **receptions** and cocktail parties.

The British often use expressions such as "drop in anytime" and "come see me soon". However, do not take these literally. To be on the safe side, always telephone before visiting someone at home. If you receive a written invitation to an event that says "RSVP", you should respond to the sender as soon as possible, whether you are going to attend or not.

Body Language and Dress Code

British people are not very keen on displaying affection in public. Hugging, kissing, and touching are usually for family members and very close friends. You should also avoid talking loudly in public or going to extremes with hand gestures during the course of communication. The British like a certain amount of personal space. Do not stand too close to another person or put your arm around someone's shoulder.

When it comes to clothes, there are no limits and restrictions on how to dress. Just make sure that you respect the general rules when in formal situations. Observation will reveal that people in larger cities dress more formally, especially in London. Men and women wear wools and **tweeds** for casual occasions. **Slacks**, sweaters, and jackets are appropriate for men and women. Do not wear a **blazer** to work—it is country or weekend wear. On formal occasions, always select an **outfit** that fits the **dress code**. When attending a holiday dinner or cultural event, such as a concert or theatre performance, it is best to dress formally.

General Advice

Men should open doors for women and stand when a woman enters a room, although it is generally accepted for men and women both to hold the door open for each other, depending on who goes through the door first.

It is important to respect the British desire for privacy. Don't ask personal questions about family background and origin, profession, marital status, political preferences, or money issues. It is extremely impolite to violate a queue, so never push ahead in a line. It is also very rude to try to sound British or **mimic** their accent.

Remember that humour is ever-present in English life. It is often **self-deprecating**, **ribbing**, sarcastic, sexist or racist. Try not to take offense.

Cultural etiquette dictates that when invited to someone's home, you should bring a small gift for the hostess. Give flowers, chocolates, wine, champagne or books. Feel free to express your gratitude and delight with the visit on the next day with a note or a telephone call.

British Etiquette Rules for Women

Women in Britain are entitled to equal respect and status as men, both at work and daily life. The British have the habit to use "affectionate" names when addressing someone, so do not take any offense if they call you "love", "dearie", or "darling". These are commonly used and not considered rude.

It is acceptable for a foreign woman to invite an English man to dinner. It is best to stick with lunch. Also, if you would like to pay for your meal, you should state it at the outset. Remember that when in public, it is proper to cross your legs at the ankles, instead of at the knees.

Vocabulary

Brit	n.	英国人
reserved	adj.	矜持的
prolonged	adj.	持续很久的
punctuality	n.	准时，守时
reception	n.	招待会
tweed	n.	粗花呢
slacks	n.	休闲裤

Chapter 3 **Communication—Etiquette Here and There**

blazer	*n.*	夹克
outfit	*n.*	全套服装
dress code		着装要求
mimic	*v.*	模仿
self-deprecating	*adj.*	自贬的，自嘲的
ribbing	*n.*	（友善的）玩笑

Exercises

I. **Decide whether the following statements are true or false, and mark T or F accordingly.**

_____ 1. Although the four countries in the UK share many customs, each has its own set of traditions and history.

_____ 2. In reality, British people are reserved and cold.

_____ 3. For formal dinners, lunches, or appointments, it's best to arrive a few minutes early.

_____ 4. People in large cities dress more informally, especially in London.

_____ 5. It is generally accepted for men and women both to hold the door open for each other, depending on who goes through the door first.

II. **Match the word partners to form collocations.**

1. decent   A. occasion
2. appropriate   B. rule
3. casual   C. manner
4. cultural   D. title
5. general   E. event

III. **Fill in the blanks with the appropriate forms of the words in the box.**

| prolonged | punctuality | reception | slacks |
| outfit | mimic | self-deprecating | |

1. He could _____ anybody, and he often reduced Isabel to helpless laughter.

2. If you feel overdressed during your first interview, hit the sale racks for a blazer and matching _____ or skirt.

3. They suffered _____ sexual and psychological abuse and had miscarriages, according to a city councilman.

4. Indian weddings are traditionally divided into three parts: the pre-wedding, the wedding, and the _____.

5. In recent years the underground's finances have improved even though its _____ and reliability leave much to be desired.

6. Roberts is a gifted public speaker—relaxed, often funny, sometimes _____—and he began his speech with a warm remembrance of his mentor.

7. Her standard _____ is a jacket with baggy trousers or calf-length skirt and flat-heeled, clodhopper shoes.

IV. Write an essay of about 200 words to make a comparison between British social etiquette and Chinese social etiquette in terms of greetings, punctuality, dress code, etc.

Further Reading

Text II   English Etiquette*

Whilst the English **penchant** for manners and socially appropriate behaviour is renowned across the world, the word "etiquette" to which we so often refer actually originates from the French "estiquette"—"to attach or stick". Indeed, the modern understanding of the word can be linked to the Court of the French King Louis XIV, who used small **placards** called etiquettes, as a reminder to **courtiers** of accepted "house rules" such as not walking through certain areas of the palace gardens.

Every culture across the ages has been defined by the concept of etiquette and accepted social interaction. However, it is the British—and the English in particular—who have historically been known to place a great deal of importance in good manners. Whether it be in relation to speech, timeliness, body language or dining, politeness is key.

---

* Retrieved from Historic UK website.

Chapter 3 **Communication—Etiquette Here and There**

British etiquette dictates courteousness at all times, which means forming an orderly queue in a shop or for public transport, saying "excuse me" when someone is blocking your way and saying "please" and "thank you" for any service you have received is **de rigueur**.

The British reputation for being reserved is not without merit. Overfamiliarity of personal space or behaviour is a big no-no! When meeting someone for the first time a handshake is always preferable to a hug, and a kiss on the cheek is reserved for close friends only. Asking personal questions about salary, relationship status, weight or age (particularly in the case of more "mature" ladies) is also frowned upon.

Traditionally, one of the best examples of the British etiquette is the importance placed on punctuality. It is considered rude to arrive late to a business meeting, medical appointment or formal social occasion such as a wedding. As such it is advisable to arrive 5–10 minutes early to appear professional, prepared and **unflustered** as a mark of respect to your host. Conversely, should you arrive too early to a dinner party, this could also appear slightly rude and ruin the atmosphere for the evening if the host is still completing his preparations. For the same reason an unannounced house call is often frowned upon for risk of inconveniencing the home owner.

Should you be invited to a British dinner party it is customary for a dinner guest to bring a gift for the host or hostess, such as a bottle of wine, a **bouquet** of flowers or chocolates. Good table manners are essential (particularly if you want to be invited back!) and unless you are attending a barbeque or an informal **buffet** it is frowned upon to use fingers rather than **cutlery** to eat. The cutlery should also be held correctly, i.e. the knife in the right hand and the fork in the left hand with the **prongs** pointing downwards and the food pushed onto the back of the fork with the knife rather than "scooped". At a formal dinner party when there are numerous **utensils** at your place setting it is customary to begin with the utensils on the outside and work your way inward with each course.

As the guest it is polite to wait until everyone at the table has been served and your host starts eating or indicates that you should do so. Once the meal has begun it is impolite to reach over someone else's plate for an item such as seasoning or a food **platter**; it is more considerate to ask for the item to be passed to you. Leaning your elbows on the table whilst you are eating is also considered rude.

Slurping or making other such loud noises whilst eating is completely frowned upon. As with yawning or coughing it is also considered very rude to chew open-mouthed or talk when there is still food in your mouth. These actions imply that a person was not brought up to adhere to good manners, a criticism against not only the offender but his family too!

Social Classes

Rules of etiquette are usually unwritten and passed down from generation to generation, although in days gone by it was common for young ladies to attend a finishing school to ensure their manners were up to scratch. Knowing the rules of etiquette is an **attribute** which was felt particularly crucial in securing a suitable husband!

Whilst today good manners and etiquette are seen as a sign of respect, particularly to those more senior (in either age or position), in Victorian England when the class system was alive and well, etiquette was often used as a social weapon in the interests of social advancement or exclusion.

The Evolution of Etiquette

More recently, a rise in multiculturalism, a changing economy and the introduction of social and gender specific equality laws have all played a part in Britain moving away from its rigid class system of old and therefore a more informal attitude to social etiquette has arisen. However, today—like the rest of the world—Britain has been influenced by the importance of **corporate** etiquette, with a shift in focus from the social or household setting to an emphasis on business etiquette and **protocol**. With the whole concept of etiquette being dependent on culture, for a business to succeed internationally it is important to be aware that what is considered good manners in one society may be rude to another. For instance, the "okay" gesture—made by connecting the thumb and forefinger in a circle and holding the other fingers straight, is recognised in Britain and North America as a signal to question or confirm that a person is well or safe. However, in parts of southern Europe and South America this is an offensive gesture.

Thus the etiquette of business has become a set of written and unwritten rules of conduct that make social interactions run more smoothly, whether during interaction with a co-worker or contact with external or international colleagues.

Indeed, the rise in online business and social media sites has even seen the creation of a worldwide "online society", **necessitating** its own rules of

Chapter 3 Communication—Etiquette Here and There

conduct, commonly referred to as "netiquette", or network etiquette. These rules regarding the protocol for such communications as email, forums and blogs are constantly being redefined as the Internet continues to evolve. So whilst the traditionally accepted behaviours of old may not have the influence they once did, it could be argued that etiquette is as crucial in today's far-reaching society as it has ever been.

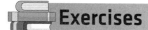

Vocabulary

penchant	*n.*	特别的喜好
placard	*n.*	标语牌
courtier	*n.*	朝臣
de rigueur	*adj.*	时尚的
unflustered	*adj.*	从容不迫的
bouquet	*n.*	花束
buffet	*n.*	自助餐
cutlery	*n.*	餐具
prong	*n.*	（叉子等的）尖头
utensil	*n.*	器皿
platter	*n.*	（盛食物的）大浅盘
slurp	*v.*	出声地喝（或吃）
attribute	*n.*	特性
corporate	*adj.*	公司的
protocol	*n.*	礼节
necessitate	*v.*	使成为必需

Exercises

Unit 3

English Pubs—How to Engage in Non-verbal and Verbal Communication

A pub can be a magical place.

—Rhys Ifans

 Test Your Knowledge

Discuss the following questions with your partner.

1. What comes to your mind when you hear the words "pubs, clubs and bars"?
2. What do you like about pubs, clubs and bars?
3. What do you dislike about pubs, clubs and bars?

Text I Seven Differences Between American and British Pubs*

It's no coincidence that British soap operas are almost always centered around the local drinking establishment. For the pub is so deeply engrained in Britain's sense of community, such an intrinsic part of the culture, that for those who leave their shores no adequate replacement can ever be found. Sure, America has its fair share of quality **watering holes**, but there is nothing quite like sitting by the blazing fire of a cozy British pub while sipping contentedly on a pint of real ale.

Britain Has Pubs, America Has Bars

Generally speaking, or generally drinking, if you will, America has more

---

* Retrieved from BBC America website.

Chapter 3 **Communication—Etiquette Here and There**

of a bar scene than a pub culture. Particularly popular is the sports bar, where thousands of giant TV screens simultaneously broadcast billions of seemingly never-ending games. Such places are **rowdy**, loud and full of frat bros loaded on light beer. British pubs are quiet, relaxing environments, and although there are pubs in America, they don't serve the same function as they do in the UK. This is because Brits occupy pubs in the same way Americans occupy coffee shops. Brits will happily go to a pub during the day (without fear of judgment) to work, read, take meetings or simply enjoy a drink.

History

Most British pubs take their charm from the old buildings in which they're housed. No two are ever the same, but many share **quaint** and **quintessential** characteristics like low ceilings held aloft by wooden beams, stone floors, log fireplaces, **mahogany** shelving littered with **bric-a-brac** and a regular named Dave. These public houses have scarcely changed in centuries, and the walls could teach you a thousand lessons about love, life and knowing your limits. In Nottingham alone, three pubs claim to date from before the mid-15th century. Meanwhile, if you happen to stumble across somewhere in the US claiming to be "Ye Olde Traditional Pub", the chances are slim that it was built any earlier than the turn of the 20th century. That's not to say that old pubs don't exist in America; it's just that they're **few and far between**.

The Cat & Custard Pot vs. Johnny's Bar

British pubs are usually bestowed with such imaginative and wondrous names (The Pig & Whistle, The Drunken Duck, The Swan with Two Necks) that most of the time they don't even allude to the concept of friends gathering to enjoy a drink, but rather **conjure** images resembling some magical creature from a Brothers Grimm fairytale. American drinkeries, on the other hand, tell it like it is with wholly colorless names such as "Mike's Tavern", "Jeffrey's Taproom", or even the simple yet uninspiring "Bar".

The Fruit Machine

In every corner of every pub in every British town, you will find a fruit machine. This is not a vending machine from which **punters** may dispense fresh fruit for their consumption; rather it is a slot machine much like the ones found in Las Vegas and Atlantic City. **Colloquially** known as a "gambler", the machine is a confusing clusterjam of flashing fruits and strange beeping that only the person with the lowest IQ in the pub can understand.

英国社会与文化

British Pubs Are Family-Friendly

Most British pubs are family-friendly and even have a playground out back for the kids. Usually there's a separate area inside the pub marked "Family Room" where children are permitted. This ensures that the little **tykes** don't displease the kid-loathing adults drowning their sorrows at the bar. Meanwhile, I don't recall ever having seen a child in a bar in the United States.

Age

As we all know, the legal drinking age in the UK is 18, which means the **clientele** frequenting British pubs are much younger than those in American bars. Add to this some British **lackadaisical** door security, and you've got kids who couldn't get into an R-rated movie without an accompanying adult buying drinks, making the pub look more like a youth club than a fully licensed **taproom**. In America, however, almost every bar will have a **bouncer** on the door who won't let you in unless you have valid identification proving you're 21 or over. Even if you're 63 and look terrible for your age, you'll still be asked for ID. Interestingly, in the UK it's actually legal for someone as young as 16 to drink beer, cider or wine in a pub so long as it's with a meal and they are accompanied by an adult over 18 who purchases the alcohol.

Closing Times

Until the 2003 Licensing Act changed the law, British pubs had to close at 11:00 pm on both weekdays and weekends. After the law came into force at the end of 2005 it permitted licensees to theoretically operate 24 hours a day if they applied for a license. However, here we are a decade later, and you'd still struggle to get a drink at a British pub after 11:00 pm. Bars in America, on the other hand, will happily keep serving until the **wee hours** so long as **revelers** keep ordering (at least this is what it feels like, in actuality bars in most states call last orders at 2 am, although many go later).

Vocabulary

watering hole		酒吧
rowdy	*adj.*	吵闹的
quaint	*adj.*	古雅的
quintessential	*adj.*	典型的
mahogany	*n.*	红木
bric-a-brac	*n.*	小装饰品

Chapter 3 Communication—Etiquette Here and There

few and far between		稀少
conjure	v.	呈现于脑际
punter	n.	顾客
colloquially	adv.	口语地
tyke	n.	小淘气
clientele	n.	顾客群
lackadaisical	adj.	无精打采的
taproom	n.	酒吧
bouncer	n.	（夜总会）保安
wee hours		凌晨
reveler	n.	狂欢者

Exercises

I. **Decide whether the following statements are true or false, and mark T or F accordingly.**

_____ 1. The pub is deeply engrained in Britain's sense of community.

_____ 2. British pubs are rowdy, loud and full of frat bros loaded on light beer.

_____ 3. British pubs have undergone significant changes in centuries.

_____ 4. American bars have colorless names.

_____ 5. A fruit machine is a vending machine from which customers can get fresh fruit for their consumption.

_____ 6. In Britain, almost every pub has a bouncer on the door.

II. **Match the word partners to form collocations.**

1. intrinsic
2. adequate
3. relaxing
4. wondrous
5. valid

A. name
B. identification
C. replacement
D. part
E. environment

III. Fill in the table with the information about British pubs and American bars.

	British Pubs	American Bars
Atmosphere		
History		
Name		
Family-Friendliness		
Legal Drinking Age		
Closing Time		

IV. Introduce the characteristics of bars or pubs in China to the class. In what ways can we incorporate some British elements into Chinese bar culture? Please elaborate and give a presentation for about 3 minutes.

Further Reading

Text II What Is Britain Without the Pub?*

London—After a long day of working from home, all four of them in one **cramped terraced house** in East London, the roommates wait for salvation via text message.

Today, it comes from Lucie Audibert, a trainee lawyer. "I'm going for a pint at the Ufton Arms if you want to join." She passes Victor Tricaud, an analyst, as she heads downstairs—he hasn't seen the text yet—but it won't be long before he joins her.

Eventually, all four roommates will make their way from their shared apartment to the garden out back: The Ufton Arms, named for the road out front.

They spent the better part of 10 hours on a recent weekend assembling a pub bench in their garden. Naturally, the holes in the wooden slats weren't **aligned**, so they bought a **cordless** power drill and made new holes, determined to finish.

---

* Retrieved from *The New York Times* website.

Chapter 3 Communication—Etiquette Here and There

They already had pint glasses—stolen from their local pub, an honored tradition. Someone found a YouTube video for "Pub Background Noise Sound Effects".

"We thought about making a sign, but that was getting a little too pathetic," said Ms. Audibert, sipping a pint of her favorite—Beavertown's Neck Oil IPA—on a Saturday afternoon so sunny it was cruel. As the four of them live in the same household, they are not violating social distancing rules by sitting together in their backyard.

"It's not much of a pub," Mr. Tricaud said laughing. "It's more of a mental recreation of the pub."

In the midst of a pandemic that has sickened over 65,000 people in Britain and killed almost 8,000, the desire to sit inside a **musty** room and share an uncleaned glass of beer with friends ranks low among national priorities. That doesn't make it any easier.

It may seem **trivial**, but the closing of pubs is **unprecedented** for Britain. Never before in the history of the country have the pubs been closed outright.

"I do accept that what we're doing is extraordinary. We're taking away the ancient, **inalienable** right of freeborn people of the United Kingdom to go to the pub," Prime Minister Boris Johnson said when he announced the closures of all pubs, restaurants, bars and cafés on March 20. (Three days earlier, when Mr. Johnson had recommended that the public avoid pubs and other social venues, his own father responded, "Of course I'll go to a pub if I need to go to a pub.")

Even the 20th-century wars could not close down the pubs.

"During the two world wars, sometimes there was a shortage of beer and the pubs had to close for that reason," said Paul Jennings, a historian and author of several books about pub culture and alcohol consumption in Britain. He added that some pubs, particularly those in London, may have closed during The Great Plague of 1665, but that "there is no real **precedent** for closing all of them like this".

Historically, pubs were open 24 hours a day, but that started to change in the early 19th century, when they would briefly close on Sundays for church services. Everything changed during World War I, Mr. Jennings explained, as the government at the time claimed that drunkenness was undermining the war effort. ("It probably wasn't," Mr. Jennings said.)

Pubs were then ordered to stay closed until at least late morning, then to briefly close again in the afternoon and to close for the night around 9 pm. The days of grabbing a 6 am pint on the way to work ended with the war, too.

Those general opening hours largely stayed the same through World War II. "Churchill was keen to make sure they still had a beer supply," Mr. Jennings said. "It was seen as good for morale."

During the 1980s, Margaret Thatcher's free market government gradually removed most restrictions on operating hours, once again allowing pubs to open all day. Today, pubs operate on "agreed hours" when they apply for their license with their local council authority. Most close by midnight.

Pub culture has evolved from its original days of old men drinking a pint or 10 in the afternoon. Women are at the pub, children are at the pub, and many pubs are now as focused on food, if not more, than drink. Many a meat-heavy Sunday meal, the "Sunday roast", has moved from family dining rooms to the pub.

But as easy as it is to **lament** the loss of the storied British tradition of drinking, pub closures are being **acutely** felt by business owners and workers across Britain. By last count, there were about 48,000 pubs employing around 450,000 people, all of whom are without work indefinitely. (The government has said it will revisit the closures next week.)

Pubs have been granted permission to sell food for **carryout**, but no alcohol.

"This is pretty much the worst time in my life," said Rosie Wesemann, who has owned The Scolt Head, a pub in East London, with her brother for the past 11 years. Ms. Wesemann has had to **furlough** all 40 of her employees.

Rishi Sunak, the chancellor of the Exchequer, has announced a multibillion-dollar rescue package that will cover 80% of the wages for the staff, up to about $2,900 a month, provided they are kept on by their employer. But the program's requirements make it inaccessible for many pub owners like Ms. Wesemann.

"We need 30,000 pounds to pay everyone their salary this month," she said, or about $37,000, "and we don't have a month's worth of wages sitting in our bank account." Ms. Wesemann said she applied for a bank loan two weeks ago.

Many pubs in Britain are searching for other income streams, whether through virtual quizzes or online home-brew classes or just becoming full-time carryout restaurants. Ms. Wesemann said she felt that the limited revenue from food sales was not enough to put her employees at risk.

"It's just not worth it to make a couple burgers," she said, adding that food delivery apps take a **hefty** cut. "You need to be selling a lot."

Chapter 3 **Communication—Etiquette Here and There**

Ms. Wesemann worries most about her older customers. For as long as she can remember, The Scolt Head has hosted a weekly "Freedom Club", inviting residents aged 60 and older to meet at the pub on Tuesdays to see a film or make **marmalade**. It's the only time some of them leave their house.

"These are really isolated people. It's not just those who are desperate for a pint of Guinness," Ms. Wesemann said. "Now, they're even more isolated, and that's heartbreaking."

Sean White, the owner of the Queen's Head in Pinner, a northwestern suburb of London, was emotional over having to close his own pub—it's been open for more than 300 years. But he also worried about how the closures would affect communities across the country.

"Up and down England, there are small towns and villages with one pub," Mr. White said. "If that one pub closes, you change the whole fabric of society."

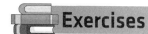

cramped	*adj.*	狭小的
terraced house		排屋
aligned	*adj.*	对齐的
cordless	*adj.*	无电线的
musty	*adj.*	有霉味的
trivial	*adj.*	无关紧要的
unprecedented	*adj.*	史无前例的
inalienable	*adj.*	不可剥夺的
precedent	*n.*	先例
lament	*v.*	对……感到悲痛
acutely	*adv.*	强烈地
carryout	*n.*	外卖
furlough	*v.*	停职
hefty	*adj.*	高额的；(数目，数量)相当大的
marmalade	*n.*	橘子酱

Exercises

Chapter 4

British Media—Broadcasting, Newspapers and Television

Introduction

The United Kingdom is not only famous for its glorious history and its contribution to the promotion of the civilization of the world, but also enjoys the reputation for the advancement of the media industry. Mass media communicates to a large group. The technologies through which communication takes place include a variety of outlets. In an age of explosion of digital communication technology, mass media could be classified into eight industries: books, the Internet, magazines, movies, newspapers, radio, recordings, and television. In view of history and representativeness, radio, newspapers and television are chosen as topics of this chapter.

Unit 1

The Broadcasting History of BBC

The power of radio is not that it speaks to millions, but that it speaks intimately and privately to each one of those millions.

—Hallie Flanagan

Test Your Knowledge

I. **The following is based on the annual report of the BBC in 2020–2021, the most-used brand in the UK for media. Check what you know about the BBC.**

1. It is used by _____ of UK adults and _____ of young adults on average per week.

   A. 70%; 80% B. 80%; 90%

   C. 90%; 80% D. 80%; 70%

2. It is at the heart of UK life—the public choose the BBC around _____ million times a day.

   A. 100 B. 150

   C. 200 D. 250

3. It is used by an average of five million adults every single minute of the day and night, across TV, radio and online, and by a total of _____ million people across all ages over 24 hours.

   A. 40 B. 45

   C. 50 D. 55

4. It delivered £2.63 of direct economic impact for every £1 spent with _____ of that economic impact outside London, compared to a sector average of 20%.

   A. 50% B. 60%

   C. 40% D. 30%

5. Audiences trusted us to guide them through the pandemic, with _____ naming the BBC as their number one source for information/news on COVID-19 (next nearest—13%).

Chapter 4 British Media—Broadcasting, Newspapers and Television

A. 45%   B. 55%
C. 65%   D. 75%

II. The BBC has ten radio stations serving the whole UK. Of the ten national stations, five are major stations. Match the programmes with their radio channels.

1. BBC Radio 1
2. BBC Radio 2
3. BBC Radio 3
4. BBC Radio 4
5. BBC Radio 5 Live

A. 24-hour news, sport and talk programmes
B. classical and jazz music together with some spoken-word programming of a cultural nature
C. adult contemporary, country and soul music amongst many other genres
D. current affairs, factual and other speech-based programming, including drama and comedy
E. new music and popular styles and being notable for its chart show

Intensive Reading

Text I   The Growth of Alternative Media*

Both the US and British radio industries started at approximately the same time in 1922. As a result of the significantly different size of each nation, the US radio industry grew faster: The number of broadcasting **licences** issued by the US Department of Commerce rose from 30 in 1922 to 556 in the following year. In the UK, the number of licences was severely restricted and eventually ended with radio broadcasting in the control of the British Broadcasting Corporation, subsequently the BBC. This was entirely **consistent** with the political policies of the government of the day, which was to exercise firm control of what it recognised could become a powerful medium.

The UK government decided that it would finance this public service, thus ensuring that its control was absolute. The US authorities in their tradition of free enterprise were happy to free the newly licensed radio industry to operate commercially and this led directly to the situation where practically every

---

* Excerpted from John Hill. *The British Newspaper Industry*. London: Palgrave Macmillan, 2016: 80–90.

community in the US had its own local station.

Rather than have a multitude of stations, the British pattern meant that national programming was the order of the day, which suited the government, simplifying, as it did, the exercise of control. However, for technical reasons, it was not possible to **transmit** the same content to different areas at the same time, so, in the beginning, the BBC was a series of local radio stations. It was not until the early 1930s that it became possible to have simultaneous transmission to all BBC listeners and the service became truly national. It was not until 1967 that the BBC **proceeded** to provide local content once again when it launched Radio **Leicester** as the first part of the BBC local radio network.

In the US, the radio industry was experiencing problems of a different kind. While most of its output was entertainment in the form of recorded music, news broadcasting was starting to occupy more airtime in response to a public desire to be better informed. This raised problems with newspaper owners, who found that the **wire services** such as Associated Press, United Press and International News Services were supplying the radio stations, and newspaper managers believed that this was undercutting their products. The wire services resisted pressure from the newspaper companies, which was just as well because the newspaper groups began to purchase radio stations within their areas of influence. The next major development was the 1933 decision of the radio stations to largely cease providing their own news and rely on the news services of National Broadcasting Company (NBC) and Columbia Broadcasting System (CBS).

Radio revenues continued to rise at a steady rate, from $40 million in the late 1920s to $80 million during the Great Depression, and this continued right through the World War II. In many ways, this era represented the golden years of the US radio industry, which was destined to begin to come to an end immediately after the end of the war, when television stations were licensed. By 1948, there were 34 television stations operating in 21 different cities.

The World War II provided a **boost** to radio listener figures both in the US and in the UK as the populations sought news of the progress of the Allies. Although the broadcasting schedules in the UK were severely restricted (the BBC service did not begin until six o'clock in the evening), it was regarded as being of vital importance to the maintenance of morale in a country which was being subjected to total war. The **fledgling** British television service had been closed down following the outbreak of war, so newspapers and radio were the only sources of news for the general population. As radio had the immediacy which

Chapter 4 British Media—Broadcasting, Newspapers and Television

newspapers lacked, it soon became the news source **of choice**.

Immediately after the war ended, the BBC set about **reinstating** the National Service, which was re-titled the Home Service. Recognising the growing importance of entertainment programming, the BBC launched the Light Programme and, in the following year, the Third Programme to cater for serious drama and classical music. These changes remained in place until 1967, when the stations were re-named Radio 4 for the Home Service, Radio 3 for the Third Programme and Radio 2 for the Light Programme. To **counteract** the popularity of pirate radio stations, Radio 1 came into being. This structure remained in place until 1967 when the Regional Service was replaced with 20 Local Radio stations.

Vocabulary

licence	*n.*	许可证；执照
consistent	*adj.*	与……一致的；相符的
transmit	*v.*	播送；传输
proceed	*v.*	开始；继续进行
Leicester	*n.*	莱斯特郡（英国中部城市）
wire service		新闻通讯社
boost	*n.*	增长；提高
fledgling	*adj.*	新的；无经验的
of choice		特别的；精选的
reinstate	*v.*	恢复
counteract	*v.*	抵制；抵消

Exercises

I. Choose the best option to answer each question or complete each statement.

1. The issue of broadcasting licences was strictly controlled in the UK because _____.

    A. it was the policy of the government at that time

    B. the government feared that the media might be too powerful to be under control

    C. the radio industry did not grow very fast

D. the British Broadcasting Company took charge of it

2. What ended the golden years of the US radio industry?

   A. The emergence of television stations.

   B. The end of the World War II.

   C. A twist of fate.

   D. The end of the Great Depression.

3. Which of the following best describes pirate radio stations?

   A. Pirate radio stations are operated by pirates.

   B. Pirate radio stations broadcast without a valid licence.

   C. Pirate radio stations are radio stations whose signals run cross a national boundary.

   D. Pirate radio stations are very popular among young people.

4. The Light Programme of the BBC refers to the following programme EXCEPT _____.

   A. programme that is not serious and doesn't need much mental effort

   B. entertainment programme

   C. programme that is free from worry and cheerful

   D. programme that caters for the masses

5. Which of the following is **NOT** the problem the radio industry in the US experienced?

   A. The public wanted more information.

   B. The news agency provided news to radio stations.

   C. Providing news service on air caused discontent among newspaper owners.

   D. Newspaper groups began to buy radio stations in their sphere of influence.

II. Summarize the differences in radio industry between the UK and the US in your own words.

	The UK	The US
Issuing of Broadcasting Liscences		
Finance		
Number of Stations		
Problems		

Chapter 4 British Media—Broadcasting, Newspapers and Television

III. Fill in the blanks with the appropriate forms of the words in the box.

ahead of	obligation	consumer	priority	regional
range	lockdown	current	access	impartial
demonstrate	previous	counter	source	

These pages **1.** _____ ways in which the BBC met its **2.** _____ to provide impartial news and information over the last year. Today, the BBC provides an unrivalled level of local, **3.** _____, national and international news and **4.** _____ affairs. We remain the most trusted **5.** _____ of news in this country and we play an important role in helping to **6.** _____ the misinformation and confusion that now so often proliferate. BBC News continues to come out far **7.** _____ any other news provider when news **8.** _____ are asked to name the one source they are most likely to turn to for **9.** _____, trusted and accurate news. Whilst figures are down on the year, as the **10.** _____ survey was conducted at the start of the first **11.** _____ when the UK turned to the BBC at a moment of national emergency, the BBC continues to be seen as the most impartial and trusted news provider across a(n) **12.** _____ of measures. Strengthening impartiality is a key **13.** _____. The importance of what we do to ensure that everyone has **14.** _____ to news and information they can trust has been repeatedly highlighted this year.

Further Reading

Text II Swashbuckling Sounds: The History of Pirate Radio Stations*

—The Ups and Downs of Pirate Radio Stations in the UK

These days, it's easier than ever for musicians to reach thousands, even millions of listeners. Whether you're looking for an outlet for your brand, or you're just trying to see how people respond to your sound, you can submit music to online radio stations, post videos on YouTube and more.

Of course, this doesn't mean that it's not difficult to become a famous musician

---

* Retrieved from Radio Fidelity website.

in 2019. The difference is that struggling artists can find the opportunities they need to get their voice heard.

In the 1950s, 60s and beyond; however, it was far more challenging to make your way into the industry. Countless musicians were **beholden** to record companies and radio stations who refused hundreds of demo tapes every month.

In the UK, the British Broadcasting Corporation maintained a monopoly over the radio for many years. With the support of the British government, the BBC determined exactly what radio station listeners could tune into each day.

Enter the dawn of pirate radio.

Pirate radio stations are a crucial part of British music culture. The history of pirate radio stations is **inextricably** linked with the development of countless genres, including hip-hop, garage, punk, and grime. What's more, pirate radio stations gave us access to some of the most **pivotal** figures in the UK music history. So, where did the original pirate radio ships come from? How did the rebellious radio revolutionaries behind pirate radio get their start? Let's find out.

Hoisting the Flag: The History of Pirate Radio

The history of pirate radio spans several decades. However, for many experts, the golden age of "offshore" broadcasting was the mid-60s. During this time, there were at least a dozen stations floating in the seas around the UK, transmitting **unregulated** radio signals to the UK.

The British Broadcasting Corporation did its best to keep listeners happy with traditional tunes and gardening tips.

However, in the meantime, countless music lovers and teenagers across the UK were **fiddling with** their radio stations, trying to find the pirates that would bring them the rock-and-roll music and **unfiltered** conversations they were looking for.

Today, "pirate radio" generally refers to modern radio **freebooters**. However, back in the 1960s, offshore stations were defined by actual pirate radio ships. Companies took to the seas to avoid the legislation of the UK government and the BBC.

UK pirate radio history was inspired by groups in Denmark and Sweden, who also broadcasted shows from the sea through stations like Radio Mercur or Radio Nord in the late 1950s and early 1960s.

The first well-known pirate radio ship in the UK was launched by a man

Chapter 4 British Media—Broadcasting, Newspapers and Television

called Ronan O'Rahilly.

Determined to launch the career of musician, Georgie Fame, PR expert O'Rahilly **conspired** to create his pirate radio station. Radio Caroline was named after the daughter of President John F. Kennedy, and it began on a Danish passenger ferry (Frederica).

With financial backing from a handful of investors, O'Rahilly rigged the boat with AM transmitters and a considerable mast, so that the team could broadcast from 6 am to 6 pm every day.

Radio Caroline earned a **cult**-like **following** of dedicated listeners. By 1966, the company had more than 23 million listeners across London and the UK.

What's more, the well-known pirate radio ship also inspired countless other organisations to launch their own off-shore stations too. Pirate radio became the site of some of the most important musical innovations in Britain.

It introduced pop to the airwaves in the 1960s, launched the career of countless hip-hop, R&B, and other underground genres, and even changed the way that the BBC broadcasted eventually.

Unfortunately, though pirate radio stations have always been popular with listeners, they were constantly battling the **scrutiny** of government bodies.

In 1967, the British government passed the Marine Broadcast Offences Act, which made it increasingly difficult for organisations to broadcast from the water.

Stations That Made UK Pirate Radio History

For many **avid** fans, the history of pirate radio stations started with Radio Caroline in the UK.

However, Caroline was far from the only offshore station bringing music to listeners who didn't appreciate the gentle approach of the BBC.

Inspired by "the boat that rocked the world", Radio Caroline, countless new organisations began to make names from themselves out of **repurposed** rigs. Radio Atlanta, Radio Invicta, Radio 270, and Radio London (Wonderful Radio London) all emerged over the years.

Let's take a look at three of the best-known pirate radio ships in British history:

1. Radio Atlanta

Radio Atlanta (the station that eventually merged with Radio Caroline), started as the brainchild of Alan Crawford, an Australian music publisher. Crawford purchased a boat named the MV Mi Amigo in 1964 and fitted it with some of the best broadcasting equipment on the market.

Atlanta ran on the same frequency as Caroline at first, intending to steal its audience. Eventually, however, the group changed its rate from 197 metres to 201 metres.

Most of Radio Atlanta's broadcasts were recorded in London and transmitted from the ship. When advertising revenue and audiences couldn't keep Atlanta **afloat**, the company decided to join forces with Radio Caroline.

2. Radio London

Otherwise known as Wonderful Radio London, or the "Big L", this well-known pirate radio ship broadcast on 266 metres, and played some of the most well-loved music of the day. The organization started in 1964 and ran every day until 1967.

Radio London was managed from a former US **minesweeper** ship called MV Galaxy, and it was **anchored** at Frinton-on-Sea, near Essex.

Interestingly, unlike many of its rivals, Wonderful Radio London quickly became a **legitimate** operation, with primary offices on Central London. However, most of the programmes shared by this station were recorded and presented live from a ship-based studio.

3. Kiss FM

Kiss FM might not have had its own pirate radio ship, but it wasn't any less of a **buccaneering** broadcaster in the eyes of its fans. The organization launched in October of 1985, long after the original Marine Broadcast Offences Act was first introduced.

The show broadcast on 94 FM and was founded by Gordon Mac McNamee.

Across Greater London, Kiss FM achieved a dedicated following with nearly half a million listeners—all while operating as a pirate radio station. The show became the best place to go for urban music and hip-hop content before it was rebranded in 1998.

The history of pirate radio was so significant in the UK that the company at the very top of UK broadcasting—the BBC eventually started to **replicate** the pirate style. BBC Radio 1 launched in 1967 in response to the growing demand for pirate radio stations.

Chapter 4 British Media—Broadcasting, Newspapers and Television

The programmes were designed to **emulate** the experiences of pirate radio, with some of the most famous DJs from pirate stations **on the air**. People like John Peel, Tony Blackburn, and Kenny Everett joined the BBC to broadcast popular music and shows to the masses.

Vocabulary

swashbuckling	*adj.*	历经艰险的；惊心动魄的
beholden	*adj.*	对……表示感谢的
inextricably	*adv.*	不可分开地，密不可分地
pivotal	*adj.*	关键的
hoist	*v.*	升起（旗、帆等）
unregulated	*adj.*	未受控制的，无管理的
fiddle with		调试；摆弄
unfiltered	*adj.*	未过滤的
freebooter	*n.*	劫掠者；海盗
conspire	*v.*	合谋
cult	*n.*	狂热崇拜；（特定群体的）偶像
following	*n.*	追随者，拥护者
scrutiny	*n.*	详细审查
avid	*adj.*	渴望的；热心的
repurpose	*v.*	改换用途
afloat	*adj.*	经济上周转得开的；能维持下去的
minesweeper	*n.*	扫雷舰
anchor	*v.*	抛锚；泊（船）
legitimate	*adj.*	合法的
buccaneering	*adj.*	海盗的
replicate	*v.*	复制
emulate	*v.*	效仿，模仿
on the air		在广播

Exercises

Unit 2

Britain's Big Three: Quality or Popular Papers

If you don't read the newspaper, you're uninformed. If you read the newspaper, you're mis-informed.

—Mark Twain

  Test Your Knowledge

I. **Choose the best answer based on your current knowledge.**

1. What is the size of a typical broadsheet in the UK?

   A. 29½ × 23½ inches.

   B. 30 × 22¾ inches.

   C. 22¾ × 12 inches.

2. How is the size of the broadsheet paper measured?

   A. As it appears folded on a newsstand.

   B. It measures when unfolded.

   C. In horizontally-folded form.

3. What is the size of a standard tabloid paper in the UK?

   A. Generally half the size of the broadsheet paper.

   B. Twice the size of the broadsheet paper.

   C. No standard.

II. **Categorize the following characteristics as broadsheets or tabloids.**

   A. traditional, prestigious, hard-hitting journalism

   B. a great deal of pictures or photographs

   C. entertaining and fascinating stories, sensational crime stories or celebrity gossip

   D. the language is simple and colloquial

   E. a higher-minded approach to news-gathering and delivery

   F. educated readers opting for in-depth articles and editorials

   G. condensed stories easily consumed by everyday readers

Chapter 4 British Media—Broadcasting, Newspapers and Television

 H. focusing a great deal on politics and foreign affairs
 I. mainly serious stories
 J. the language is more formal
 K. exaggerating the truth or sometimes mixing the truth with some lies

 1. broadsheets: _____
 2. tabloids: _____

Intensive Reading

Text I A History of the Broadsheet Newspaper*

 To many, broadsheet newspapers are synonymous with the purest, most dependable form of journalism in existence. For centuries, the broadsheet has been the **go-to** outlet for news and opinion, all across the globe. But what is a broadsheet newspaper? Where did it come from? What is it by definition? And, perhaps most pressingly of all, why exactly are those pages so big?

 The genesis of the broadsheet newspaper can be traced back to 18th-century Britain. Although the reasons aren't abundantly clear, it seems that in 1712 the British government placed a tax on newspapers relating to their number of pages. To counter this, publishers made their products much larger in order to decrease page count, despite the new versions being much harder to hold.

 Before this, "newspapers" were publications published sporadically, focusing on a singular event, such as a battle or national tragedy. The idea of a more regular news **booklet** originated in the Netherlands in around 1618; these were known as "corantos" ("currents of news"). One such edition, *Courante uyt Italien, Duytslandt, &c.*, is considered to be the world's first broadsheet newspaper.

 Corantos began **popping up** in Italy, Germany and England shortly after. However, **censorship** across Europe in the 17th century was **rife**, with growth in readership **stunted** accordingly. Similarly, in North America, the United States' first newspaper, *Publick Occurrences Both Forreign and Domestick*, was buried by the colonial governor after a single 1690 issue.

---

* Retrieved from Historic Newspapers website.

The end of the 18th century saw the biggest leaps forward for the newspaper on both sides of the world. In Britain, Parliament formally **bestowed** journalists the right to report proceedings in 1771, with *The Times* being founded just over a decade later. And, with the passing of the First Amendment to the United States Constitution in 1791, the freedom of the American press was ensured, eight years after *The Pennsylvania Evening Post*, the first paper to publish the Declaration of Independence, became the country's first daily.

Between 1815 and 1850, thanks to technological advancements made possible by the Industrial Revolution, *The Times* increased its circulation tenfold, and at the same time, 400 dailies and 3,000 weeklies were being published nationwide in the USA.

While it can be said the broadsheet papers are generally twice the size of the standard tabloid paper, the actual broadsheet newspaper dimensions vary from country to country, and in some cases is exclusive to the publication itself.

The **archetypal** British broadsheet measures a **whopping** 29½ inches in length when unfolded, and 23½ inches wide. The traditional American broadsheet is slightly longer and narrower (30 × 22¾ inches), although in recent years many authoritative papers, such as *The New York Times* and *The Wall Street Journal*, have downsized to a 24-inch length to save money.

In many cases, the dimensions of a broadsheet refer to the size of the paper as it appears folded on a newsstand, which leads to *The Wall Street Journal* for example being listed as 22¾ × 12 inches.

As broadsheets are typically presented in this horizontally-folded form, publishers will always make sure that the biggest headline fits into the top half of the front page, or as it's more commonly known: "above the fold".

In 1901, Alfred Harmsworth, founder of *The Daily Mail* in England, was invited to guest edit the New Year's Day 1901 edition of the *New York World*, as a means to test his theory that a smaller newspaper, with "condensed" journalism, would be more time-efficient for both the writers and readers, **in line with** an ever-evolving society. Two years later, Harmsworth launched *The Daily Mirror* in the UK, and the tabloid newspaper was officially born.

The Mirror was eventually followed in Britain by other tabloids like *The Sun* and *The Daily Star*, **capitalizing on** the popularity of the **format**, which strayed from the more traditional, prestigious, hard-hitting journalism found in broadsheet papers in favor of a "something for everyone" approach, utilizing **astrology, gossip columns**

Chapter 4 British Media—Broadcasting, Newspapers and Television

and **agony aunts**, as well as a more frequent use of images.

In America, publications such as *The National Enquirer* and *The Globe* **took a leaf from the same book** as their transatlantic counterparts, focusing on **salacious** hearsay and celebrity exposés, with an added dash of the **paranormal**, at the expense of authenticity. Indeed, the term "tabloid" in the United States is generally used to refer to these supermarket-sold weeklies, whereas in Britain, it is categorized as a **bona fide** newspaper.

The difference between how broadsheets and tabloids are viewed on either side of the Atlantic can best be illustrated by the shift (or lack thereof) of long-established broadsheet publications to the tabloid format (or, as they prefer to call it, "compact" form).

Such is the popularity of tabloid journalism in the United Kingdom that nearly all remaining nationally circulated newspapers are now tabloid size, following the shrinking of *The Daily Mail* in 1971, *The Daily Express* in 1977, *The Times* in 2004 and both *The Observer* and *The Guardian* in 2018, all historically UK broadsheet newspapers. The official line for this is that a smaller-sized paper makes it easier for **commuters** to read on public transport, and that the new dimensions have no effect on content or legitimacy.

As it stands, the only remaining broadsheet-size newspapers to be published nationwide in Britain are *The Daily Telegraph*, *The Financial Times* and *The Sunday Times*.

The story in the United States is a wholly different one. Despite a public transport system which easily rivals Britain's, particularly in New York, almost all of the major newspapers in the US remain broadsheets, be they newspapers of public record like *The New York Times* and *The Washington Post*, the most widely-circulated paper in the country *USA Today*, or small, more local publications like *The Miami Herald*, *The Philadelphia Inquirer* and *The Denver Post*.

Vocabulary

go-to	*adj.*	（为解决某个问题或做某件事情）必找的（人）
booklet	*n.*	小册子
pop up		突然出现
censorship	*n.*	审查；审查制度
rife	*adj.*	普遍的；流行的
stunt	*v.*	阻碍……的正常生长或发展

bestow	v.	授予
archetypal	adj.	典型的；原型的
whopping	adj.	巨大的
in line with		符合；与……一致
capitalize on		利用；使用
format	n.	（出版物的）版式，开本
astrology	n.	占星学；星座
gossip column		（报纸杂志的）八卦栏；花边新闻专栏
agony aunt		知心阿姨；报纸或杂志上回答读者来信并为他们的个人问题提出建议的撰稿人
take a leaf from/out of sb's book		效仿；模仿
salacious	adj.	淫秽的，色情的
paranormal	adj.	超常的
bona fide	adj.	真正的；真诚的
commuter	n.	上下班往返的人

Exercises

I. Match the subtitles with the related paragraphs.

1. Paragraphs 2–4   A. Moving Forward
2. Paragraphs 5–6   B. Broadsheets Today
3. Paragraphs 7–8   C. Tabloids vs. Broadsheets
4. Paragraphs 9–10   D. Newspaper Beginnings
5. Paragraphs 11–13   E. Broadsheet Paper Size
6. Paragraphs 14–15   F. The Emergence of the Tabloid
7. Paragraphs 16–17   G. "Above the Fold"

II. Complete the following timeline chart based on the text.

1618	"Corantos" ("currents of news") **1.** _____ in the Netherlands. *Courante uyt Italien, Duytslandt, &c.* is considered to be **2.** _____.
1712	The British government **3.** _____.
the 17th century	**4.** _____ was rife, with growth in readership stunted accordingly.
1771	The British Parliament **5.** _____.

Chapter 4 British Media—Broadcasting, Newspapers and Television

(Continued)

1785	**6.** _____, the oldest British newspaper, was founded.
1783	*The Pennsylvania Evening Post* **7.** _____.
1903	**8.** _____ was officially born in the UK.
1971, 1977, 2004, 2018	These years saw **9.** _____ of many UK broadsheet newspapers.

III. **There is one more section at the end of the article. Predict what it will be about and discuss with your partner.**

IV. **Compare your prediction with the following final part of the article.**

The Future of Broadsheets

When the New York-based *Wall Street Journal*, the country's second most-read newspaper, announced in 2005 that its overseas version would be converting to tabloid size, a conversation was started regarding whether the future of its original version, as well as many other American broadsheet newspapers, could, like many British papers, lie in a smaller, more compact format. However, this shift never happened, and any probability of it was squashed when the smaller international version itself switched back to broadsheet size a decade later.

And so, while *The Daily Telegraph* remains the last of the big broadsheet bastions in the UK, the future of the broadsheet in America looks as bright as ever, at least in terms of its paper size. Across the rest of the world the same seems to be true, with *The Times of India*, the world's most-circulated broadsheet, reaching almost three million readers each and every day.

V. **We all know that newspapers, whether broadsheets or tabloids, are experiencing difficult times these days. Where will broadsheets go in the future? How would Internet forces change them? Collect your ideas and write an essay of about 200 words entitled "The Future of Broadsheets".**

Further Reading

Text II The Era of the Press Barons*

The era of the **press barons** is often seen as a **maverick interlude** in the development of the press when newspapers became subject to the whims and **caprices** of their owners. According to this view, the press barons built vast press empires and ruled them like personal **fiefdoms**. In the hands of men like Beaverbrook and Rothermere, newspapers became mere "engines of **propaganda**", manipulated in order to further their political ambitions. As Stanley Baldwin declared in a memorable sentence, "What **proprietorship** of these papers is aiming at is power, and power without responsibility—the **prerogative** of the **harlot** throughout the ages."

The **despotic** rule of the press barons is usually compared unfavourably with a preceding "golden age" when proprietors played an inactive role and "sovereign" editors conducted their papers in a responsible manner. In some accounts, too, the era of Northcliffe and Rothermere is contrasted with the period after the World War II when journalists became more educated, independent and professional. The press barons have thus become favourite **bogeymen**: Their **indictment** has become a way of celebrating the editorial integrity of newspapers, both past and present.

But in reality the reign of the press barons did not constitute an exceptional **pathology** in the evolution of the press, but merely a continuation of tendencies already present before. Indeed, insofar as the barons may be said to have been **innovators**, it is not for the reasons that are generally given. They did not break with tradition by using their papers for political propaganda; their distinctive contribution was rather that they **downgraded** propaganda in favour of entertainment. Nor did they subvert the role of the press as a **fourth estate**; on the contrary it was they who detached the commercial press from the political parties and, consequently, from the state. What actually happened is, in some ways, the exact opposite of historical mythology.

The newspaper chains built by the press barons were not a new phenomenon. Multiple ownership of weekly newspapers had developed as early as the 18th century. Local daily chains had also emerged shortly after the regional daily

---

* Excerpted from James Curran & Jean Seaton. *Power Without Responsibility: The Press, Broadcasting, and New Media in Britain.* London: Psychology Press, 2003: 37.

Chapter 4 British Media—Broadcasting, Newspapers and Television

press was established in the mid-19th century. By 1884, for instance, a **syndicate** headed by the Scots-American steel **magnate** Carnegie controlled eight dailies and ten weeklies.

Although some papers controlled by the press barons gained a dominant market position, this too had happened before. *The Times*, for example, had dominated the respectable daily press during the early Victorian period. This recurring pattern arose from the unequal competitive relationship that developed between strong and weak papers. As soon as one paper gained a market lead, it was in a strong position to move further ahead because it had more money than its rivals from both sales and scale economies to invest in editorial development.

While the press barons reached a growing audience as a consequence of a rapid increase in circulation, this was also not new. There had been a sustained growth of newspaper consumption ever since the 17th century, and this growth was already accelerating before the press barons made their mark.

The large empires created by the press barons may thus be viewed as a continuation of three well-established trends—chain ownership, an expanding market and a tendency for a few papers to become dominant. All that happened was that some of these trends became more **pronounced** during the period of their **ascendancy**. In the first place there was, between 1890 and 1920, a rapid growth of newspaper chains which incorporated national as well as regional papers. By 1921 the three Harmsworth brothers controlled newspapers with an **aggregate** circulation of over six million—probably the largest press group in the Western world at the time.

Between the wars, concentration of press ownership entered a new phase, with the **spectacular** consolidation of the regional chains. The percentage of provincial evening **titles** controlled by the five big chains rose from 8% to 40% between 1921 and 1939; their ownership of the provincial morning titles also increased, from 12% to 44% during the same period. The power of the chains was extended further by the **elimination** of local competition. Between 1921 and 1937, the number of towns with a choice of evening paper fell from twenty-four to ten, while towns with a choice of local morning paper declined from fifteen to seven.

The principal pace-setters in the expansion of the regional chains were the Berry brothers, Lords Camrose and Kemsley. Their group grew from four daily and Sunday papers in 1921 to twenty daily and Sunday papers in 1939. This was achieved only after a **long-drawn-out** and costly "war" with Lord Rothermere, which was eventually resolved in a series of local treaties in which the three lords divided up different parts of the country between them.

There was also, during the inter-war period, an enormous increase in the sales of national dailies which for the first time overtook that of local dailies. Between 1920 and 1939 the combined circulation of the national daily press rose from 5.4 million to 10.6 million, while that of the local daily and weekly press remained relatively static. This major expansion of the London-based press meant that some proprietors gained enormous audiences even when they owned relatively few papers. This applied in particular to Lord Beaverbrook, controller of the *Daily Express*, the leading popular daily of the late 1930s.

These changes meant that, after the death of Lord Northcliffe in 1922, four men—Lords Beaverbrook, Rothermere, Camrose and Kemsley—became the dominant figures in the inter-war press. In 1937, for instance, they owned nearly one in every two national and local daily papers sold in Britain, as well as one in every three Sunday papers that were sold. The combined circulation of all their newspapers amounted to over thirteen million.

Vocabulary

press baron		报业巨头，报业大王
maverick	*adj.*	行为不合常规的，特立独行的
interlude	*n.*	（两事件之间的）间歇；插入事件
caprice	*n.*	任性；反复无常
fiefdom	*n.*	封地；采邑
propaganda	*n.*	宣传；鼓吹
proprietorship	*n.*	所有权；私营企业
prerogative	*n.*	特权
harlot	*n.*	妓女
despotic	*adj.*	专横的
bogeyman	*n.*	怪物，妖怪
indictment	*n.*	控告，谴责
pathology	*n.*	病态；反常
innovator	*n.*	改革者，创新者
downgrade	*v.*	降低
fourth estate		第四等级（新闻界的别称）
syndicate	*n.*	企业联合组织；财团

Chapter 4 British Media—Broadcasting, Newspapers and Television

magnate	*n.*	巨头，大亨
pronounced	*adj.*	显著的，明显的
ascendancy	*n.*	优势；支配地位
aggregate	*adj.*	总数的，总计的
spectacular	*adj.*	惊人的；庞大的
title	*n.*	（书刊的）一种，一本
elimination	*n.*	消灭，干掉（尤指敌人或对手）
long-drawn-out	*adj.*	拖长的；持续很久的

Unit 3

Television: An Idiotic Thing?

The world is at your door—It's here for everyone to view, conjured up in sound and sight, by the magic rays of light that bring television to you.

—Anonymous

Test Your Knowledge

I. Match the ways of delivering with the types of TV.

1. "over the air" by terrestrial radio waves
2. along coaxial cables
3. reflected off of satellites held in geostationary Earth orbit

A. cable TV
B. direct broadcast satellite, or DBS, TV
C. traditional broadcast TV

II. Match the electronic devices in the left column with the times they were introduced in the right column.

1. digital high-definition (HDTV) systems
2. RCA (Radio Corporation of America) demonstrated the first all-electronic TV
3. cable TV systems
4. recording or playback machines; VCR (Video Cassette Recorder)
5. colour TV

A. in 1932
B. in the late 1940s
C. in the 1950s
D. in the 1980s
E. in the 1990s

Chapter 4 British Media—Broadcasting, Newspapers and Television

Intensive Reading

Text I The Age of Show Business*

A dedicated graduate student I know returned to his small apartment the night before a major examination only to discover that his solitary lamp was broken beyond repair. After a **whiff** of panic, he was able to restore both his **equanimity** and his chances for a satisfactory grade by turning on the television set, turning off the sound, and with his back to the set, using its light to read important passages on which he was to be tested. This is one use of television—as a source of **illuminating** the printed page.

But the television screen is more than a light source. It is also a smooth, nearly flat surface on which the printed word may be displayed. We have all stayed at hotels in which the TV set has had a special channel for describing the day's events in letters rolled endlessly across the screen. This is another use of television—as an electronic **bulletin board**.

Many television sets are also large and sturdy enough to bear the weight of a small library. The top of an old-fashioned RCA **console** can handle as many as thirty books, and I know one woman who has securely placed her entire collection of Dickens, Flaubert, and Turgenev on the top of a 21-inch Westinghouse. Here is still another use of television—as bookcase.

I bring forward these quixotic uses of television to ridicule the hope harbored by some that television can be used to support the literate tradition. Such a hope represents exactly what Marshall McLuhan used to call "rear-view mirror" thinking: the assumption that a new medium is merely an extension or **amplification** of an older one; that an automobile, for example, is only a fast horse, or an electric light a powerful candle. To make such a mistake in the matter at hand is to **misconstrue** entirely how television redefines the meaning of public discourse. Television does not extend or amplify literate culture. It attacks it. If television is a continuation of anything, it is of a tradition begun by the telegraph and photograph in the mid-19th century, not by the printing press in the 15th.

What is television? What kinds of conversations does it permit? What are

---

* Excerpted from Neil Postman. *Amusing Ourselves to Death: Public Discourse in the Age of Show Business*. London: Penguin Books, 1985: 83–85.

the intellectual tendencies it encourages? What sort of culture does it produce?

These are the questions to be addressed in the rest of this book, and to approach them with a minimum of confusion, I must begin by making a distinction between a technology and a medium. We might say that a technology is to a medium as the brain is to the mind. Like the brain, a technology is a physical **apparatus**. Like the mind, a medium is a use to which a physical apparatus is put. A technology becomes a medium as it employs a particular **symbolic code**, as it finds its place in a particular social setting, as it **insinuates** itself into economic and political contexts. A technology, in other words, is merely a machine. A medium is the social and intellectual environment a machine creates.

Of course, like the brain itself, every technology has an inherent bias. It has within its physical form a **predisposition** toward being used in certain ways and not others. Only those who know nothing of the history of technology believe that a technology is entirely neutral. There is an old joke that **mocks** that naive belief. Thomas Edison, it goes, would have revealed his discovery of the electric light much sooner than he did except for the fact that every time he turned it on, he held it to his mouth and said, "Hello? Hello?"

Not very likely. Each technology has an agenda of its own. It is, as I have suggested, a metaphor waiting to unfold. The printing press, for example, had a clear bias toward being used as a linguistic medium. It is conceivable to use it exclusively for the reproduction of pictures. And, one imagines, the Roman Catholic Church would not have objected to its being so used in the 16th century. Had that been the case, the Protestant Reformation might not have occurred, for as Luther **contended**, with the word of God on every family's kitchen table, **Christians** do not require the **Papacy** to interpret it for them. But in fact there never was much chance that the press would be used solely, or even very much, for the **duplication** of **icons**. From its beginning in the 15th century, the press was perceived as an extraordinary opportunity for the display and mass distribution of written language. Everything about its technical possibilities led in that direction. One might even say it was invented for that purpose.

The technology of television has a bias, as well. It is conceivable to use television as a lamp, a surface for texts, a bookcase, even as radio. But it has not been so used and will not be so used, at least in America. Thus, in answering the question "What is television?" we must understand as a first point that we are not talking about television as a technology but television as a medium.

Chapter 4 British Media—Broadcasting, Newspapers and Television

There are many places in the world where television, though the same technology as it is in America, is an entirely different medium from that which we know. I refer to places where the majority of people do not have television sets, and those who do have only one; where only one station is available; where television does not operate around the clock; where most programs have as their purpose the direct **furtherance** of government **ideology** and policy; where commercials are unknown, and "**talking heads**" are the principal image; where television is mostly used as if it were radio. For these reasons and more television will not have the same meaning or power as it does in America, which is to say, it is possible for a technology to be so used that its **potentialities** are prevented from developing and its social consequences kept to a minimum.

Vocabulary

whiff	n.	一点点；些许
equanimity	n.	平静；镇定
illuminate	v.	照射；照亮
bulletin board		公告牌；布告栏
console	n.	控制台；仪表盘
amplification	n.	扩大；增强
misconstrue	v.	误解，曲解
apparatus	n.	设备；器具
symbolic code		符号代码
insinuate	v.	巧妙地（或许不诚实地）进入
predisposition	n.	倾向
mock	v.	嘲笑
contend	v.	声称；主张
Christian	n.	基督徒
Papacy	n.	罗马教皇职位；天主教会
duplication	n.	复制品；复制
icon	n.	圣像（如基督、圣母玛利亚等）
furtherance	n.	促进；助成
ideology	n.	意识形态；思想体系
talking head		（电视上的）发言者头部特写
potentiality	n.	潜力，潜能

英国社会与文化

Exercises

I. Choose the best option to answer each question or complete each statement.

1. For what purpose was the printing press invented?
   A. The exhibition and wide spread of written words.
   B. The reproduction of pictures of holy persons.
   C. The realization of its technical potential.
   D. The implementation of religious reform.

2. Which of the following does the author argue against?
   A. Television is a continuation of the creation of the telegraph and photograph.
   B. Television as a new medium is an extension of print media.
   C. The appearance of television bears a new meaning of public communication.
   D. Television can be used as a light source, an electronic bulletin board or a bookcase.

3. The following are distinctions made by the author between a technology and a medium **EXCEPT** that _____.
   A. a technology signifies real things that can be touched, seen, and felt, etc., whereas a medium is the reverse
   B. a technology is a container filled with medium
   C. it is compared to the relationship between the brain and the mind
   D. a medium sets the social context for a technology

4. The author tells the old joke about Thomas Edison to _____.
   A. admit the mistakes Edison made in the invention of the electric light
   B. make fun of the discovery story
   C. dismiss the belief that a technology is unbiased
   D. show that people who know little of the history of technology, like Thomas Edison, were simple-minded

5. How does the author consider the "rear-view mirror" thinking?
   A. He laughs at it.
   B. He hopes for it.
   C. He partly agrees with it.
   D. He assumes that it is right.

Chapter 4 British Media—Broadcasting, Newspapers and Television

II. **Match the boldfaced words with their meanings.**

1. The technology of television has a **bias**, as well.

2. the display and mass **distribution** of written language

3. It is **conceivable** to use television as a lamp.

4. There is an old joke that mocks that **naive** belief.

5. ...**sturdy** enough to bear the weight of a small library

6. a metaphor waiting to **unfold**

7. to **ridicule** the hope harbored by some

8. I bring forward these **quixotic** uses of television.

9. the hope **harbor**ed by some

10. a **dedicated** graduate student

A. strong and not easily damaged

B. from the character Don Quixote in the novel by Miguel de Cervantes, whose adventures are a result of him trying to achieve or obtain things that are impossible

C. a strong feeling in favour of or against one group of people, often not based on fair judgement

D. working hard at sth because it is very important to you

E. to make sth known to other people

F. to keep feelings or thoughts in your mind for a long time

G. the act of giving or delivering sth to a number of people

H. lacking experience of life, knowledge or good judgement and willing to believe that people always tell you the truth

I. that you can imagine or believe

J. to make sb/sth look silly by laughing at him/her or it

III. **Read the following introduction to two different views about recreational activities and answer the question: According to the text about television, whose vision does Postman think we ought to pay closer attention to?**

Postman's book *Amusing Ourselves to Death* opens with a Foreword that examines two literary dystopian (反乌托邦的) visions. George Orwell in *1984* warned about a tyrannical state where government overreach is responsible for the death of free speech and thought. Unlike George Orwell, Aldous Huxley in *Brave New World* foresaw that we would eventually be destroyed by that which we love most: entertainment, leisure, and laughter.

Further Reading

Text II The Medium Is the Message*

In a culture like ours, long accustomed to splitting and dividing all things as a means of control, it is sometimes a bit of a shock to be reminded that, in operational and practical fact, the medium is the message. This is merely to say that the personal and social consequences of any medium—that is, of any extension of ourselves—result from the new scale that is introduced into our affairs by each extension of ourselves, or by any new technology. Thus, with automation, for example, the new patterns of human association tend to eliminate jobs, it is true. That is the negative result. Positively, automation creates roles for people, which is to say depth of involvement in their work and human association that our preceding mechanical technology had destroyed. Many people would **be disposed to** say that it was not the machine, but what one did with the machine, that was its meaning or message. In terms of the ways in which the machine altered our relations to one another and to ourselves, it mattered not in the least whether it turned out **cornflakes** or **Cadillacs**. The restructuring of human work and association was shaped by the technique of **fragmentation** that is the essence of machine technology. The essence of automation technology is the opposite. It is integral and decentralist in depth, just as the machine was fragmentary, centralist, and superficial in its patterning of human relationships.

The instance of the electric light may prove illuminating **in this connection**. The electric light is pure information. It is a medium without a message, as it were, unless it is used to spell out some verbal ad or name. This fact, characteristic of all media, means that the "content" of any medium is always another medium. The content of writing is speech, just as the written word is the content of print, and print is the content of the telegraph. If it is asked, "What is the content of speech?", it is necessary to say, "It is an actual process of thought, which is in itself nonverbal." An abstract painting represents direct **manifestation** of creative thought processes as they might appear in computer designs. What we are considering here, however, are the psychic and social consequences of the designs or patterns as they amplify or accelerate existing processes. For the

---

* Excerpted from Marshall McLuhan. *Understanding Media: The Extensions of Man.* New York: The New American Library, 1964: 7–10.

Chapter 4 British Media—Broadcasting, Newspapers and Television

"message" of any medium or technology is the change of scale or pace or pattern that it introduces into human affairs. The railway did not introduce movement or transportation or wheel or road into human society, but it accelerated and enlarged the scale of previous human functions, creating totally new kinds of cities and new kinds of work and leisure. This happened whether the railway functioned in a tropical or a northern environment, and is quite independent of the **freight** or content of the railway medium. The airplane, on the other hand, by accelerating the rate of transportation, tends to **dissolve** the railway form of city, politics, and association, quite independently of what the airplane is used for.

Let us return to the electric light. Whether the light is being used for brain surgery or night baseball is a matter of indifference. It could be argued that these activities are in some way the "content" of the electric light, since they could not exist without the electric light. This fact merely underlines the point that "the medium is the message" because it is the medium that shapes and controls the scale and form of human association and action. The content or uses of such media are as diverse as they are **ineffectual** in shaping the form of human association. Indeed, it is only too typical that the "content" of any medium blinds us to the character of the medium. It is only today that industries have become aware of the various kinds of business in which they are engaged. When IBM discovered that it was not in the business of making office equipment or business machines, but that it was in the business of processing information, then it began to navigate with clear vision. The General Electric Company makes a considerable portion of its profits from electric light bulbs and lighting systems. It has not yet discovered that, quite as much as A.T. & T., it is in the business of moving information.

The electric light escapes attention as a communication medium just because it has no "content". And this makes it an invaluable instance of how people fail to study media at all.

For it is not till the electric light is used to spell out some brand name that it is noticed as a medium. Then it is not the light but the "content" (or what is really another medium) that is noticed. The message of the electric light is like the message of electric power in industry, totally radical, **pervasive**, and decentralized. For electric light and power are separate from their uses, yet they **eliminate** time and space factors in human association exactly as do radio, telegraph, telephone, and TV, creating involvement in depth.

A fairly complete handbook for studying the extensions of man could be made up from selections from Shakespeare. Some might **quibble** about whether or not he was referring to TV in these familiar lines from *Romeo and Juliet*:

> But soft! what light through **yonder** window breaks?
>
> It speaks, and yet says nothing.

In *Othello*, which, as much as *King Lear*, is concerned with the **torment** of people **transformed** by illusions, there are these lines that **bespeak** Shakespeare's intuition of the transforming powers of new media:

> Is there not charms
>
> By which the property of youth and **maidhood**
>
> May be abus'd? Have you not read Roderigo,
>
> Of some such thing?

In Shakespeare's *Troilus and Cressida*, which is almost completely devoted to both a psychic and social study of communication, Shakespeare states his awareness that true social and political navigation depends upon anticipating the consequences of innovation:

> The **providence** that's in a **watchful** state
>
> Knows almost every grain of Plutus' gold,
>
> Finds bottom in the uncomprehensive deeps,
>
> Keeps place with thought, and almost like the gods
>
> Does thoughts **unveil** in their dumb cradles.

The increasing awareness of the action of media, quite independently of their "content" or programming, was indicated in the annoyed and **anonymous stanza**:

> In modern thought, (if not in fact)
>
> Nothing is that doesn't act,
>
> So that is reckoned wisdom which
>
> Describes the **scratch** but not the **itch**.

Vocabulary

be disposed to		倾向于
cornflake	*n.*	玉米片

Chapter 4 British Media—Broadcasting, Newspapers and Television

Cadillac	*n.*	凯迪拉克轿车
fragmentation	*n.*	破碎；分裂
in this connection		在这一点上
manifestation	*n.*	表现；表现形式
freight	*n.*	货物
dissolve	*v.*	解除；消失
ineffectual	*adj.*	无效的，不起作用的
pervasive	*adj.*	弥漫的，遍布的
eliminate	*v.*	清除，消除
quibble	*v.*	争辩
yonder	*adj.*	那边的
torment	*n.*	（尤指精神上的）折磨，痛苦
transform	*v.*	使改变
bespeak	*v.*	显示，证明
maidhood	*n.*	少女时代
providence	*n.*	上帝；天意
watchful	*adj.*	注意的；警惕的
unveil	*v.*	（首次）公开，揭示
anonymous	*adj.*	匿名的，不知名字的
stanza	*n.*	（诗的）节，段
scratch	*n.*	挠痒
itch	*n.*	痒；渴望

Exercises

Chapter 5

A Country of Countries—Geography and Tourist Attractions

Introduction

As the first country to complete the Industrial Revolution, Britain used to be the most powerful country and the largest colony, but its national strength was seriously damaged after the two world wars, especially after the British Empire was disintegrated and the world hegemony was replaced by the United States. However, as one of the four largest economies in Europe and a highly developed capitalist country, Britain once again attracted the attention of the world because of its announcement of Brexit in 2017. What kind of country is Britain? What is the difference among England, Scotland, Wales and Northern Ireland? What do we mean by Great Britain?

Let us further explore the ancient and fresh British culture by understanding British geography, the history of their languages and people; experiencing the tradition and culture of Britain through the iconic River Thames, Stonehenge, White Cliff of Dover and so on. Choose your favorite UK destination by getting to know the major cities such as London, Belfast, Edinburgh and Cardiff. Don't just take the traveler's mind. Take the cultural learner's perspective, and understand Britain's past, present and future at its roots.

英国社会与文化

Geographical Divisions of United Kingdom

You tell your king that William Wallace will not be ruled...and nor will any Scot while I'm alive. Go back to England and tell them there that Scotland's daughters and sons are yours no more. Tell them Scotland is free.

—Movie: *Brave Heart*

 Test Your Knowledge

Search for relevant information to answer the following questions.

1. Who are the earliest inhabitants of Britain, of whom the English people have written records?
2. As for the four constituent nations of the UK, what is the local term for the population of each nation?
3. Since they are considered as the British citizens, do they have their own passports?

Intensive Reading

Text I The Differences Among the UK, Britain, Great Britain and England*

Lot of people get confused by different terms for the political or geographic body that includes England; some people will use Great Britain and the UK **interchangeably**. There are, however, some key differences among the United Kingdom, Britain, Great Britain and England.

Roman Britannia, or "Britain"

The name "Britain" comes from an old Roman name "Britannia", used for the regions we'd now identify as England and Wales. Britannia was the territory

---

* Retrieved from Infoplease website.

Chapter 5 **A Country of Countries—Geography and Tourist Attractions**

under Roman rule, which ended at Hadrian's Wall (which divided Scotland, or "Caledonia", from Britannia).

This should not be confused with Brittany in France. They are connected, though. Brittany was, at one time, called "Lesser Britain" (as opposed to "Great Britain") since it was settled by Britons from across the Channel.

England

England is a country that is part of the United Kingdom. England is the largest and most **populous** nation in the UK. It is bounded by Wales and the Irish Sea to the west and Scotland to the north. The English Channel, the Strait of Dover, and the North Sea separate it from Europe to the east. The Channel Islands like the Isle of Wight, off the southern mainland in the English Channel are considered part of England. The Isles of Sicily, in the Atlantic Ocean off the southwestern tip of the mainland, are also considered part of England.

Scotland

Scotland occupies the northern third of the island of Great Britain. It is bounded by England in the south and on the other three sides by water: by the Atlantic Ocean on the west and north and by the North Sea on the east. Scotland is divided into three physical regions—the Highlands; the Central Lowlands, containing two-thirds of the population; and the Southern Uplands. The western Highland coast is intersected throughout by long, narrow sea lochs, or fjords. Scotland also includes the Outer and Inner Hebrides and other islands off the west coast and the Orkney and Shetland Islands off the north coast.

Wales

Wales is a country that is part of the United Kingdom. It is bordered by England to the east, the Irish Sea to the north and west, and the Bristol Channel to the south. It had a population in 2011 of 3,063,456 and has a total area of 20,779 km^2 (8,023 sq mi). Wales has over 1,680 miles (2,700 km) of coastline and is largely mountainous with its higher peaks in the north and central areas, including Snowdon (Yr Wyddfa), its highest summit. The country lies within the North Temperate Zone and has a changeable, maritime climate.

Northern Ireland

Northern Ireland is a part of the United Kingdom that is variously described as a country, province, territory or region. Located in the northeast of the island of Ireland, Northern Ireland shares a border to the south and west with the Republic of Ireland. In 2011, its population was 1,810,863, constituting about 30% of the island's population and about 3% of the UK's population. The Northern Ireland Assembly (colloquially referred to as Stormont after its location), established by the Northern Ireland Act 1998, holds responsibility for a range of devolved policy matters, while other areas are reserved for the British government. Northern Ireland cooperates with the Republic of Ireland in several areas.

Great Britain

The island of Great Britain, also called "Albion" by the Romans, consists of three somewhat **autonomous regions** that include England, Scotland and Wales. It is located east of Ireland and northwest of France in the Atlantic Ocean. The term also includes several offshore islands, including the Hebrides in Scotland.

The United Kingdom

The United Kingdom (commonly abbreviated UK) is a country that includes England, Scotland, Wales and Northern Ireland. Its official name is the United Kingdom of Great Britain and Northern Ireland. While England, Wales, Scotland and Northern Ireland are called countries, there exist regulations and policies in those states that are determined by the UK. The capital city of the United Kingdom is London, although the different countries maintain **parliaments** in Cardiff (Wales), Edinburgh (Scotland), and Belfast (Northern Ireland).

The UK formerly **encompassed** the entire island of Ireland, and the islands were **collectively** referred to as the British Isles. But, in the early 20th century much of Ireland won **autonomy** as the Irish Free State, and later won independence as the Republic of Ireland.

The United Kingdom **comprises**, quite literally, the united kingdoms of Scotland and England. They shared **monarchs** for generations, but were distinct entities. That changed when the Scottish king James Stuart (James I of England and James VI of Scotland) inherited the throne of England from Elizabeth I. James was the grandson of Margaret Tudor, sister of Henry VIII. As Elizabeth I was childless, this made him her successor.

A century later, his descendant, Queen Anne of England, Scotland, and Ireland, would pass the Acts of Union. In England and Scotland both, the Parliament passed an act of union formalizing a melding of the two states. The result was the United Kingdom of Great Britain. This would later include Ireland after then Acts of Union of 1800.

Chapter 5 A Country of Countries—Geography and Tourist Attractions

Welsh people were long considered part of the Kingdom of England. They would not establish their own Parliament until the late 1990s.

The term UK also includes several dependencies and territories, nations that are politically distinct but rely on the UK for essential services. These include Gibraltar, the Isle of Man, and other smaller islands.

The Commonwealth of Nations

The **Commonwealth** of Nations is a voluntary association of 52 states or countries that were formerly part of the British Empire. This does not include the United States.

16 members of the Commonwealth of Nations recognize the United Kingdom's monarch as their own king or queen, but remain politically independent. These are identified as Commonwealth realms.

33 other Commonwealth countries are republics, which means they don't recognize a monarch. However, they still participate in the partnership.

The Commonwealth has no constitution. The Singapore Declaration of Commonwealth Principles, however, states that the Commonwealth is "a voluntary association of independent **sovereign** states each responsible for its own policies, consulting and co-operating in the common interests of their peoples and in the promotion of international understanding and world peace".

Vocabulary

interchangeably	*adv.*	可交换地
populous	*adj.*	人口稠密的
autonomous region		自治区
parliament	*n.*	议会，国会
encompass	*v.*	包围，环绕
collectively	*adv.*	集体地；共同地
autonomy	*n.*	自治；自治权
comprise	*v.*	是……的组成部分；构成
monarch	*n.*	君主，君王
Commonwealth	*n.*	英联邦
sovereign	*adj.*	（国家）有主权的，完全独立的

Exercises

I. Decide whether the following statements are true or false, and mark T or F accordingly.

_____ 1. The full spelling of the UK is the United Kingdom of Great Britain.

_____ 2. Great Britain is the largest and most populous nation in the UK.

_____ 3. Scotland is bounded by England in the south and on the other three sides by water: by the Atlantic Ocean on the west and north and by the North Sea on the east.

_____ 4. Even though Wales, Scotland and Northern Ireland are called countries, the UK cannot determine those states using regulations and policies.

_____ 5. The UK includes several dependencies and territories, nations that are politically distinct but rely on the UK for essential services.

_____ 6. The Commonwealth of Nations including the United States, is a voluntary association of 52 states or countries that were formerly part of the British Empire.

II. Translate the following sentences into Chinese.

1. The UK formerly encompassed the entire island of Ireland, and the islands were collectively referred to as the British Isles.

2. In England and Scotland both, the Parliament passed an act of union formalizing a melding of the two states.

3. The term UK also includes several dependencies and territories, nations that are politically distinct but rely on the UK for essential services.

4. 16 members of the Commonwealth of Nations recognize the United Kingdom's monarch as their own king or queen, but remain politically independent.

5. The Singapore Declaration of Commonwealth Principles, however, states that the Commonwealth is "a voluntary association of independent sovereign states each responsible for its own policies, consulting and co-operating in the common interests of their peoples and in the promotion of international understanding and world peace".

III. Please make some study and research about the British geography and history by yourself, take notes if you can, and tell your partner something about the rise and fall of the British Empire.

Further Reading

Text II People and Language*

Ethnic Groups

For centuries people have migrated to the British Isles from many parts of the world, some to avoid political or religious persecution, others to find a better way of life or to escape poverty. In historic times migrants from the European mainland joined the **indigenous** population of Britain during the Roman Empire and during the invasions of the Angles, Saxons, Jutes, Danes, and Normans. The Irish have long made homes in Great Britain. Many Jews arrived in Britain toward the end of the 19th century and in the 1930s.

After 1945 large numbers of other European refugees settled in the country. The large immigrant communities from the West Indies and South Asia date from the 1950s and 1960s. There are also **substantial** groups of Americans, Australians, and Chinese, as well as various other Europeans, such as Greeks, Russians, Poles, Serbs, Estonians, Latvians, Armenians, Turkish Cypriots, Italians, and Spaniards. Beginning in the early 1970s, Ugandan Asians (expelled by Idi Amin) and immigrants from Latin America, Southeast Asia, and Sri Lanka have sought refuge in Britain. People of Indian, Pakistani, and Bangladeshi origin account for more than half of the total ethnic minority population, and people of West Indian origin are the next largest group. The foreign-born element of the population is disproportionately concentrated in inner-city areas, and more than half live in Greater London.

Languages

All the traditional languages spoken in the United Kingdom ultimately **derive from** a common Indo-European origin, a tongue so ancient that, over the **millennia**, it has split into a variety of languages, each with its own **peculiarities** in sounds, grammar, and vocabulary. The distinct languages in what became

---

* Retrieved from Britannica website.

the United Kingdom originated when languages from the European continent developed independently in the British Isles, cut off from regular communication with their parent languages.

Of the surviving languages the earliest to arrive were the two forms of Celtic: the Goidelic (from which Irish, Manx, and Scottish Gaelic derive) and Brythonic (from which the old Cornish language and modern Welsh have developed). Among the contemporary Celtic languages Welsh is the strongest: About one-fifth of the total population of Wales are able to speak it, and there are extensive interior upland areas and regions facing the Irish Sea where the percentage rises to more than half. Scottish Gaelic is strongest among the inhabitants of the islands of the Outer Hebrides and Skye, although it is still heard in the nearby North West Highlands. Because less than 2% of Scots are able to speak Gaelic, it has long since ceased to be a national language, and even in northwestern areas, where it remains the language of religion, business, and social activity, Gaelic is losing ground. In Northern Ireland very little Irish is spoken. Similarly, Manx no longer has any native speakers, although as late as 1870 it was spoken by about half the people of the Isle of Man. The last native speakers of Cornish died in the 18th century.

The second link with Indo-European is through the ancient Germanic language group, two branches of which, the North Germanic and the West Germanic, were destined to make contributions to the English language. Modern English is derived mainly from the Germanic **dialects** spoken by the Angles, Saxons, and Jutes (who all arrived in Britain in the 5th century) and heavily influenced by the language of the Danes (Vikings), who began raiding the British Isles about 790 and subsequently colonized parts of northern and eastern England. The Humber became an important linguistic as well as a geographic boundary, and the English-speaking territory was divided into a Northumbrian province (roughly corresponding to the kingdom of Northumbria) and a Southumbrian province (in which the most important kingdoms were Mercia, Wessex, and Kent). In the 8th century Northumbria was foremost in literature and culture, followed for a short time by Mercia; afterward Wessex predominated politically and linguistically until the time of King Edward the Confessor.

Although the French-speaking Normans were also of Viking stock, the English population initially regarded them as much more of an **alien** race than the Danes. Under the Norman and Angevin kings, England formed part of a continental empire, and the prolonged connection with France retained by its

Chapter 5 A Country of Countries—Geography and Tourist Attractions

new rulers and landlords made a deep impression on the English language. A **hybrid** speech combining Anglo-Saxon and Norman French elements developed and remained the official language, sometimes even **displacing** Latin in public documents, until the mid-14th century, when late Middle English, a language heavily influenced by Norman French, became the official language. This hybrid language subsequently evolved into modern English. Many additions to the English language have been made since the 14th century, but the Normans were the last important linguistic group to enter Britain.

Vocabulary

indigenous	*adj.*	本土的
substantial	*adj.*	大量的
derive from		来自
millennia	*n.*	千年期
peculiarity	*n.*	独特性
dialect	*n.*	方言，土话
alien	*adj.*	陌生的；外国的
hybrid	*adj.*	混合的；混合而成的
displace	*v.*	取代；置换

Exercises

英国社会与文化

Unit 2

Historical Heritage and Landscape

Stonehenge was built possibly by the Minoans. It presents one of man's first attempts to order his view of the outside world.

—Stephen Gardiner

Test Your Knowledge

I. Match the names of the tourist attractions with the corresponding pictures.

1. 　　　　　　　　　　***A.*** Westminster Abbey

2. 　　　　　　　　　　***B.*** Big Ben

3. 　　　　　　　　　　***C.*** Tower Bridge

4. 　　　　　　　　　　***D.*** 10 Downing Street

Chapter 5 A Country of Countries—Geography and Tourist Attractions

II. Match the Chinese translations of the scenic spots with their English names.

1. 大英博物馆   A. Roman Baths
2. 罗马浴场   B. British Museum
3. 爱丁堡城堡   C. The Elephant House
4. 大象咖啡馆   D. Edinburgh Castle
5. 环球剧场   E. Arthur's Seat
6. 亚瑟王座   F. Globe Theatre

Intensive Reading

Text I Stonehenge-Era Pig Roasts United Ancient Britain, Scientists Say*

A new study of bones discarded after prehistoric barbeques is providing unexpected insight into the first "pan-British" gatherings.

A surprising study of leftovers from 4,500-year-old pig roasts reveals that prehistoric **ceremonial** sites around Stonehenge served as "pan-British" centers that helped bring together **disparate** populations of Neolithic peoples from across the island for the first time. The study was published today in the journal *Science Advances*.

During the late Neolithic period in Britain (around 2800–2400 BC), large feasts were held at ceremonial centers in southern England such as Durrington Walls, where the builders of Stonehenge likely lived, and Marden, the largest circular earthworks in Britain.

Excavations at Durrington Walls, for example, have shown that enormous feasts took place there during the winter, when **celebrants** roasted and ate large quantities of pork and the occasional cow. Of the 8,500 bones recovered at Durrington, for instance, pigs outnumbered cattle ten to one.

The presence of large amounts of pig bones at other similar ceremonial sites in the region reinforces the idea that the prehistoric pork roast was a late

---

* Retrieved from National Geographic website.

Neolithic phenomenon in southern England. Researchers, however, remained unsure whether the purpose of these feasts was to unify a local population—much like a community barbeque—or to **forge** alliances between neighboring groups.

Now, a chemical analysis of the pig bones is revealing an unexpected result: The ceremonial sites, and the feasts hosted there, served as **lynchpins** of vast social networks across the island "demonstrating a level of interaction and social complexity not previously appreciated".

Pigs as Proxy

In recent years, scientists have tried to answer the question of how **far-flung** the feasters were with **strontium isotope** analysis, a technique that identifies a unique chemical signature that reflects the geological area which a human or animal lived in. Previous isotopic studies of **cremated** human remain at Stonehenge and cattle bones from Durrington Walls suggest that both may have come to the ceremonial sites from considerable distances—some as far as modern Wales.

Until now, however, researchers never bothered with analyzing the isotopic signatures of pig bones recovered from sites like Durrington Walls, assuming that the pigs would have been bred locally near the feasting centers where they were **butchered** and eaten, and therefore would provide little useful information on where the feasters themselves came from. Cattle would have been driven by humans across great distances and could therefore be used as a **proxy** for human movement, they reasoned, but long-distance pig herding?

"I was worried that the pigs wouldn't tell us where these people were coming from," says Richard Madgwick, a lecturer in **archaeological** science at Cardiff University and lead author on the *Science Advances* article.

However, the new isotopic analysis of 131 pig remains from four different late Neolithic ceremonial sites (Durrington Walls, Marden, Mount Pleasant, and West Kennet Palisade Enclosures) reveals that the vast majority of pigs consumed at the sites were not raised locally, but rather brought by feasters from many different areas in Britain, including Wales and Scotland—at distances of at least 30 miles and potentially more than 350 miles.

The fact that these ceremonial centers drew people from many different areas in Britain, and often from considerable distances, suggests that these feasting sites weren't just for local or regional gatherings, but rather evidence for the first "pan-British" events in history.

Chapter 5 A Country of Countries—Geography and Tourist Attractions

Swine Drives

The results are also making researchers re-think their assumptions about pigs as proxies for human movement. "I was indeed quite surprised," at the number of pigs brought into the Neolithic ceremonial centers from great distances, says Christophe Snoeck, a post-doctoral researcher at the Vrije Universiteit Brussel who performed the strontium analysis on human remains from Stonehenge but was not involved in the current study. Snoeck also praised the fact that multiple isotopes—not just strontium—were analyzed in the pig remains, providing a richer insight into where the pigs were raised and what they ate.

For instance, the study notes that the pigs from Durrington Walls came from very different environments based on strontium, oxygen, and **sulfur** isotope signatures, but had a similar carbon isotope signature, which suggests they ate a similar diet. Madgwick believes that this may reflect the enormous scale of the feasts at Durrington Walls, which meant that feasters weren't raising pigs on scraps in small household operations, but rather driving large stocks of swine through prehistoric forests to **forage**.

"The feasters weren't Neolithic couch potatoes," Madgwick says, noting that people were going to "great lengths" to bring pigs to the ceremonial feasts.

This makes sense to Mark Essig, author of *Lesser Beasts: A Snout-to-Tail History of the Humble Pig*, who has studied hog droving in the United States. "It's a false assumption that you can't herd a pig," he says, noting that in the 19th century, the animals were regularly moved on foot between central Kentucky and coastal South Carolina.

"These pigs weren't Wilbur or Babe. Pigs in the Neolithic looked like wild **boar** or **feral** pigs—skinnier with longer legs. They would have been **agile** and hearty enough to make a long journey on foot."

Vocabulary

ceremonial	*adj.*	仪式的，礼节的；(职务) 礼仪性的，象征性的
disparate	*adj.*	不同的，不相干的，全异的
excavation	*n.*	挖掘，发掘
celebrant	*n.*	宗教庆典的主持者；宗教庆典的参加者
forge	*v.*	创造，缔造（关系、形式、环境）
lynchpin	*n.*	关键
far-flung	*adj.*	遥远的

英国社会与文化

strontium isotope		锶同位素
cremate	v.	焚烧，火化（尸体），（尤指）火葬
butcher	v.	屠宰；宰杀
proxy	n.	代理人，代表
archaeological	adj.	考古学的；考古的
sulfur	n.	硫；硫磺
forage	v.	觅食；搜寻
boar	n.	野猪
feral	adj.	野生的（尤指喂养后逃脱的）
agile	adj.	敏捷的，灵活的

Exercises

I. **Choose the best answer to each question.**

1. In the late Neolithic period in Britain, what were held at ceremonial centers in southern England?

   A. Large banquets.　　B. Fireworks.
   C. Big parties.　　D. Dance parties.

2. Which of the following makes people believe that celebrants roasted and ate large quantities of pork at Durrington Walls?

   A. Scientists unveiled the fossils of pork and beef at Durrington Walls.
   B. According to the historian, many books have recorded the feast of Durrington for having a pork barbeque.
   C. The number of pig bones counted 90% of 8,500 bones discovered at Durrington.
   D. Anthropologists admitted that there was evidence of pigs and many other cattle.

3. Which of the following is the ratified purpose of the winter feasts at Durrington Walls?

   A. To forge alliances between tribes like Anglos and Saxons during the early period of time.
   B. To unify a local population.
   C. To hold a community potluck or barbeque.
   D. To serve as lynchpins of vast social networks across the island "demonstrating a level of interaction and social complexity not previously appreciated".

138

Chapter 5 **A Country of Countries—Geography and Tourist Attractions**

    4. What has been done to make analysis towards the far-flung feasts?

        A. Strontium isotope analysis.

        B. Analyzing the element of carbon-14 in the ruins at Durrington.

        C. Using X-ray machines and analyzing the X-ray plates.

        D. Scientists used laboratories to analyze the remains in the soil.

II. Translate the following sentences into Chinese.

    1. A new study of bones discarded after prehistoric barbeques is providing unexpected insight into the first "pan-British" gatherings.

    2. Of the 8,5000 bones recovered at Durrington, for instance, pigs outnumbered cattle ten to one.

    3. The presence of large amounts of pig bones at other similar ceremonial sites in the region reinforces the idea that the prehistoric pork roast was a late Neolithic phenomenon in southern England.

    4. Researchers, however, remained unsure whether the purpose of these feasts was to unify a local population—much like a community barbeque—or to forge alliances between neighboring groups.

III. Hubei Provincial Museum is a primary institution of cultural relics collection, exhibition and promotion as well as an important research center of archaeological exploration, discovery and relic protection in the province. It is said that the discovery of the chime bell set has rewritten the history of world music. Please write an essay describing your favorite museum with special historical discoveries. You should write at least 200 words.

Text II The White Cliffs of Dover—Things to See and Do*

Introduction of the White Cliffs of Dover

    The famous White Cliffs of Dover are a chalk formation in the southeast

---

* Retrieved from National Trust website.

of the island of Great Britain. The cliffs look out on the narrowest part of the English Channel, which stretches between Great Britain and the continent of Europe.

A cliff is a mass of rock that rises very high and is almost vertical, or straight up-and-down. Cliffs are very common landscape features. They can form near the ocean (sea cliffs), high in mountains, or as the walls of **canyons** and valleys. Waterfalls **tumble** over cliffs.

Cliffs are usually formed because of processes called **erosion** and **weathering**. Weathering happens when natural events, like wind or rain, break up pieces of rock. In coastal areas, strong winds and powerful waves break off soft or **grainy** rocks from harder rocks. The harder rocks are left as cliffs.

The tiny pieces of rocks broken off by weathering are called **sediment** or **alluvium**. Erosion is the process of transportation of this sediment. On sea cliffs, sediment becomes part of the seafloor and is washed away with the waves. On inland cliffs, sediment is often carried away by rivers or winds.

Larger rocks broken off by sediment are called **scree** or **talus**. Scree builds up at the bottom of many inland cliffs as rocks tumble down. These piles are called scree slopes or talus piles. Some scree slopes can be so large that soil and sediment can build up between the rocks, allowing trees and other vegetation to grow on the slope.

Ever Changing Views

The views from the White Cliffs of Dover are perpetually changing. When it is gloriously sunny and the sea is calm and smooth as glass you can wander across the cliffs and take in the breath-taking views across the Channel. On the clearest of days you may even be able to see the buildings in France.

On a winter's day make sure you wrap up warm and with rosy cheeks experience the peaceful **tranquility** of a **hazy** cliff top walk. Even when the weather takes a turn for the worse and it pours with rain the view from the Visitor Centre is striking. Watch as the waves crash over the sea wall and the ferries heave in the violence of a storm.

Cliff Top Wildlife

Fields of Flowers

Amongst the wealth of wildflowers on the cliffs there is a surprising variety of **orchids**, the most nationally rare being the Early Spider Orchid, with yellow-

Chapter 5 A Country of Countries—Geography and Tourist Attractions

green to brownish green petals with a flower that looks like the body of a large spider. This small plant flowers for just two months in April and May.

Very similar in appearance to an orchid but not from the same family is the Oxtongue Broomrape. Best recognized by its yellow to straw colored stems bearing yellow, white or blue snapdragon-like flowers, this delicate flower can be seen dotting the cliff top walk from June to September.

Another plant that **adorns** the cliff top is Viper's-bugloss. This highly **flamboyant** plant is easily seen due to its vivid shades of blue and purple with rough petals and red tongue-like **stamens**. Viper's-bugloss can sometimes be overlooked in its longer flowering period of June to September.

Beautiful Butterflies

Such a wealth of wildflowers attracts an abundance of insect life, including around 30 different species of butterflies. So keep your eyes peeled for the graceful flutter of wings on your cliff top walk.

Perhaps one of our most rare butterflies is the Adonis Blue. The male of this species has vibrant blue wings which are lined with a white margin, whereas the females are a rich chocolate brown. In contrast to the jewel like top, the undersides of the wings are a malty brown with a string of black spots and a row of orange near the margin. These can be seen on the wing in two **broods**, from mid-May to late June and then again from early August to the end of September.

Things to Do

A Little Walk

We have a wheelchair friendly footpath that leads to a viewing point, ideal if you just want a short walk to see the iconic cliffs. This all weather path is built with a **staggered** incline, allowing a few **breathers** on the way up and is ideal if the weather is bad. At the top is one of the best views of the cliffs with the rolling green hilltops and sheer chalk edge, dropping to the sea below.

Guided Tours to Historical Places

Here at the White Cliffs of Dover we are able to offer not only a wonderful walk with breath-taking views, but also guided tours around two historical places.

The first place that you come to, only a mile and a half from the Visitor Centre, is Fan Bay Deep Shelter. After an extraordinary volunteer effort we opened the World War II tunnel complex and two World War I Sound Mirrors in

英国社会与文化

2015 and now take you on a fantastic hard hat head torch lit adventure.

The second special place to be reached on the cliff walk is South Foreland Lighthouse. This Victorian marvel is a Tardis that has witnessed an incredible amount of history, science and innovation. The infamous Mrs. Knott's tea room offers delicious treats and with kite flying and games the lighthouse also holds fun for all the family.

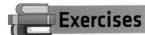

Vocabulary

canyon	n.	峡谷
tumble	v.	翻滚
erosion	n.	侵蚀，腐蚀
weathering	n.	风化作用
grainy	adj.	颗粒状的
sediment	n.	沉积；沉积物
alluvium	n.	冲击层；冲击土
scree	n.	岩屑堆
talus	n.	岩堆，岩屑堆；山麓堆积
tranquility	n.	宁静，安静
hazy	adj.	雾蒙蒙的；朦胧的
orchid	n.	兰花
adorn	v.	装饰
flamboyant	adj.	艳丽的；火焰似的
stamen	n.	雄蕊
brood	n.	一窝幼雏；（一次孵或生的）一窝动物
staggered	adj.	交错的；错开的
breather	n.	短时间的休息

Exercises

Chapter 5 A Country of Countries—Geography and Tourist Attractions

Unit 3

A Tour to Major Cities: Landmarks and Spectaculars

What would I put in a museum? Probably a museum! That's an amusing relic of our past.

—John Hodgman

 Test Your Knowledge

I. Search for relevant information to answer the following questions.

1. What are the names for the countries of Great Britain? Point out the categories each of them may fall into.
2. What are the location, size and landform features of Britain?
3. What role did Britain play in shaping the modern world?
4. What are the large mountain ranges and the highest mountain peaks of Britain?
5. What are the large rivers and lakes you know in Britain? Point out their length or size.
6. Can you find the four big seaside-resort towns of Britain on the map and tell where they are located?
7. What is the climate like in Britain? Point out its three features.
8. What natural resources is Britain blessed with?
9. Among Britain's natural resources, which is the most important to the country's economy? Tell its distribution.
10. What special animals and birds can be found in Britain?

II. Could you illustrate some famous landmarks of London?

III. Translate the following geographical names into Chinese.

1. the United Kingdom of Great Britain and Northern Ireland
2. the Strait of Dover
3. the English Channel

4. Greenwich
5. the Channel Islands
6. the Thames River
7. the Severn River
8. Lake Neigh
9. Lake District
10. the Isle of Man
11. Edinburgh
12. Glasgow
13. Cardiff

Intensive Reading

Text I Six of London's Best Small Museums and Why You Should Visit Them Now*

Beyond the capital's famous museums are over 100 smaller cultural institutions, many at threat of closing due to the impact of coronavirus. From the Garden Museum to Pitzhanger Manor, here are six hidden gems to discover now.

For museum-lovers, London is hard to beat. Some of the world's best museums are here, and no other city boasts as many **entries** in the world's top 10 most-visited. Tate Modern, the National Gallery, the British Museum and Natural History Museum are ranked among the most popular on the planet. But London's reputation as a museum capital is not just because of the big names. Crammed into all corners of the city are well over 100 small museums that bring millions of art, culture and history fans flocking to explore them each year. That is, until 2020—the year the global pandemic arrived.

International visitors have all but dried up, and the hesitancy of domestic visitors to visit museums is reflected in largely **lackluster** booking figures. For London's small museums, which nearly all rely on admission fees, shops and cafés for their income, this has dealt them a financial blow. Many are facing a

---

* Retrieved from National Geographic website.

Chapter 5 A Country of Countries—Geography and Tourist Attractions

fight for survival.

So, as they begin to reopen after **lockdown** (employing resourceful social distancing and safety measures), now's the time to start ticking them off. Small museums can be fun and fascinating, and visiting now will provide a much-needed financial **lifeline** to these important institutions in these precarious times, helping to ensure London's rich museum scene continues to thrive. Here are six of the best to get started with.

The Garden Museum

A calm **oasis** away from the **hustle and bustle** of city life, the Garden Museum is a real treat for **horticulturalists** and **amateur** gardeners alike. Housed in a **converted** medieval church in Lambeth with a sleek modern extension, the museum celebrates all the charms of British gardens through historical objects, art and temporary exhibitions. After exploring the displays, visitors should enjoy the inner courtyard of **exotic** plants. There are even two Victorian mausoleums hiding among the foliage.

Pitzhanger Manor

The Regency country manor in which this west London museum is set would be worth a visit in its own right, but this is no ordinary house. It was built by one of Britain's most **visionary** architects, Sir John Soane, as a rural retreat when Ealing was just a village. It was the "laboratory" where he put all of his most innovative ideas into practice, and today it's open to visitors after a major **restoration**. It's a pure joy to explore, a magnificent temple to the tastes of the early 19th century. Plus, a new gallery for **contemporary** art alongside just adds to the draw.

Charles Dickens Museum

Literary history was made in this five-storey townhouse in Holborn. It was here that Charles Dickens wrote *Oliver Twist* and *Nicholas Nickleby,* turning the author into an international superstar by the time he moved out in 1839. To visit now is to step back in time to early Victorian London, as the museum is presented as Dickens and his young family lived in it. You can nose around everything from the study where he penned these iconic novels, to the **wine cellar** and servants' washhouse.

Florence Nightingale Museum

Easily missed in the grounds of St. Thomas' Hospital, on the south side of Westminster Bridge, this small museum is the very definition of a hidden gem.

英国社会与文化

Once located, visitors explore the life and pioneering career of the Lady with the Lamp (said lamp from the Crimean War is one of the highlight objects). New for 2020 is an immersive display looking at her legacy in the bicentenary of her birth. It would be a tragic irony if the museum celebrating the founder of modern nursing falls victim to the current health crisis.

Museum of London Docklands

Often overshadowed by its larger sister museum in the Square Mile, the Museum of London Docklands punches well above its weight. Fascinating displays on the history of London as a port city are fused with full-sized replicas of a 19th-century **ramshackle** riverside district. (Not many museums allow you to sit in a sailor's tavern!) It's one of London's most family-friendly museums, but there is plenty here for all ages. Entry is free, so donations will be welcome.

The Brunel Museum

This tiny museum is a celebration of an engineering feat briefly regarded as the Eighth Wonder of the World. The Thames Tunnel, designed by Marc Isambard Brunel, was the world's very first underwater tunnel, opening in 1843. The turbulent story of the project is explored, but the real treat is a visit to the Grand Entrance Hall. Recently reborn as a performance venue deep beneath London, this **cavernous** space is half the size of Shakespeare's Globe. Descend to the bottom to be just inches from the hurtling trains now using the Tunnel.

Vocabulary

entry	n.	进入，加入；登记，录入
lackluster	adj.	萎靡不振的；乏善可陈的
lockdown	n.	（对人或者交通工具的）活动限制；封锁
lifeline	n.	命脉；救生索
oasis	n.	（困苦中）令人快慰的地方（或时刻）；（沙漠中的）绿洲
hustle and bustle		熙熙攘攘；忙碌
horticulturalist	n.	园艺家
amateur	adj.	业余的；非专业爱好的
converted	adj.	经过改造的，修改的
exotic	adj.	奇异的；异国风情的
manor	n.	庄园；领地
visionary	adj.	有眼力的；远见卓识的
restoration	n.	（对建筑或艺术品的）修复；修复物

Chapter 5 **A Country of Countries—Geography and Tourist Attractions**

contemporary	*adj.*	当代的，现代的
wine cellar		酒窖
ramshackle	*adj.*	（建筑物等）摇摇欲坠的，破败不堪的
cavernous	*adj.*	大而空的；像洞穴的

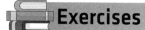

Exercises

I. Choose the best option to each question.

1. What is the main idea of the article?

A. The big museums' survival strategies during the pandemic.

B. The introduction of best small museums in the city of Manchester.

C. A collection of introductory description of six of London's best small museums that visitors might be very interested in.

D. A comparison and contrast between the six different small museums in London.

2. Which of the following statements is true?

A. Florence Nightingale Museum is a very small museum in memory of the famous doctor Florence Nightgale who led a pioneering career of reforming the hospital system in the UK.

B. One of the museums worth visiting in Ealing, London is the West London Museum built by the architect, Sir John Soane.

C. The Brunel Museum is a celebration of an engineering feat named Channel Tunnel, which has the longest undersea portion of any tunnel in the world.

D. Charles Dickens Museum is a five-storey townhouse located in Holborn where Dickens published his masterpieces of *Nicholas Nickleby* and *Oliver Twist*.

3. What makes Museum of London Docklands so special?

A. It displays a lot of historical photos of London as a port city thousands years ago.

B. It is not entrance free, but allows visitors to stand in a sailor's tavern.

C. It is much larger than its sister museum in the Square Mile.

D. The museum has full-sized replicas and people of all ages can visit this family-friendly museum.

4. According to passage, which of the following is **NOT** a reason that small museums are facing a fight for survival?

147

A. Most of the small museums are closed after lockdown due to the government's strict rules of social distancing and safety measures.

B. International visitors have dried up.

C. Without any sponsor or financial support from big firms, running a small museum would definitely face a lot of financial crisis during and after the global pandemic.

D. The small museums are too hard to be found geographically to attract and hold the hesitant domestic visitors.

II. Translate the following statements into Chinese.

1. International visitors have all but dried up, and the hesitancy of domestic visitors to visit museums is reflected in largely lackluster booking figures.

2. A calm oasis away from the hustle and bustle of city life, the Garden Museum is a real treat for horticulturalists and amateur gardeners alike.

3. Literary history was made in this five-storey townhouse in Holborn. It was here that Charles Dickens wrote *Oliver Twist* and *Nicholas Nickleby*, turning the author into an international superstar by the time he moved out in 1839.

4. Fascinating displays on the history of London as a port city are fused with full-sized replicas of a 19th-century ramshackle riverside district.

5. The Thames Tunnel, designed by Marc Isambard Brunel, was the world's very first underwater tunnel, opening in 1843. The turbulent story of the project is explored, but the real treat is a visit to the Grand Entrance Hall.

Further Reading

Text II How to Experience Belfast's Cultural Scene like a Local*

The Northern Irish capital has blossomed into a true cultural hotspot, **replete** with bold street art, galleries and a string of hip **boutiques**.

Art and Soul

Belfast is best explored on foot, so strike out and get your bearings in the Cathedral Quarter, a **rejuvenated** trade and **warehousing** district that today

---

* Retrieved from National Geographic website.

Chapter 5 A Country of Countries—Geography and Tourist Attractions

claims the best bars, restaurants and galleries in the city. Among its highlights are Belfast Exposed, a **pull-no-punches** photography gallery with its roots in the divided city of the 1980s, and the MAC (Metropolitan Arts Centre), the big fish of the city's cultural scene, which has run a varied program of visual art, theatre and dance since it opened in 2012. The permanent work in the MAC's foyer is worth a nose, too; Irish artist Mark Garry's piece sees 400 metal wires weave **a spectrum of** color through the space.

If urban art's your thing, a two-hour tour led by local artists shares the inside track on the city's street art scene. There's an ever-changing **itinerary**, but pieces like Smug's **riveting** portrait of a chef on High Street Court, and MTO's *Son of Protagoras*, which portrays a **crouching** figure bearing a dove **pierced** by a pair of arrows, already feel iconic.

Night owl? The first Thursday of every month sees up to 20 galleries welcoming visitors for celebrations of visual art. From 18:00 to 21:00, you can visit galleries like Platform or Artisann Gallery, have a drink and meet some of the artists. Pick your own route or join an organised bus tour; coaches leave from Linen Hall Library.

Shop'til You Drop

Victoria Square is the city's best mall, but Belfast is a city that rewards **hunter-gatherers**. For a ladies' fashion fix, call in at Envoy of Belfast on Wellington Street, a boutique offering labels like Simone Rocha and Paul Harnden. Men should **make a beeline for** The Bureau and its stylish independent labels.

"If you can't get it in Sawers, you can't get it anywhere", the local saying goes. Swing by Northern Ireland's oldest deli to stock up on regional **nibbles** like Abernethy butter or Ewing's smoked salmon. Cheese **fiends** shouldn't miss Mike's Fancy Cheese—its **honking** Young Buck is one of the best blue cheeses on the island.

Beyond the centre, the Lisburn Road is dubbed Belfast's "style mile"—but do your research to prevent the waste of a taxi fare. DeJa Vu, with its designer **cast-offs**, is a reliable bet.

Finally, if you need a one-stop shop for local crafts, applied art and design, hit up Space Craft. The College Street hub sells everything from lampwork glass earrings to hand-painted silk scarves and tableware.

The Best Places to See Art in Belfast

The following are the best places to see art in Belfast as suggested by Adam Turkington, owner/manager of Seedhead Arts, a Belfast-based arts **consultancy**.

The Black Box

I think this is the most important arts organization in the city. It's been a petri dish for outsider art, as well as small and interesting events and festivals in Belfast for the past 12 years.

Duel of Belfast, Dance by Candlelight

This **mural** by Conor Harrington is one of the oldest pieces on our street art tour. It echoes our history and the idea of fighting over things that don't matter while everything is collapsing around us.

Golden Thread Gallery

This is a really well **curated** contemporary arts space on Great Patrick Street. You'll find small experimental stuff—and, well, really big, ambitious, experimental stuff. It's always on my list.

CS Lewis Square

Celebrating the local author with Narnia-inspired statues, this square has transformed this part of the city along with the East Side Visitor Centre. It's a short walk from Boundary Brewing, which I'd consider Ireland's best **brewery**.

Sunflower Public House

There's music every night at this spot on the corner of Kent Street and Union Street. There's plenty of street art on display in the bar, as well as on the surrounding streets.

Top tip: Sunday trading rules mean many bigger shops don't open until 1 pm, so Belfast can feel like a ghost town in the mornings. Use the time to see big-hitters like Titanic Belfast (book ahead) or the Ulster Museum.

Vocabulary

replete	*adj.*	充满；充足
boutique	*n.*	时装店；精品店
incorporate	*v.*	包含
rejuvenated	*adj.*	恢复活力的
warehousing	*n.*	仓储
pull-no-punches	*adj.*	毫无保留的；不客气的
a spectrum of		连续的；连串的
itinerary	*n.*	行程；旅行日程

Chapter 5 A Country of Countries—Geography and Tourist Attractions

riveting	*adj.*	吸引人的
crouch	*v.*	蜷缩，蹲下
pierce	*v.*	扎；刺破；穿透
hunter-gatherer	*n.*	采集者；狩猎者
make a beeline for		径直朝……走去，走直路
nibble	*n.*	点心，小吃
fiend	*n.*	对……有嗜好的人；着魔者
honking	*adj.*	（车辆喇叭）鸣响般的
cast-off	*n.*	遗弃之人或物
consultancy	*n.*	咨询公司；顾问工作
mural	*n.*	壁画
curated	*adj.*	仔细挑选并展览的
brewery	*n.*	啤酒厂；啤酒公司

Chapter 6

Entertainment—Sports, Movies and TV Series

Introduction

How would the Britons enjoy their leisure time? Why are they fascinated with sports, especially football, tennis and cricket? Why are British films so popular and successful? What are the popular TV series worthwhile for us to appreciate? How did the Britons successfully hold three Olympic Games in London to manifest the Olympic spirit? What are the remarkable performances of the brilliant athletes? In this chapter, we intend to help you learn further about the Britons' common ways of entertainment, like sports, films and TV series. Besides, you could also feel the pride and excitement of Britons and their fascination with sports and competition from their experiences of holding three Olympic Games successfully in London.

英国社会与文化

Sports: Widespread Participation

I've missed more than 9,000 shots in my career. I've lost almost 300 games. 26 times, I've been trusted to take the game-winning shot and missed. I've failed over and over and over again in my life. And that is why I succeed.

—Michael Jordan

 Test Your Knowledge

I. **Discuss the following questions with your partner.**

1. What kind of sports would young people in the UK participate in?

2. What reasons do people have for participating in various kinds of sports? Please illustrate at least three reasons for a certain sport.

3. What qualities do you think a good sportsman should possess?

II. **Match the following sports with their descriptions.**

A. rugby   1. The players have not necessarily any personal connection with the town for whose team they play. Many players travel thousands of miles to attend the Wembley Stadium Championship games at the end of each season.

B. rowing   2. Today, all union teams of this sport have 15 players positioned in two lines. Since the players do not wear protective clothing, bruises and injuries are frequent.

C. football   3. A first-class match lasts for up to three days, with six hours' play on each afternoon.

D. golf   4. The courses of this sport are usually meeting places of the business community, which are very desirable for bank managers.

E. cricket   5. This sport, in fours or eights, occupies a leading place in the sporting life of schools and universities which have suitable water nearby.

Chapter 6 Entertainment—Sports, Movies and TV Series

Intensive Reading

Text I Sports in the UK*

Sports of all kinds play an important part in many people's lives. There are several sports that are particularly popular in the UK. Many sporting events take place at major stadiums such as Wembley Stadium in London and the Millennium Stadium in Cardiff.

Local governments and private companies provide sports **facilities** such as swimming pools, tennis courts, football pitches, dry ski slopes and **gymnasiums**. Many famous sports, including cricket, football, lawn tennis, golf and rugby, began in Britain.

The UK has hosted the Olympic Games on three occasions: 1908, 1948 and 2012. The main Olympic site for the 2012 Games was in Stratford, East London. The British team was very successful, across a wide range of Olympic sports, finishing third in the medal table.

The **Paralympic** Games for 2012 were also hosted in London. The Paralympics have their origin in the work of Dr. Sir Ludwig Guttman, a German refugee, at the Stoke Mandeville hospital in Buckinghamshire. Dr. Guttman developed new methods of treatment for people with **spinal** injuries and encouraged patients to take part in exercise and sport.

Cricket

Cricket originated in England and is now played in many countries. Games can last up to five days but still result in a draw! The **idiosyncratic** nature of the game and its complex laws are said to reflect the best of the British character and sense of fair play. You may come across expressions such as "rain stopped play", "batting on a sticky wicket", "playing a straight bat", "bowled a **googly**" or "it's just not cricket", which have passed into everyday usage. The most famous competition is the Ashes, which is a series of test matches played between England and Australia.

Football

Football is the UK's most popular sport. It has a long history in the UK and

---

* Excerpted from Jenny Wales. *Life in the United Kingdom: A Guide for New Residents* (3rd ed.). London: TSO, 2013: 84.

the first professional football clubs were formed in the late 19th century.

England, Scotland, Wales and Northern Ireland each have separate leagues in which clubs representing different towns and cities compete. The English Premier League attracts a huge international audience. Many of the best players in the world play in the Premier League. Many UK teams also compete in competitions such as the UEFA (Union of European Football Associations) Champions League, against other teams from Europe. Most towns and cities have a professional club and people take great pride in supporting their home team. There can be great **rivalry** between different football clubs and among fans.

Each country in the UK also has its own national team that competes with other national teams across the world in tournaments such as the FIFA (Fédération International de Football Association) World Cup and the UEFA European Football Championships. England's only international tournament victory was at the World Cup of 1966, hosted in the UK.

Football is also a popular sport to play in many local communities, with people playing amateur games every week in parks all over the UK.

Rugby

Rugby originated in England in the early 19th century and is very popular in the UK today. There are two different types of rugby, which have different rules: union and league. Both have separate leagues and national teams in England, Wales, Scotland and Northern Ireland (who play with the Republic of Ireland). Teams from all countries compete in a range of competitions. The most famous rugby union competition is the Six Nations Championship between England, Ireland, Scotland, Wales, France and Italy. The Super League is the most well-known rugby league (club) competition.

Horse Racing

There is a very long history of horse racing in Britain, with evidence of events taking place as far back as Roman times. The sport has a long association with royalty. There are **racecourses** all over the UK. Famous horse racing events include: Royal Ascot, a five day race meeting in Berkshire attended by members of the Royal Family; the Grand National at Aintree near Liverpool; and the Scottish Grand National at Ayr. There is a National Horseracing Museum in Newmarket, Suffolk.

Chapter 6 Entertainment—Sports, Movies and TV Series

Golf

The modern game of golf can be traced back to 15th-century Scotland. It is a popular sport played socially as well as professionally. There are public and private golf courses all over the UK. St. Andrews in Scotland is known as the home of golf. The Open Championship is the only "Major" tournament held outside the United States. It is hosted by a different golf course every year.

Tennis

Modern tennis evolved in England in the late 19th century. The first tennis club was founded in Leamington Spa in 1872. The most famous tournament hosted in Britain is The Wimbledon Championships, which takes place each year at the All England Lawn Tennis and **Croquet** Club. It is the oldest tennis tournament in the world and the only "Grand Slam" event played on grass.

Water Sports

Sailing continues to be popular in the UK, reflecting their maritime heritage. A British sailor, Sir Francis Chichester, was the first person to sail **single-handed** around the world passing the Cape of Good Hope (Africa) and Cape Horn (South America), in 1966/1967. Two years later, Sir Robin Knox-Johnston became the first person to do this without stopping. Many sailing events are held throughout the UK, the most famous of which is at Cowes on the Isle of Wight.

Rowing is also popular, both as a leisure activity and as a competitive sport. There is a popular yearly race on the Thames between Oxford and Cambridge Universities.

Motor Sports

There is a long history of motor sport in the UK, for both cars and motor cycles. Motor car racing in the UK started in 1902. The UK continues to be a world leader in the development and **manufacture** of motor-sport technology. A Formula 1 Grand Prix event is held in the UK each year and a number of British Grand Prix drivers have won the Formula 1 World Championship. Recent British winners include Damon Hill, Lewis Hamilton and Jensen Button.

Skiing

Skiing is increasingly popular in the UK. Many people go abroad to ski and there are also dry ski slopes throughout the UK. Skiing on snow may also be possible during the winter. There are five ski centres in Scotland, as well as Europe's longest dry ski slope near Edinburgh.

英国社会与文化

Vocabulary

facility	n.	设施
gymnasium	n.	体育馆
Paralympic	n.	残奥会
spinal	adj.	脊髓的；脊柱的
idiosyncratic	adj.	特殊的
googly	n.	外曲线球；变向曲线球
rivalry	n.	竞争；较劲
tournament	n.	锦标赛；联赛
racecourse	n.	赛马场；跑马场
croquet	n.	槌球戏；循环球戏
single-handed	adv.	单独地；单枪匹马地
manufacture	n.	制造；制造业

Exercises

I. Decide whether the following statements are true or false, and mark T or F accordingly.

_____ 1. There are many sports that are originated from Britain, including football, tennis, cricket, golf and rugby.

_____ 2. Dr. Guttman made great contribution to the Paralympic Games by developing new methods of treatment.

_____ 3. The Olympic Games have been held in Britain for three times: in 1908, 1948 and 2016 respectively.

_____ 4. It is a pity that Britain has never won any championship in the international tournaments of football.

_____ 5. The Six Nations Championship is a well-known rugby league competition.

_____ 6. The Wimbledon Championships is the oldest tennis tournament in the world.

_____ 7. St. Andrews in Scotland is regarded as the home of tennis.

_____ 8. Sir Francis Chichester was the first British sailor to sail around the world on his own.

_____ 9. Europe's longest dry ski slope is near Edinburgh in Scotland.

Chapter 6 Entertainment—Sports, Movies and TV Series

II. Fill in the blanks with the appropriate forms of the words in the box.

> idiosyncratic   separate   watering   significant
> respectively   increasingly   attend   originate
> associate   tournament   manufacture   hold
> audience   fascinate   popularity   continue
> complicated

There is no doubt that sports have played a(n) **1.** _____ role in the UK. The Olympic Games have been **2.** _____ in London in 1908, 1948 and 2012 **3.** _____. As for the sports **4.** _____ by the British people, football should rank the first. Not only in the UK, but also **5.** _____ from all over the world watch the English Premier League. Cricket **6.** _____ in England and games can last up to five days but still result in a draw, due to its **7.** _____ nature and **8.** _____ rules. There are two different types of rugby: union and league, both of which have **9.** _____ leagues and national teams in the UK. Horse racing is closely **10.** _____ with royalty, and Royal Ascot is **11.** _____ by members of the Royal Family. Golf and tennis also enjoy **12.** _____ in the UK and have well-known **13.** _____ called "The Open Championship" for golf and "Wimbledon" for tennis. Sailing and rowing belong to the category of **14.** _____ sports, which are also very popular. The UK **15.** _____ to be a world leader in the development and **16.** _____ of motor-sport technology. Skiing has **17.** _____ attracted the interest of people at home and abroad.

III. Match the famous British sporting events with the descriptions.

   A. The Ashes   1. the only "Major" golf tournament held outside the United States

   B. The UEFA Champions League   2. a football competition between teams in Europe

   C. The FIFA World Cup   3. a football competition between countries across the world

   D. Royal Ascot   4. a rowing competition held on the River Thames

   E. The Open Championship   5. the oldest tennis tournament in the world

F. The Wimbledon Championships

G. The Oxford and Cambridge University Boat Race

H. Formula 1 Grand Prix

6. a cricket competition between England and Australia

7. a five-day race meeting in Berkshire attended by members of the Royal Family

8. a motor sport held in the UK each year

IV. Match the expressions with their explanations.

A. rain stopped play

B. bat on a sticky wicket

C. play a straight bat

D. bowl a googly

E. It's just not cricket.

F. result in a draw

1. to fight to a standoff

2. to be in a difficult situation in which you find it hard to deal with your problems

3. to do something that you did not expect and is difficult for you to deal with

4. a game is suspended because of heavy rain

5. to do things in an honest and simple way because you have traditional ideas and values

6. It is not fair, honest or moral.

Further Reading

Text II Association Football or Soccer*

Although there have been games recorded around the world involving balls being kicked around a field, the modern rules of Association Football, **aka** soccer, can be traced back to mid-19th century England. By **standardising** the many different rules that existed at that time, the great public schools of England could at last compete with each other on a fair and level playing field.

The history of football being played in England dates back many centuries.

---

* Retrieved from Historic UK website.

Chapter 6 Entertainment—Sports, Movies and TV Series

Medieval or mob football was often played between neighbouring towns and villages, with a mass of players from opposing teams clashing to deliver an inflated pig **bladder** from one end of town to the other. Kicking or **punching** the bladder, or ball, was permitted, as was doing the same to your opponents... these medieval matches were **chaotic** and had very few rules.

Mob football can still be seen throughout England today, generally played on Shrove Tuesday. Royal Shrovetide Football takes place at Ashbourne, Derbyshire, with other Shrove Tuesday Football Games being played at Atherstone, Warwickshire and Corfe Castle in Dorset, to name but a few.

Disturbed by the adverse effect that football was having on the good citizens of London, King Edward II banned the game from the city. Later in 1349, his son Edward III banned football entirely, concerned that the game was **distracting** men from practising their **archery**. Following the massive loss of life suffered as a consequence of the Black Death, England needed as many archers as possible in order to achieve Edward's military ambitions in both France and Scotland.

Known for his sporting **prowess** in his early years, Henry VIII is believed to have owned the first pair of soccer boots, when in 1526 the royal footwear collection was recorded as including "...45 **velvet** pairs and 1 leather pair for football". Perhaps due to his increased waistline and hence his inability to compete at the highest level, Henry later banned the game in 1548, claiming that it **incited** riots.

The reputation of football as a violent game appears again and again throughout the 16th and 17th centuries in documented accounts, not only from England, but by this time the popularity of the sport appears to have spread to Ireland, Scotland and Wales.

It was in the slightly more civilised surroundings of Cambridge University that in 1848, representatives from the major public schools of England met to agree the laws that would standardise the games played between them. The Cambridge Rules were duly noted and formed the code that was adopted by the football teams of Eton, Harrow, Rugby, Shrewsbury and Winchester public schools. This also ensured that when the students **eventually** arrived at Cambridge, they all played the same game!

These were not the only rules in place for the game at that time, however, as throughout the 1850s, many clubs not associated with the universities or schools continued with their own version of football. Yet another set of rules, known as the Sheffield Rules were used by a number of clubs in the north of England.

It took a hard headed Yorkshireman to finally bang heads together and produce the first comprehensive set of rules for the game. Born in Hull, Ebenezer Cobb Morley had moved to London at the age of 22, to further his career as a **solicitor**. A keen sportsman and captain of the Barnes Club, Ebenezer **instigated** a meeting on the morning of 26th October 1863 at the Freemason's Tavern in Great Queen Street, London, that would **ultimately** lead to the formation of the Football Association, or the FA as it is perhaps better known today.

It took five further meetings at the Freemasons, between October and November that year, for the FA to produce the first comprehensive rules of football. Even then at the last meeting, the FA treasurer from Blackheath withdrew his club, angered by the removal of two draft rules; the first would have allowed players to pick up and run with the ball in hand, the other **prohibited** a player from tripping up and holding onto an opponent. Other clubs also withdrew their support from the FA and went on to join with Blackheath to form the Rugby Football Union; the term soccer was now commonly used to **distinguish** between the two codes of football.

Meanwhile, showing true Yorkshire grit, Ebenezer along with the eleven remaining clubs, went on to **ratify** the original thirteen laws of the game. Although some northern clubs remained loyal to the Sheffield Rules well into the mid-1870s, the FA continued to **tweak** its laws until there was little difference between the two games.

Today the laws of the game are governed by the International Football Association, which was formed in 1886 after a meeting in Manchester between the Football Association, the Scottish Football Association, the Football Association of Wales and the Irish Football Association. The first ever international football match was played on 30th November 1872 between Scotland and England. Played at the West of Scotland Cricket Club ground at Hamilton Crescent in Glasgow, the match finished in a 0–0 draw and was watched by around 4,000 spectators.

Today the game is played across the world by millions, with billions more armchair supporters preferring to watch the game on television. It appears that the "beautiful game" remains close to its historic violent roots however, when in 1969 it caused a four-day war between El Salvador and Honduras and later in May 1990, when a match between Dinamo Zagreb and Red Star Belgrade **deteriorated** into rioting.

As that well-known Liverpool FC manager and footballing legend Bill

Chapter 6 Entertainment—Sports, Movies and TV Series

Shanklyso **eloquently** put it, "some people believe football is a matter of life and death. I am very disappointed with that attitude. I can assure you it is much, much more important than that."

Vocabulary

aka	*abbr.*	又名，亦称（also known as）
standardise	*v.*	使……标准化，使……统一
medieval	*adj.*	中世纪的
bladder	*n.*	可充气的囊袋
punch	*v.*	用拳猛击
chaotic	*adj.*	混乱的，无秩序的
distract	*v.*	使分心
archery	*n.*	箭术
prowess	*n.*	英勇，勇猛
velvet	*adj.*	天鹅绒的
incite	*v.*	煽动；刺激
eventually	*adv.*	最后；终于
solicitor	*n.*	律师；法务官
instigate	*v.*	使（正式）开始；使发生
ultimately	*adv.*	最后；基本上
prohibit	*v.*	阻止，禁止
distinguish	*v.*	区分，辨别
ratify	*v.*	核准；认可
tweak	*v.*	（非正式）稍微调整
deteriorate	*v.*	恶化；变坏
eloquently	*adv.*	富于表现力地

Exercises

英国社会与文化

Unit 2

What's So Fascinating of British Films?

To make a great film you need three things—the script, the script and the script.

—Alfred Hitchcock

 Test Your Knowledge

I. Match the types of film with their features.

1. animated film
2. cartoon
3. comedy
4. costume drama
5. documentary
6. drama
7. horror
8. romantic comedy
9. sci-fi
10. thriller

A. a short humorous film in which the characters are drawn
B. a film that is set in the future and there are some imaginary scientific developments
C. a type of film which combines comedy with a love story
D. a film with a very exciting story that often involves a crime
E. a film that tries to make the audience laugh
F. a film that tells a true story, often shown on television
G. a film in which the characters are drawn, made by computer or made from models
H. a historical film, often made famous by the clothes the actors wear
I. a film which tries to make the audience very frightened
J. a serious film

II. Choose one British film that you are most fascinated with, make a brief introduction of its title, type, plot and so on, but do not reveal the ending. Then make your own comment on this film.

Chapter 6 Entertainment—Sports, Movies and TV Series

Intensive Reading

Text I The Highest-Grossing British Films of All Time*

—The Trouble of Working out Homegrown Success on a Hollywood Scale

What makes a British film British? British financing? A British cast and crew? Danny Dyer?

The official BAFTA (British Academy of Film and Television Arts) definition defines it as any film with "significant British involvement" that is also **certified** as British by the BFI (British Film Institute). Getting more complicated, the BFI **grants** a film "British status" (for the purposes of tax **relief**) if it scores at least 16 points out of a possible 31 in a cultural test to assess its Britishness. Things get stickier still when you actually read the list of questions and poke into some of the **loopholes**.

Gravity, for example, was given BAFTA in 2014 for Outstanding British Film—qualifying because it was filmed in an English studio, and because Mexican director Alfonso Cuaron happened to have a house in London at the time. The same year, *Mandela: Long Walk to Freedom* was **nixed** because it was a non-British story, based on a non-British book and co-financed by a country (South Africa) that wasn't on a qualifying **shortlist**—despite having a mostly British cast, crew, director and production.

In short, it's almost impossible to work out exactly what **constitutes** a British film—which makes it tricky to work out which British films have taken the most at the box office. Sticking to the industry guidelines, the following films make up the top 10 (only about three of which actually seem like British films):

Star Wars: The Force Awakens (2015)

Worldwide gross: $2,068,223,624

Avengers: Infinity War (2018)

Worldwide gross: $2,046,452,723

Harry Potter and the Deathly Hallows Part 2 (2011)

Worldwide gross: $1,341,511,219

---

*   Retrieved from Den of Greek website.

Beauty and the Beast (2017)

Worldwide gross: $1,263,521,126

Skyfall (2012)

Worldwide gross: $1,108,561,013

The Dark Knight Rises (2012)

Worldwide gross: $1,084,939,099

Rogue One: A Star Wars Story (2016)

Worldwide gross: $1,056,057,273

The Dark Knight (2008)

Worldwide gross: $1,004,558,444

Harry Potter and the Philosopher's Stone (2001)

Worldwide gross: $974,755,371

Harry Potter and the Deathly Hallows Part 1 (2010)

Worldwide gross: $960,283,305

Star Wars: *The Force Awakens* tops the list, letting Britain claim ownership of the third highest-grossing film of all time—beaten only by *Avatar* and *Titanic*. Disney and Lucasfilm (and J. J. Abrams) might seem as American as they come, but the film qualified for a British passport by being mostly filmed at Pinewood Studios, using Industrial Light & Magic (ILM)'s London office for the bulk of the digital effects, and by having a largely Brit cast and crew.

London's superior studio facilities at Pinewood, Elstree, Shepperton and Leavesden (not to mention Twickenham's recent $50 million investment in Liverpool) give the British film industry a massive boast—with UK technical crews and production talent now working on more than half of the highest grossing Hollywood productions made in the 20 years.

Still, the list can be a bit **deceiving**. For most of us, when we think about "British film", we don't **immediately** think about *Star Wars*. Britain has a long history of making great independent films that aren't **beholden** to Hollywood—with most **exhibiting** the kind of left-field, **understated**, **quirky** charm that leans into whatever **weirdness** defines the national character.

Avengers Infinity War might technically be a British film, but it feels every inch like an American movie because it's based on American comics, starring American actors, from an American studio.

Chapter 6 Entertainment—Sports, Movies and TV Series

A more suitable list might be the following—counting down the highest grossing independent British films that were financed in the UK:

The King's Speech (2011)

Worldwide gross: $414,211,549

Slumdog Millionaire (2009)

Worldwide gross: $377,910,544

Four Weddings and a Funeral (1994)

Worldwide gross: $245,700,832

Paddington (2014)

Worldwide gross: $268,047,808

The Full Monty (1997)

Worldwide gross: $257,938,649

Paddington 2 (2017)

Worldwide gross: $226,882,399

The Woman in Black (2012)

Worldwide gross: $127,730,736

The Inbetweeners Movie (2011)

Worldwide gross: $88,025,781

The Inbetweeners 2 (2014)

Worldwide gross: $63,852,235

A Fish Called Wanda (1988)

Worldwide gross: $62,493,712

The King's Speech made the leap across the Atlantic so successfully in part because it won so many Oscars (**ditto** for *Slumdog Millionaire*) and others like *Paddington* and *The Woman in Black* worked because they had such a big crossover appeal. How the comedy of *The Inbetweeners* worked on foreign audiences is less clear—although the bulk of the box office for both movies came from the UK and Australia.

Finally, there's the **inflation** problem. *Avatar* might officially be the highest grossing film of all time, but that's mostly just because it cost more to see it in 2009 than it would have done in 1939. Adjusting the all-time gross list for inflation, James Cameron's film only ranks at number 15—with *Gone with the Wind* taking the top spot.

Taking all of international film-going history into account, *Star Wars: The Force Awakens* still comes out as the highest grossing (official) British film, none of the independents makes the top 300 and *Thunderball* beats *Skyfall* by almost 200 places.

Deciding what constitutes a British film is hard enough, but working out which one made the most money is almost impossible. The good news is that the British film industry is doing better now than it's ever done before—**generating** more than $3 billion for the UK and recently **outperforming** the **pharmaceutical** sector in employment and revenue.

A lot of key professionals are worried about the effect Brexit might have on the industry's continued success—since the business relies heavily on people from other countries being able to work in the UK for long stretches—but with more Bond, more Marvel, more *Star Wars* and many more independents already in the works at British studios, there's likely to be plenty of boom still to come before we have to start worrying about the bust.

Vocabulary

highest-grossing	*adj.*	创票房最高纪录的；高票房的
certify	*v.*	证明
grant	*v.*	（合法地）授予
relief	*n.*	减免
loophole	*n.*	漏洞
nix	*v.*	拒绝
shortlist	*n.*	最后候选人名单
constitute	*v.*	构成
deceiving	*adj.*	有欺骗性的
immediately	*adv.*	立即
beholden	*adj.*	欠……人情的
exhibit	*v.*	展现出
understated	*adj.*	不惹眼的；低调的，朴素的
quirky	*adj.*	古怪的
weirdness	*n.*	不可思议
ditto	*adj.*	相似的

Chapter 6 Entertainment—Sports, Movies and TV Series

inflation	*n.*	通货膨胀
generate	*v.*	产生
outperform	*v.*	胜过
pharmaceutical	*adj.*	制药的

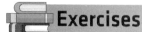
Exercises

I. **Choose the best answer to each of the following questions.**

1. How can a film be possibly certified as British by the BFI?

   A. It should have scored at least 16 points in a literal test.

   B. It should have significant British involvement like being filmed in an English studio, or the director having housing estates in the UK.

   C. It should have a mostly British cast, crew, director and production.

   D. It should be based on British comics, starring British actors, and from an British studio.

2. Which is **NOT** the reason why *Star Wars: The Force Awakens* is qualified for a British passport?

   A. It was mostly filmed at Pinewood Studios.

   B. It used ILM's London office for the bulk of the digital effects.

   C. Its director happened to have a house in London at that time.

   D. It had a largely Brit cast and crew.

3. Which of the following is **NOT** the place for the British superior studio facilities to give the British film industry a massive boast?

   A. Hollywood.   B. Pinewood.

   C. Elstree.   D. Shepperton.

4. How did the author describe the independent British films not beholden to Hollywood?

   A. They are based on American comics, starring American actors, and from an American studio.

   B. They have a mostly British cast, crew, director and production.

   C. They are mostly filmed at London's superior studio facilities.

   D. They are mostly left-field, understated and quirky.

5. Which one is true according to the passage?

   A. *The King's Speech* was very popular across the Atlantic due to the problem of inflation.

B. *Paddington* tops the list because it has won so many Oscars.

C. The director of *Gravity* happened to have a house in London in 2014.

D. When it comes to the "British film", we would immediately think about *Star Wars*.

6. What's the author's attitude towards the future of British film industry?

A. Worried.

B. Suspicious.

C. Optimistic.

D. Pessimistic.

II. **Fill in the blanks with the appropriate forms of the phrases in the box.**

> poke into   in short   in part   stick to
> make up for   not to mention   cut down   make the leap
> take the most advantage   take into account

1. Shanghai plans to build a vast underground network of malls, restaurants, and parking lots to _____ a lack of space above ground.

2. Do you think our civilization will survive long enough to _____ to deeper space?

3. The new age of machinery, _____, could not have been born without a new source of both movable and constant power.

4. She and her family have been forced to move out of Missouri, _____ because of cyber attacks.

5. When buying an apartment, people usually _____ its price, position, surroundings and so on.

6. Some people complain about the unfairness, merely because they cannot _____ out of it.

7. Lots of periodicals in foreign languages have been subscribed to, _____ those in Chinese.

8. Dieting and exercising can bring your weight under control but you must _____ your plan with perseverance.

9. Even the most harmless small talk can _____ areas we might rather not talk about.

10. In a recession, consumers could be expected to _____ on nonessentials like toys.

III. Watch one of the films mentioned in this passage, describe one scene that has impressed you the most and make your own comment for at least 200 words. Please cite specific examples to support your point of view.

Further Reading

Text II British Film History*
—The Mystery That Started It All

The very first motion picture camera **patented** in the world was patented in England by French-born Louis Aimé Augustin Le Prince in 1888. The first films were made on a **sensitised** paper roll a little over 2 inches wide. In 1889, Prince was able to obtain **celluloid** roll film from Eastman when it was introduced in England. Prince started commercial development of his motion picture camera in early 1890 with an updated version. He arranged for a demonstration to M. Mobisson, the Secretary of the Paris Opera. On September 16, 1890, Prince boarded a train at Dijon bound for Paris with his motion picture camera and films. He never arrived in Paris. No trace of Prince or his motion picture camera were ever found. The mystery was never solved. Two **fragments** of film are all that has survived from Prince and his camera. Both taken in 1888, one was at 10 frames per second and one at 20 frames per second.

Everything basically stood still for the next 5 years. In 1895, George Trajedis, a Greek showman, approached R. W. Paul who owned an optical instrument works in Saffron Hill, to manufacture some Edison **Kinetoscope** projectors. Edison had not patented them in the UK. Once they were made, Edison refused to sell films for **pirated** machines, so Paul approached Birt Acres to help construct a camera to shoot their own films. They obtained film from the American Celluloid Co. of Newark, N. J. and started filming their own with Birt Acres as the cameraman. Their first screening was at the London headquarters of the Royal Photographic Society, 14 Hanover Square on January 14, 1896.

On February 20, 1896, French magician Felicien Trewey had the first screening before a paying audience using a Lumiere Cinematopraphe at the

---
* Retrieved from Learn About Movie Posters website.

Regent Street Polytechnic in London. He had a three week engagement and charged one shilling. The first showing outside of London was by Birt Acres at Cardiff Town Hall on May 5, 1896. The first commercial showing of a film that they produced was the Oxford and Cambridge University Boat Race which was shown at Earl's Court on May 27, 1896.

Over the next few years, William Friese-Greenmade excellent advancements toward the creation of the British cameras. Unfortunately his technology was not successfully incorporated into any practical application. G. A. Smith devised the first colour system, **Kinemacolor**, in 1908. By 1909, Pathe and Gaumont began flooding the British market with films and the UK fell rapidly behind.

World War I brought the UK film industry almost to a halt. Immediately after the war, though efforts were made to resume production and pick up the industry, films remained very live theatre oriented, filming a play exactly as it had been performed on stage and with the same actors and sets. British film industry did not keep pace with the advances being made abroad and quickly became technically out of date. The British public wanted to see American films, and by 1918, there was no money left for home production.

This continued on a downward trend until production stopped in 1924. Finally the Parliament stepped in to help by passing the Cinematographers Trade Bill, which was designed to ensure there was a **guaranteed** home market for British made films. It limited the number of movies coming from other countries to give home studios a chance. The result was more British movies, but the majority of them were of very poor quality.

The **advent** of sound offered more challenges to the British film industry's financial stability. In 1929 for example, 138 films were made and the growth looked **promising**. In 1933, J. Arthur Rank, who had started by making religious films, founded British National. In 1935, he went into partnership with C. M. Woolf to take over Pinewood Studios.

At the same time, Oscar Deutsch was building up the Odeon chain of cinemas. But by 1937, the boom turned into a **slump**. The year before, the British film industry had over produced, making 220 pictures. The result was poorly made, rushed films that were not worth watching and nobody wanted. This had a **backlash** effect and opened the door to the American industry, and American companies started buying the British production companies so they would qualify under the home market **quota**.

Chapter 6 Entertainment—Sports, Movies and TV Series

Soon with the start of World War II, the industry took another turn. Many of the studio employees were engaged in the war, reducing available manpower. Half the studio space was **requisitioned** for military purposes, and only an average of 60 films were produced annually. The British public demanded more realistic films, so British studios turned to documentaries and war related movies.

After the war, the Rank Organization became the dominant force in the industry. The shift was to make British films more acceptable to the audiences outside of the UK. In addition, television caused such a **tremendous** decline in attendance that British theaters were closing in record numbers. Studios **switched** to producing TV shows and TV movies to stay **afloat**. Even though there were a few bright spots over the next few decades like Hammer Films, the British production on its own was rather **bleak**.

In the late 50s, 60s and 70s, restrictions on the US studios soon had US studios looking at the UK as a production ground, almost like US studio **outposts**. There was such an **influx** of US production in the UK that American finances virtually took over the British industry. Some of this produced a large group of British actors that in the US were thought of as US actors instead of British... These included such fine actors as: Albert Finney, Alan Bates, Tom Courtney, Richard Harris, Julie Christie, Richard Todd, Laurence Harvey, Richard Burton, Peter Finch, Peter Sellers, Terrence Stamp, Donald Pleasance, Paul Scofield and directors such as Richard Attenborough, Brian Forbes and Ken Russell.

The late 70s and 80s saw British production turning to more television production and branching into more special effects studios for major US studios like *Superman*, *Star Wars* and the *James Bond* series. But by the late 80s, there seemed to be a major decline in US production in the UK.

With this **vacuum** being created, there seems to have started a **renewal** of independently made British movies. Through the 90s, British production has increased with such hits as *Trainspotting, Brassed Off, Elizabeth, The Full Monty,* etc. Hopefully the trend will continue to stabilize with more solid British production.

Vocabulary

patent	*v.*	授予专利
sensitised	*adj.*	（照相胶卷）感光的
celluloid	*n.*	[美俚] 电影（胶片）

fragment	*n.*	片段或不完整部分
Kinetoscope	*n.*	活动电影放映机
pirated	*adj.*	盗版的
Kinemacolor	*n.*	彩色电影
guaranteed	*adj.*	有保证的
advent	*n.*	出现
promising	*adj.*	有前途的
slump	*n.*	低潮期
backlash	*n.*	反冲
quota	*n.*	配额
requisition	*v.*	征用
tremendous	*adj.*	极大的
switch	*v.*	改变（立场、方向等）
afloat	*adj.*	经济上周转得开的
bleak	*adj.*	无希望的；黯淡的
outpost	*n.*	前哨
influx	*n.*	汇集
vacuum	*n.*	空缺，空白
renewal	*n.*	复兴

Exercises

Chapter 6 Entertainment—Sports, Movies and TV Series

Unit 3

Charms of Popular TV Series—*Sherlock, Downton Abbey* and *Doctor Who*

I think it's brought the world a lot closer together, and will continue to do that. There are downsides to everything; there are unintended consequences to everything. The most corrosive piece of technology that I've ever seen is called television—but then, again, television, at its best, is magnificent.

—Steve Jobs

Test Your Knowledge

I. **Discuss the following questions with your partner.**

1. How long do you watch TV every day?
2. What was the last show you really got into?
3. Have you ever binge-watched a show?
4. Do you like to put TV in the background when you're doing homework?

II. **Match the terms with their explanations.**

A.	boxed set	1.	a free government-funded TV channel that doesn't usually show commercials
B.	cable TV	2.	a television show that tells a story over many episodes or seasons
C.	channel	3.	one part of a TV series, usually 30 to 60 minutes long
D.	commercial	4.	a television channel that paying customers receive via coaxial or fibre-optic cable
E.	episode	5.	a collection of TV series episodes, music albums or movies on a set of DVD or Blu-ray discs
F.	public television	6.	a TV series about a group of people who keep getting into comical situations

G. reality TV	**7.** a public or private broadcaster of TV shows
H. season	**8.** a set of related episodes shown over one single period of weeks or months
I. series	**9.** a program that documents supposedly unscripted real-life situations, often starring unknown individuals rather than professional actors
J. sitcom	**10.** an advertisement on television or radio

Intensive Reading

Text I Best Films and TV Shows Based on the British Royal Family*

There's no shortage of royalty-related programming out there—here's some you may have missed.

If this year's royal weddings have got you wishing there be more opportunities to see the **monarchy** in action, it's worth checking out these royal-related films and TV shows:

The Crown

Based on the award-winning play *The Audience* by showrunner Peter Morgan, this **lavish**, Netflix Original drama will eventually **chronicle** the life of Queen Elizabeth II (Claire Foy) from the 1940s to the modern day. The series begin with an inside look at the early reign of the queen, who ascended the throne at age 25 after the death of her father, King George VI.

The first two series drew critical **acclaim** with *The Guardian* saying that: "Netflix can rest assured that its £100m gamble has paid off. This first series, about good old British phlegm from first to last, is the service's crowning achievement so far."

The third series, set in the 1960s and 1970s, is out later this year, with Olivia Colman taking over from Claire Foy in the lead role.

---

* Retrieved from The Week website.

Chapter 6 **Entertainment—Sports, Movies and TV Series**

The Queen

Before *The Crown*, *The Queen* saw Peter Morgan turn his hand at writing a feature-length film set during the **aftermath** of the death of Princess Diana. Helen Mirren plays a **taciturn** yet **remorseful** Queen Elizabeth II struggling to come to terms with the overwhelming public response to Diana's death, while Michael Sheen plays then-Prime Minister Tony Blair, who pushes the royals for an official expression of grief.

The film holds a 97% approval rating on Rotten Tomatoes and Mirren's performance earned her an Oscar for Best Actress.

The Windsors

Here's something to watch if you like your royal TV shows a little more **frivolous**. *The Windsors* **transposes** today's royals into a soap opera situation and imagines what their lives and loves might be like.

The series has been criticised for storylines such as Kate Middleton catching **ebola** and Princesses Eugenie and Beatrice becoming **radicalised**.

Reviews have been mixed, with *The Guardian* saying: "High-brow humour this is not. But, despite a number of cast and crew comparing the show to *Spitting Image*, *The Windsors* doesn't feel like satire: more a comic drama that makes the odd comment about monarchy."

The King's Speech

In this Oscar-winning film, Colin Firth plays the future King George VI, who employs Australian speech therapist Lionel Logue (Geoffrey Rush) to cure him of his **debilitating stammer**.

The two men become close friends as the new king counts on Logue to help him make his first wartime radio broadcast after the UK's declaration of war on Nazi Germany in 1939.

The New York Times hailed the film's leads saying: "With their volume turned up, the appealing, **impeccably** professional Mr. Firth and Mr. Rush rise to the acting occasion by twinkling and **growling** as their characters warily circle each other before settling into the **therapeutic** swing of things and unknowingly preparing for the big speech that partly gives the film its title."

The Madness of King George

Directed by Nicholas Hytner and adapted by Alan Bennett from his own play, this 1994 comedy tells the true story of George III's **deteriorating** mental health, and his equally declining relationship with his eldest son, the Prince of Wales, particularly focusing on the period around the Regency Crisis of 1788–1789.

The film was a critical success. "Under Hytner's guidance, the cast, composed of some of the best actors in British cinema, rises to the occasion," said *Variety*. "Boasting a rich period look, almost every shot is filled with handsome, emotionally charged composition."

In 1999, the British Film Institute voted the film the 42nd greatest British film of all time.

The Other Boleyn Girl

This 2008 film, directed by Justin Chadwick, presents a **dramatised** account of the lives of 16th-century **aristocrats** Mary Boleyn (Scarlett Johansson), one-time mistress of King Henry VIII (Eric Bana), and her sister, Anne (Natalie Portman), who became the monarch's second wife.

Describing it as "an enjoyable movie with an entertaining angle on a **hard-to-resist** period of history", *The San Francisco Chronicle* highlighted Natalie Portman's performance, which "shows a range and depth unlike anything she's done before", and "is the No. 1 element that tips *The Other Boleyn Girl* in the direction of a recommendation".

Victoria

While *The Crown* looks at the life and times of the current monarch, ITV's hit drama *Victoria* **delves** into the life of another famous British queen. The story begins with the death of King William IV in 1837, **propelling** the young princess onto the throne at the tender age of 18, and chronicles her relationships with the **influential** forces around her. Strong performances by Jenna Coleman as the young queen and Rufus Sewell as influential Prime Minister Lord Melbourne won the show critical praise, and saw it renewed for a third outing later this year.

Vocabulary

monarchy	*n.*	君主；女王
lavish	*adj.*	非常大方的
chronicle	*v.*	翔实记载
acclaim	*n.*	称誉；高度评价
aftermath	*n.*	后果；余波
taciturn	*adj.*	沉默寡言的

Chapter 6 Entertainment—Sports, Movies and TV Series

remorseful	*adj.*	极为后悔的
frivolous	*adj.*	无聊的
transpose	*v.*	调换
ebola	*n.*	埃博拉病毒
radicalised	*adj.*	激进的
debilitating	*adj.*	使衰弱的
stammer	*n.*	口吃；结巴
impeccably	*adv.*	无可挑剔地
growl	*v.*	咆哮
therapeutic	*adj.*	治疗的
deteriorating	*adj.*	日益恶化的
dramatised	*adj.*	生动的
aristocrat	*n.*	贵族
hard-to-resist	*adj.*	人见人爱的；无法抗拒的
delve	*v.*	探究
propel	*v.*	促使
influential	*adj.*	有影响的；有势力的

Exercises

I. **Decide whether the following statements are true or false, and mark T or F accordingly.**

_____ 1. *The Queen* portrays the life of Queen Elizabeth II in a chronological order.

_____ 2. The role of Queen Elizabeth II has been played by Claire Foy and Helen Mirren in TV series and films.

_____ 3. King George VII once suffered from the problem of stammer but later overcame it with the help of a speech therapist.

_____ 4. *The Windsors* received a very high acclaim on Rotten Tomatoes and the actress of the heroine earned an Oscar.

_____ 5. The Regency Crisis happened from 1788 to 1789, during which period George III suffered from serious mental health problems.

_____ 6. Natalie Portman made an excellent performance in the film *The Other Boleyn Girl*, and received high appreciation from the media.

_____ 7. Queen Victoria ascended to the throne at the age of 25 after the death of King William.

II. Choose the best answer to each question.

1. What is true about *The Crown*?

    A. The series of *The Crown* start with Queen Elizabeth II's governance from the 1940s to the present.

    B. *The Guardian* held a critical attitude towards the series and didn't think much of it.

    C. Claire Foy played the role of Queen Elizabeth II in the third series.

    D. Queen Elizabeth II was 25 when she inherited the Crown from her father and ascended the throne.

2. Which one is **NOT** true about *The Queen*?

    A. Queen Elizabeth II showed her regret and sympathy for the death of Princess Diana to cope with the overwhelming public response.

    B. Helen Mirren played the lead role of Princess Diana in *The Queen*, which enabled her to earn an Oscar for Best Actress.

    C. Peter Morgan once wrote a feature-length film to memorize Princess Diana.

    D. After Princess Diana died in the car accident, the Prime Minister Tony Blair expressed grief on behalf of the government.

3. Which one is **NOT** true about *The King's Speech*?

    A. King George VI once suffered from troublesome stammer but later overcame this problem with the help of a speech therapist.

    B. The film got its title partly because of the King's first wartime radio broadcast to declare war on Nazi Germany.

    C. The film received high approval and won an Oscar.

    D. The media evaluated this film with high acclaim for the performances of the two actors who played the roles of the King and the speech therapist.

4. What can we learn according to the passage?

    A. The role of Queen Elizabeth II has appeared in *The Crown*, *The Queen* and *Victoria*.

    B. Queen Victoria ascended to the throne at an earlier age than Queen Elizabeth II.

C. All the films and TV series mentioned in this passage were a great success and warmly welcomed by the audience.

D. Lord Melbourne and Lionel Logue once served as Prime Minister in British history.

III. Fill in the blanks with the appropriate forms of the phrases in the box.

> take over   in the lead role   turn one's hand   come to terms with
> count on   turn up   settle into   rise to the occasion
> in the direction of   delve into

1. If you cannot _____ it, eventually you will breach the policies and be forced to leave the business in disgrace.

2. Unless a better job does _____, the chances are the days start getting longer and time becomes harder to fill.

3. In 2006, she starred _____ in the film adaptation of the 1981 Broadway musical *Dreamgirls*, for which she earned two Golden Globe nominations.

4. "When I _____ the research and talked to scientists," she said, "I was able to put these findings into context and see the big picture."

5. Once a vehicle had _____ automated travel, the driver would be free to release the wheel, open the morning paper or just relax.

6. If you _____ to something such as a practical activity, you learn about it and do it for the first time.

7. Ever since the earliest days of AI, there have been concerns that some day software will _____ the world, leaving the fate of humans unknown.

8. People _____ hospitals and health facilities to respond, swiftly and efficiently, as the lifeline for survival and the backbone of support.

9. Athletes with disabilities must _____ just like their Olympic counterparts.

10. I slunk off _____ the cocktail table—the only place in the garden where a single man could linger without looking purposeless and alone.

IV. Search for relevant information about one member of the current British Royal Family, and tell what has interested you the most in about 200 words.

Further Reading

Text II Do You Love British TV Series? Showmax Got You Covered*

British TV is known for its excellent quality acting and **compelling** storylines. From **gritty** detective dramas to **enchanting** fantasy, these series on Showmax will have you **enthralled** from start to finish.

Keep scrolling to see if your favourite is listed. Even if it isn't, we know you'll find something you like on this list.

The Nevers

In the last years of Victoria's reign, London is beset by "The Touched": People, mostly women who suddenly manifest abnormal abilities—some charming, some disturbing. Among them are Amalia True (Laura Donnelly from *Outlander*), a mysterious, quick-fisted widow, and Penance Adair (Ann Skelly from *Vikings*), a brilliant young inventor. They are the champions of this new underclass, making a home for the Touched, while fighting the forces of...well, pretty much all the forces—to make room for those whose history as we know has no place. This is a series you will **thoroughly** enjoy.

The Capture

Holliday Grainger takes on the role of Detective Inspector Rachel Carey in this dark crime **thriller**. It's her job to find and arrest Lance Corporal Shaun Emery (Callum Turner) after he's accused—again—of being caught committing a serious crime on camera. The problem is that while Emery **proclaims** his innocence and there is **footage** of him with his now-murdered **barrister**, DI Carey believes that he's innocent and she starts her own **off-the-books** investigation into Emery's claims that he has been framed (complete with video footage) for the second time. Her methods aren't clean, and the evidence she discovers will shock you...because the exact same thing is happening in the real world right now. *The Capture* scored 92% on Rotten Tomatoes and universal critical acclaim.

The Bay

Morven Christie plays Detective Constable Lisa Armstrong in Season 1 (there is a different story in Season 2 and a new lead character in Season 3) and

---

* Retrieved from Bella Naija website.

Chapter 6 Entertainment—Sports, Movies and TV Series

she is backed into a corner with her new case. She's part of a social worker team as Family Liaison Officer at the West Lancashire Police Service. After sex with a stranger in an alleyway during a **bachelorette** party, Lisa discovers that the man she hooked up with is at the centre of a missing children's case the very next day.

While the man is a person of interest as the police investigate his missing stepchildren, Lisa could simply provide an **alibi** for him...because she was with him when the kids disappeared. Instead, she keeps the info to herself and makes life difficult for herself and her hook-up. You want to see dirty **underhanded** policing? Wait till you see what Lisa does when the pressure starts mounting.

A Confession

What makes this drama miniseries so entertaining is the fact that it's real—this really happened. Martin Freeman portrays Detective **Superintendent** Stephen Fulcher, an honest, hard-working cop who sticks to the rules—until a young woman goes missing and the clock starts ticking. While hunting a kidnapper and potential murderer, he strays from police procedure to get crucial evidence. He gets the results he wants—but when his superiors and the lawyers in the case discover how the evidence was obtained, everyone, even the families of the victims, has to choose a side.

His Dark Materials

In this adaptation of Philip Pullman's classic fantasy novels, Lyra's search for a kidnapped friend uncovers a **sinister** plot involving stolen children and sets off a quest to understand a mysterious phenomenon called Dust.

Season 2 begins after Lord Asriel has opened a bridge to a new world. There, in a strange and mysterious abandoned city, Lyra meets Will, a boy from our world who is also running from a troubled past.

The epic fantasy's cast includes child stars Dafne Keen (*Logan*) and Amir Wilson as Lyra and Will, supported by Golden Globe winner Ruth Wilson (*The Affair, Luther*) and Oscar nominee Lin-Manuel Miranda (*Hamilton*). *His Dark Materials* has an 80% critics' rating on Rotten Tomatoes, with Slate calling it "proof that TV is now the best medium for bringing epic literary fantasy to the screen". The first two seasons are on Showmax.

The Victim

Scottish thriller *The Victim* centres on Anna Dean, a **grieving** mother who finds herself on trial for attempted murder after exposing the supposed new

英国社会与文化

identity and address of the man she believes murdered her son 15 years ago. The four-part miniseries stars Golden Globe nominee and Emmy winner Kelly Macdonald (*Boardwalk Empire*), who won the Best Actress Award at BAFTAs Scotland for her role. Nominated for a 2020 BAFTA, *The Victim* has a 91% critics' rating on Rotten Tomatoes, where the critics' **consensus** calls it "a **riveting** and relevant drama".

The Luminaries

Based on Eleanor Cattin's Booker Prize-winning novel, *The Luminaries* is an epic story of love, murder and revenge set on the Wild West Coast of New Zealand during the gold rush. It's not quite British, but if you love Brit drama, you'll enjoy this.

Starring Eve Hewson (*The Knick, Behind Her Eyes, Robin Hood*), Teen Choice nominee Himesh Patel (*Yesterday, Tenet*), and Golden Globe nominee Eva Green (*Penny Dreadful, Casino Royale*), the six-part series was hailed by *Time* as "enchanting, **enthralling**" and *The Guardian* as "simply **addictive** TV...glorious escapism...a must-see full of **intrigue**, opium and political **machinations**."

📖 Vocabulary

compelling	adj.	引人注目的
gritty	adj.	坚韧不拔的
enchanting	adj.	迷人的
enthralled	adj.	被迷住的
thoroughly	adv.	彻底地
thriller	n.	（尤指关于罪案或间谍的）惊险小说（或戏剧、电影）
footage	n.	连续镜头
barrister	n.	律师
off-the-books	adj.	私下的
bachelorette	adj.	单身女郎的
alibi	n.	不在场证明或辩解
underhanded	adj.	卑劣的；不光明的
superintendent	n.	（英国的）警司
sinister	adj.	邪恶的
grieving	adj.	（因某人去世而）悲痛的
consensus	n.	一致看法，共识
riveting	adj.	吸引人的

Chapter 6 Entertainment—Sports, Movies and TV Series

enthralling	*adj.*	扣人心弦的
addictive	*adj.*	使人上瘾的
intrigue	*n.*	阴谋，密谋策划；秘密关系
machination	*n.*	阴谋，诡计

 Exercises

英国社会与文化

Unit 4

One City, Three Olympic Games

The Olympics are a wonderful metaphor for world cooperation, the kind of international competition that's wholesome and healthy, an interplay between countries that represents the best in all of us.

—John Williams

 Test Your Knowledge

I. **Search for relevant information to answer the following questions.**

1. When was the first modern Olympic Games held?
2. When was the first Winter Olympic Games held?
3. To whom did Greeks dedicate Olympic Games?
4. From which country did Olympics originate?
5. Who officially opened the 2012 Summer Olympics?
6. Who became the most decorated athlete of all time during the 2012 Summer Olympics?
7. Who is regarded as the "father of the modern Olympics"?
8. What is the Olympic motto?
9. Where is the Olympic flame traditionally lit?
10. Which five countries have participated in every Summer Olympics?

II. **Find the English words for sports featured at the Summer Olympic Games. All the words go horizontal or vertical.**

E	M	B	T	H	Y	B	E	Q	U	E	S	T	R	I	A	N	D	T	W
T	W	A	Y	V	V	F	I	O	N	H	K	Y	M	N	X	R	I	H	H
P	M	C	M	V	O	Y	H	E	A	A	W	I	W	R	O	W	I	N	G
K	A	T	R	A	M	P	O	L	I	N	E	L	X	M	S	S	Z	U	X
O	V	N	V	L	K	V	L	V	V	F	O	O	T	B	A	L	L	D	Z
I	Y	K	F	Y	F	J	I	F	Q	J	D	B	B	B	O	X	I	N	G
A	O	G	H	Y	F	Q	W	P	B	B	O	K	H	Y	X	S	D	N	E

Chapter 6 **Entertainment—Sports, Movies and TV Series**

Z	N	H	N	D	T	I	W	E	I	G	H	T	L	I	F	T	I	N	G
W	A	K	V	I	F	T	I	D	K	Q	N	M	Y	W	Y	Q	Q	Q	N
Q	T	A	W	V	E	A	B	A	D	M	I	N	T	O	N	C	N	H	P
Y	H	L	S	I	N	B	A	S	K	E	T	B	A	L	L	Z	H	H	W
V	L	L	U	N	C	L	R	B	Y	T	E	N	N	I	S	A	R	O	R
R	E	N	Z	G	I	E	P	W	H	Q	T	Z	Z	H	L	G	S	C	E
O	T	I	Z	O	N	T	C	U	V	U	N	Q	D	M	C	I	N	K	S
S	I	I	G	D	G	E	R	X	E	X	F	S	S	C	K	K	U	E	T
F	C	Y	C	L	I	N	G	E	S	Q	M	P	Z	Z	Q	D	A	Y	L
B	S	A	I	L	I	N	G	V	O	L	L	E	Y	B	A	L	L	U	I
S	I	Y	H	D	X	I	U	Y	J	V	D	I	A	S	A	X	H	O	N
S	M	V	Z	D	O	S	V	J	N	Q	O	B	Z	X	R	P	A	Y	G
C	J	U	J	H	G	Y	M	N	A	S	T	I	C	S	H	Y	Q	Y	C
X	L	V	I	H	R	C	I	E	E	R	A	O	X	J	U	D	O	S	Y
A	R	C	H	E	R	Y	S	W	I	M	M	I	N	G	G	N	S	I	N

III. Suppose your city/country is competing with several others for the right to host the next edition of the Olympic Games. You must give a speech to a panel of IOC members and tell them about the unique qualities of your city/country's culture. What would you say? How would you say it? You can use many forms of media in this presentation—digital images, performances (dance), videos, etc.

Intensive Reading

Text I London Olympic Games Then and Now: 1908 & 2012*

The 30th Olympiad of the Modern Era, aka London 2012, is here! This is the third time London has hosted the Olympics. The first time was in 1908 (4th Olympiad) and the second was in 1948 (14th Olympiad). I thought it would be fun to examine how the Olympics have changed in the past 100 years, so I'm going to compare the 1908 with the 2012 London Games.

---

* Retrieved from Library of Congress website.

Accommodations

THEN: There was no **designated** lodging for the 1,350 overseas competitors—so no Olympic Village. Organizers **distributed** booklets recommending hotels and boarding houses in the area. The US team decided to stay in the **coastal** town of Brighton—53 miles away.

NOW: Accommodations, along with **amenities**, are provided to competitors and officials in the Olympic Village. London's Olympic Village will house up to 16,000 athletes and officials at its peak. You may be wondering when the Olympic Village first made an appearance. The first Olympic Village was at the 1932 Los Angeles Games—however, it was men only! Women stayed in hotels until the 1956 Games in Melbourne, when the Olympic Village was opened to both sexes.

Duration

THEN: The 1908 London Games lasted for 6 months, from April 27 to October 31, however, the majority of the events were held from July 13–25 with the opening ceremony on July 13.

NOW: The official duration of the Olympics Games is no more than 16 days. The 2012 London Games will be held from July 27 to August 12.

Countries

THEN: There were 22 countries with 2,035 athletes participating. The majority of the countries came from Europe, but also included the countries of Canada, Russia, South Africa, and the United States. The Australasia team was made up of athletes from Australia and New Zealand. There were no Asian, Oceanic, or South American countries represented.

NOW: According to the London 2012 Organising Committee there are 10,490 athletes from 205 countries. Every region of the world (Africa, Asia, Europe, Oceania, and the Americas), except Antarctica, is represented. The Olympics have truly become a global event!

The Weather

THEN: The weather during the July events was, on the whole, considered **unfavorable**. There was rain and there was heat. A great majority of the events were held outdoors. Shepherd's Bush stadium (an outdoor venue) was where the competitions for athletics (track & field), cycling, wrestling, gymnastics, and swimming/diving were held. On the day of the 1,000 meter cycling competitions, the track was so wet that water pooled on the track and the

Chapter 6 Entertainment—Sports, Movies and TV Series

concrete came apart in places. This forced cyclists to move at a slower pace and caused a number of flat tires. Because the conditions were so poor, cyclists could not finish the race in the required time of 1 minute 45 seconds, so the officials called the race null and void; it was not replayed.

There are many more **incidents** in which the weather affected the 1908 Games. During the York Round in archery, shooting had to be **suspended** due to the rain and wind; about half of the marathon runners dropped out due to heat (also see the story of marathon runner Dorando Pietri); and during the shot put event, **contestants** had difficulty reaching their full capabilities because the iron balls were **slippery** and the turf was soaking wet.

NOW: The UK's Met Office (National Weather Service) is playing an integral role in the Olympics by providing "essential weather information for planning and **logistics**". So we should not expect any weather **inflicted catastrophes** to happen like those in 1908. If you go to its Olympics website, you will find weather forecasts, outlooks, and statistics, as well as pages about weather and sport. According to the Met Office the forecast for London during the Games includes some of the **ubiquitous** rain England is known for.

Women

THEN: Women first took part in the 1900 Paris Olympic Games, four years after the first Olympic Games in 1896. There were 22 women out of 997 athletes who competed in five sports: tennis, sailing, croquet, **equestrian**, and golf.

The 1908 Games had 36 women athletes compete. There were only 5 medal sports in which women competed: archery, figure skating (singles and pairs), rackets (doubles), tennis (singles), and indoor tennis. Sybil "Queenie" Newall took the gold medal in the National Round in archery and became the oldest woman to win a gold medal—aged 53 years and 277 days. Women also participated in an all-day demonstration of a foil (fencing) competition, swimming/diving **exhibition**, and gymnastics display.

Each Olympiad, the IOC members would vote on whether to include women's sports and events. It was not until 1951 that the women's sports became a permanent part of the Olympic Games.

NOW: Women will compete in every sport in the games of the 30th Olympiad program and each participating country has sent women athletes to compete. I do not have the grand total of 2012 women athletes; however, the 2008 Beijing Summer Olympics **boasted** 4,637 (42.7%) female athletes. I should also note that the 2012 Olympics is the first appearance of a women boxing event.

英国社会与文化

 **Vocabulary**

designated	adj.	指定的
distribute	v.	分发
coastal	adj.	沿海的；海岸的
amenity	n.	便利设施
unfavorable	adj.	不宜的；令人不快的
concrete	n.	混凝土
incident	n.	事件
suspended	adj.	暂停的
contestant	n.	竞争者
slippery	adj.	滑得抓不住的
logistics	n.	后勤
inflict	v.	造成
catastrophe	n.	大灾难；大祸
ubiquitous	adj.	普遍存在的，无所不在的
equestrian	n.	骑术；马术
exhibition	n.	表演赛
boast	v.	以有……而自豪

 Exercises

I. Choose the best option to answer each question or complete each of the following statements.

1. London held the Olympic Games in _____.

    A. 1908, 1932 and 2012

    B. 1908, 1948 and 2008

    C. 1908, 1948 and 2012

    D. 1908, 1948 and 2016

2. What was so special about the Olympic Games in 1908?

    A. Accommodations and amenities were provided to competitors and officials in the Olympic Village.

    B. The official duration of the Olympic Games was no more than 16 days.

    C. There were no Asian, Oceanic, or South American countries represented.

    D. You could go to its Olympic website to find weather forecasts, outlooks and statistics.

Chapter 6 Entertainment—Sports, Movies and TV Series

3. When and where did the Olympic Village first make an appearance?

A. 1900; Paris.

B. 1932; Los Angeles.

C. 1956; Melbourne.

D. 2008; Beijing.

4. Which of the following is **NOT** true about women athletes in the Olympic Games?

A. Women first participated in the Paris Olympic Games in 1900.

B. Women athletes were not allowed to stay in the Olympic Village until in 1956.

C. Women's sports have become a permanent part of the Olympic Games since 1908.

D. Women competed on every sport in the 2012 London Olympic Games.

5. Which of the following is **NOT** true about the Olympic Games in 2012?

A. The 2012 London Olympic Games was held from July 27 to August 12.

B. Every region of the world, including Africa, Asia, Europe, Oceania, the Americas and Antarctica, was represented.

C. Thanks to the UK's Met Office, we should not expect any weather inflicted catastrophes to happen like those in 1908.

D. A women boxing event appeared for the first time in the 2012 Olympics.

II. **Match the years with the relevant information according to the passage.**

1. 1896   *A.* The Olympic Village was opened to both sexes.

2. 1900   *B.* The first Olympic Games was held in Athens.

3. 1908   *C.* The first Olympic Village appeared at Los Angeles Games.

4. 1932   *D.* Women first took part in the Paris Games.

5. 1951   *E.* It was the first time for London to hold the Olympic Games.

6. 1956   *F.* Women's sports became a permanent part of the Olympic Games.

7. 2008   *G.* There were 10,490 athletes from 205 countries.

8. 2012   *H.* 4,637 female athletes participated in this Olympics.

III. Fill in each blank with a suitable preposition.

1. Their sense of humour and ability to get along _____ people are two characteristics that compensate for their lack of experience.
2. Can you provide me _____ some information about the different culture between China and the USA?
3. _____ its peak around AD 600, this city was one of the largest human settlements in the world.
4. Dinners are usually made up _____ meat or fish with vegetables followed by dessert, fruit and coffee.
5. According _____ the theory of relativity, nothing can travel faster than light.
6. These textbooks are, _____ the whole, small, presumably inexpensive to produce, but well set out and logically developed.
7. People often quit jobs, take new jobs, or drop _____ of the labor force to retrain themselves.
8. With rising food prices, milk can play an important role _____ improving the diets of the poor.
9. All the villagers, men and women, old and young, took part _____ the battle against the drought.
10. Congress plans to vote next month _____ whether to approve or reject the deal.

Further Reading

Text II Legacies of Past Olympic Games*

The Olympic Games are the main sporting event in the world. They are not just a sporting event, but a huge **incentive** for the development of the country in which they are held. They bring positive long-term social and economic changes, set new standards to **popularize** the Olympic values. All this rich tangible and **intangible** heritage remains in the country for many years. Therefore, countries are struggling for the right to hold games and in case of receiving this right, they announce it to be the project of national significance.

There are many examples of how the Olympic Games have changed

---

* Retrieved from ESSAY4YOU website.

radically the image of the city, its **infrastructure** and economy, in fact, to give the city new life. For example, the industrial center of Barcelona has become a global tourist resort, and Beijing has become a real exhibition of achievements of modern China.

The **legacy** of Olympic Games is huge and is expressed in different aspects of human life. Legacy is the **phenomenon** of the spiritual lifestyle, inherited and **apprehended** from previous generations. The legacy that remains after the major sporting events includes various physical facilities: roads, airports, hotels and stadiums. But that's not all, as there is so-called Olympic effect—a sharp and steady increase in trade volumes of 30% in the country when Games are held. Experts admit that with proper planning a major sporting event may serve not only the **impetus** for the development of infrastructure, but also acts as a **catalyst** for the development of socio-economic sphere, attracting necessary financing in infrastructure projects.

Thus, the Olympic Games in 1992 became a catalyst for urban renewal process and a **comprehensive** renovation throughout Barcelona. The city built ring roads which reduced the problem of **congestion** and traffic lines of constant traffic jams. The public transport system was also reorganized.

Another vivid example was Olympic Games in Beijing. While the preparation for the Games (2002–2006), China has invested nearly $40 billion just in infrastructure. China built 40 new stadiums and sports facilities, doubled the **capacity** of Beijing subway and the construction of public transportation **monorail**, built and rebuilt roads, and opened a new airport.

Olympic Games in Vancouver also led to the development of infrastructure. One of such improvements was the reconstruction of the road Sea-to-Sky Highway, which allowed increasing the capacity of the Vancouver–Whistler corridor. Another example is the construction of Canada Line, which connects Vancouver with Richmond and Vancouver International Airport, as well as the **subsequent** improvement of roads throughout Greater Vancouver.

The legacy of the Olympic Games is not limited to urban **regeneration**, transportation, facilities, tourism, economic and cultural legacy, but also includes the development of volunteer movement. Olympic Games would have been impossible without the volunteer movement activists, **submitted**, mostly by young people. Olympics are not just a sport, but also culture and education, which influence understanding and **solidarity**. All Olympic legacies often go to the youth. To unite the youth with the help of Olympic values in a broad sense, not only by sports, but also by mutual understanding and friendship is one of the main strategic objectives of any Olympic Organizing Committee.

The **evolution** of voluntary movement, during the Olympic Games, began with Stockholm (1912), Antwerp (1920), Paris (1924) and Amsterdam (1928), which used the volunteers from the association, similar to Scouts. These young men carried simple but very important tasks for the organization of the Olympic Games activities, such as mail delivery, cleaning and assistance in maintaining order during the Games.

Then more and more volunteers assisted in holding the Olympic Games: 2,191 volunteers in Helsinki (1952), 3,500 in Melbourne (1956), 6,700 in Lake Placid (1980), 4,000 in Sarajevo (1984), 34,548 in Barcelona (1992). The Beijing Olympics have broken the record for the number of volunteers: 70,000 volunteers worked at the Olympics.

Beijing Olympic volunteers provided customer services, worked in two data centers for thousands of foreigners, and helped the guests of the Olympics to focus on the streets of the **metropolis**. About 400 thousand of volunteers followed tourists to the historical and cultural sights of the capital. Many volunteers were engaged in information support services for the Olympic Games, opening and closing ceremonies, took care of foreigners, spoke foreign languages and were able to provide first aid if necessary.

Volunteer Olympic legacy is one of the most important legacies, as it **contributes** to the development of skills and abilities, helps volunteers meet new friends and feel themselves as a part of the new team. Involvement in a **spectacular** historic event is a unique chance to meet with famous athletes, **prominent** politicians and foreign guests. It gives a unique experience and skills, which can later be used by volunteers in their future lives. The Olympic Games play an important role in the development of **volunteerism** around the whole world.

Vocabulary

incentive	*n.*	刺激；激励
popularize	*v.*	普及，推广
intangible	*adj.*	无形的
infrastructure	*n.*	基础设施，公共建设
legacy	*n.*	遗产

Chapter 6 Entertainment—Sports, Movies and TV Series

phenomenon	*n.*	现象
apprehend	*n.*	领会
impetus	*n.*	动力
catalyst	*n.*	刺激因素；催化剂
comprehensive	*adj.*	综合的；广泛的
congestion	*n.*	拥塞
capacity	*n.*	容量；能力
monorail	*n.*	单轨；单轨铁路
subsequent	*adj.*	随后的
regeneration	*n.*	复建；改造
submit	*v.*	提交；主张
solidarity	*n.*	团结
evolution	*n.*	演变
metropolis	*n.*	大都会；大都市
contribute	*v.*	有助于；促成
spectacular	*adj.*	壮观的
prominent	*adj.*	杰出的，卓越的
volunteerism	*n.*	志愿精神；志愿服务

Exercises

Chapter 7 Politics—Constitutional Monarchy

Introduction

Britain is a parliamentary democracy with a constitutional monarchy. The chapter provides a brief account of British political institutions, of the public support for the continuation of the monarchy, of the allocation of power and of how the three branches of government, namely the legislature, the executive and the judiciary, check and balance each other. The chapter also explores Tereasa May's proposal of an early election without losing sight of the underlying structure of governmental institutions and the Brexit negotiation against the backdrop of the low level of psychological attachment to the EU by most Britons.

Unit 1

Constitution and Monarch: How to Justify Britain's Support for Monarchy

I know of no single formula for success. But over the years I have observed that some attributes of leadership are universal and are often about finding ways of encouraging people to combine their efforts, their talents, their insights, their enthusiasm and their inspiration to work together.

—Queen Elizabeth II

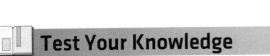

Test Your Knowledge

I. Search for relevant information to answer the following questions.

1. Who is today's monarch in Britain?
2. What do you know about the British constitution?
3. What role does the monarch play in Britain?
4. What do you know about the British Royal Family?
5. How can you justify the public support for the monarchy in Britain?

II. Match the English terms with the corresponding Chinese translations.

1. Constitutional Monarchy
2. Absolute Monarchy
3. Monarchy
4. Constitution
5. Statutory Laws
6. Common Laws
7. Conventions
8. Republic

A. 成文法
B. 君主立宪制
C. 君主专制制
D. 习惯法
E. 君主制
F. 共和政体
G. 判例法
H. 宪法

Chapter 7 Politics—Constitutional Monarchy

Intensive Reading

Text I Elizabeth II*

Elizabeth was the elder daughter of Prince Albert, duke of York, and his wife, Lady Elizabeth Bowes-Lyon. As the child of a younger son of King George V, the young Elizabeth had little prospect of **acceding** to the throne until her uncle, Edward VIII (afterward duke of Windsor), **abdicated** in her father's favour on December 11, 1936, at which time her father became King George VI and she became **heir presumptive**. The princess' education was supervised by her mother, who **entrusted** her daughters to a governess, Marion Crawford; the princess was also **grounded** in history by C. H. K. Marten, afterward **provost** of Eton College, and had instruction from visiting teachers in music and languages. During World War II, she and her sister, Princess Margaret Rose, spent much of their time safely away from the London blitz and separated from their parents, living mostly at Balmoral Castle in Scotland and at the Royal Lodge, Windsor and Windsor Castle.

Early in 1947 Princess Elizabeth went with the king and queen to South Africa. After her return there was an announcement of her **betrothal** to her distant cousin Lieutenant Philip Mountbatten of the Royal Navy, formerly Prince Philip of Greece and Denmark. The marriage took place in Westminster Abbey on November 20, 1947. On the eve of the wedding her father, the king, **conferred** upon the **bridegroom** the titles of duke of Edinburgh, **earl** of Merioneth, and **Baron** Greenwich. They took **residence** at Clarence House in London. Their first child, Prince Charles (Charles Philip Arthur George), was born on November 14, 1948, at Buckingham Palace.

In the summer of 1951 the health of King George VI entered into a serious decline, and Princess Elizabeth represented him at the Trooping the Colour and on various other state occasions. On October 7 she and her husband set out on a highly successful tour of Canada and Washington, D. C. After Christmas in England she and the duke set out in January 1952 for a tour of Australia and New Zealand, but **en route**, at Sagana, Kenya, news reached them of the king's death on February 6, 1952. Elizabeth, now queen, at once flew back to England. The first three months of her reign, the period of full **mourning** for her father, were passed in comparative **seclusion**. But in the summer, after she had moved

---

* Retrieved from Britannica website.

from Clarence House to Buckingham Palace, she undertook the routine duties of the sovereign and carried out her first state opening of Parliament on November 4, 1952. Her **coronation** was held at Westminster Abbey on June 2, 1953.

On the accession of Queen Elizabeth, her son Prince Charles became **heir apparent**; he was named prince of Wales on July 26, 1958, and was so invested on July 1, 1969.

The queen seemed increasingly aware of the modern role of the monarchy, allowing, for example, the televising of the Royal Family's domestic life in 1970 and **condoning** the formal **dissolution** of her sister's marriage in 1978. In the 1990s, however, the Royal Family faced a number of challenges. In 1992, a year that Elizabeth referred to as the Royal Family's **annus horribilis**, Prince Charles and his wife, Diana, princess of Wales, separated, as did Prince Andrew and his wife, Sarah, duchess of York. Moreover, Anne divorced, and a fire gutted the royal residence of Windsor Castle. In addition, as the country struggled with a recession, resentment over the royals' lifestyle **mounted**, and in 1992 Elizabeth, although personally **exempt**, agreed to pay taxes on her private income. The separation and later divorce (1996) of Charles and the immensely popular Diana further eroded support for the Royal Family, which was viewed by some as **antiquated** and unfeeling. The criticism intensified following Diana's death in 1997, especially after Elizabeth initially refused to allow the national flag to fly at half-staff over Buckingham Palace. In line with her earlier attempts at modernizing the monarchy, the queen subsequently sought to present a less-**stuffy** and less-traditional image of the monarchy. These attempts were met with mixed success.

Beginning in the latter part of the first decade of the 21st century, the public standing of the Royal Family **rebounded**, and even Charles' 2005 marriage to Camilla Parker Bowles found much support among the British people. In 2012 Elizabeth celebrated her "Diamond Jubilee", marking 60 years on the throne. On September 9, 2015, she surpassed Victoria's record reign of 63 years and 216 days.

Elizabeth is known to favour simplicity in court life and is also known to take a serious and informed interest in government business, aside from the traditional and ceremonial duties. Privately, she became a keen horsewoman; she kept racehorses, frequently attended races, and periodically visited the Kentucky stud farms in the United States. Her financial and property holdings made her one of the world's richest women.

Chapter 7 Politics—Constitutional Monarchy

Vocabulary

accede	*v.*	（尤指君主）即位，就任
abdicate	*v.*	退位；逊位
heir presumptive		继承人；推定继承人
entrust	*v.*	托付，委托
ground	*v.*	（在某学科上）给……以扎实的基础教育
provost	*n.*	教务长
betrothal	*n.*	婚约；订婚
confer	*v.*	授予（奖项、学位、荣誉或权利）
bridegroom	*n.*	新郎；即将（或刚刚）结婚的男子
earl	*n.*	伯爵
residence	*n.*	定居；住所
en route	*adv.*	在途中，在路上
mourn	*v.*	（因失去……而）哀悼，忧伤
seclusion	*n.*	隐居；与世隔绝
coronation	*n.*	加冕礼
heir apparent		当然继承人；法定继承人
condone	*v.*	宽恕；饶恕
dissolution	*n.*	（婚姻关系的）解除；（商业协议的）终止
annus horribilis		灾年
mount	*v.*	逐步增加
exempt	*v.*	免除（责任、付款等）；获豁免
antiquated	*adj.*	过时的，陈旧的
stuffy	*adj.*	一本正经的；古板的
rebound	*v.*	反弹，弹回

Exercises

I. Decide whether the following statements are true or false, and mark T or F accordingly.

_____ **1.** The young Elizabeth had little prospect of acceding to the throne as her father was a younger son of King George V.

_____ **2.** In the summer of 1951 the health of King George VI entered into a serious decline, and Princess Elizabeth represented him to deploy troops.

_____ **3.** The queen seemed increasingly aware of the modern role of the monarchy, however, her allowing for the televising of the Royal Family's domestic life was viewed by some as antiquated and unfeeling.

_____ 4. The public standing of the Royal Family rebounded in the latter part of the first decade of the 21st century thanks to Charles' 2005 marriage to Camilla Parker Bowles.

_____ 5. In 2012 Elizabeth celebrated her "Diamond Jubilee", which meant that she reigned over her country longer than any other British king or queen before her.

II. Put the following events in the right order according to the passage.

1. Prince Charles and his wife, Diana, princess of Wales, separated.
2. Elizabeth and her husband set out on a highly successful tour of Canada and Washington, D. C.
3. Elizabeth II's coronation was held at Westminster Abbey.
4. The first three months of Elizabeth II's reign, the period of full mourning for her father, were passed in comparative seclusion.
5. The queen seemed increasingly aware of the modern role of the monarchy, allowing, for example, the televising of the Royal Family's domestic life.

_____ → _____ → _____ → _____ → _____

III. Complete the sentences with the appropriate forms of the words in the box.

| sovereign | accede | seclude | ground | mourn |
| rebound | reside | confer | entrust | dissolve |

1. If you prepare the _____ for a future event, course of action, or development, you make it easier for it to happen.
2. The Queen would have to decide whether to grant a(n) _____ of Parliament.
3. She lived in _____ with her husband on their farm in Panama.
4. However, temperatures should _____ to near 70 by Thanksgiving.
5. When he dies, people throughout the world will _____.
6. He _____ to the throne in 1838.

Chapter 7 Politics—Constitutional Monarchy

7. In March 1889, she became the first British _____ to set foot on Spanish soil.

8. He liked the ease and glitter of the life, and the lustre _____ on him by being a member of this group of rich and conspicuous people.

9. He recently ended his _____ at the apartment complex.

10. She was _____ with the job of organizing the reception.

IV. Complete the following sentences by translating the Chinese in the brackets into English using expressions in the passage.

1. As the child of a younger son of King George V, the young Elizabeth had little prospect of _____ (登上皇位).

2. Her father became King George VI and she became _____ (法定继承人).

3. After her return there was an announcement of her _____ (订婚) to her distant cousin Lieutenant Philip Mountbatten of the Royal Navy, formerly Prince Philip of Greece and Denmark.

4. 1992 was what Elizabeth referred to as the Royal Family's _____ (多灾之年).

5. As the country struggled with a recession, resentment over the royals' lifestyle _____ (不断增加).

V. Give a brief account of Queen Elizabeth II's life experience and make your comment on what she has done to modernize the Royal Family.

Further Reading

Text II   Harry's Departure Could Do Britain's Royal Family a Favor*

The British have always had an **ambivalent** relationship with their kings and queens. In 1649, after much soul-searching, the English Parliament chopped the monarch's head off.

Charles I had believed he was on the throne by the grace of God, while

---

* Retrieved from *China Daily* website.

Parliament argued he was subject to the will of the people. His execution settled the matter once and for all and, when his son was restored to the throne a decade later, it was as a constitutional monarch.

And thus it has remained for the past three-and-a-half centuries, despite occasional **disruptions** caused by scandal, social change, dynastic disruption and even one case of temporary madness.

The present **furore** over the decision of Queen Elizabeth's grandson Prince Harry and his wife Meghan to withdraw from royal duties is among the more minor crises that the British monarchy has had to face. Yet it has provided the latest opportunity to revive a debate over whether the institution can survive in the 21st century.

Monarchy, constitutional or otherwise, is an **anachronism** based on the magical thinking that the authority of a head of state can pass from one generation to the next of a single family.

The British people, who at least until the Brexit drama could boast of their **pragmatism**, accepted monarchy because it sort of worked. The existence of a totally neutral **figurehead**, who **wielded** authority but no actual power, was regarded as a check on **overweening** politicians and a symbol of national unity among political divisions.

The current debate over whether the monarchy can survive the Harry-Meghan crisis, which is in its own way almost as **divisive** as the argument over the UK's role in Europe caused by Brexit, is really nothing new.

Although the 93-year-old queen enjoyed near-universal respect for a lifetime of public service, it is less than three decades since a poll showed three out of four Britons believed the Royal Family was falling apart.

Famously, the queen herself described 1992, a year of scandals including the break-up of the marriage of her son and heir Charles and Princess Diana, as her annus horribilis—her horrible year.

The **mawkish** outpouring of grief that seemed to **afflict** much of the population at the time of Diana's death five years later sparked criticism that Elizabeth was insensitive. Once again, the future of the monarchy seemed to be **on the line**.

At the start of her reign as queen in 1952, the young Elizabeth had responded to post-war **apathy** toward the monarchy by opening up the previously aloof Royal Family to greater public **scrutiny**.

Chapter 7 **Politics—Constitutional Monarchy**

Her great-great-grandmother Queen Victoria had faced a similar challenge after retreating from public life after the death of her husband, Albert. The British people began to complain about Victoria's absence and to question her role until she was gradually **coaxed** back into the public gaze.

Elizabeth's tactic, however, proved to be a double-edged sword. It made the ruling House of Windsor more human but it also exposed its members to the arbitrary judgments of the general public.

The popular press and much of the public act now as if they have an intimate understanding of the motivations and desires of every individual royal as if they were members of their own family. The female royals are particularly exposed to scrutiny, whether it is over their level of dedication to their royal role or the length of their **hemlines**.

The British print media has been accused of contributing to undermining the Royal Family by its **obsessive** coverage, an element that apparently drives sales in a **dwindling** market. But once again, this is nothing new.

In the golden age of Georgian satire in the early 19th century, the Royal Family was savaged in **scurrilous** and near-**obscene** caricatures that would not pass the good-taste test of any modern publication.

If history is anything to go by, the current furore will no doubt die down and the monarchy will survive, at least in the short term, largely through **inertia**. Post-Brexit, no-one is in a hurry to put any more nationally divisive issues, such as the future of the royals, to the people.

Apart from **diehard** republicans, most Britons do not obsess about replacing their constitutional monarchy with a presidential system. Anti-royal feeling is focused less on Elizabeth and her constitutional role than it is on the privileges and expenditure of royals lower down the **pecking order**.

Prince Harry's role was as a "spare", a second heir to the throne should his older brother William not survive. With the birth of William's children, Harry has dropped down to sixth in the order of succession. It is probably safe for him to go his own way.

Maybe his decision will start a trend. While the British people are not yet marching in the streets for an end to monarchy, a **slimmed-down** system that **marginalized** the lesser members of such a privileged family might have a greater chance of survival in the years to come.

Vocabulary

ambivalent	*adj.*	（忧喜参半、好坏参半等）矛盾情绪的
disruption	*n.*	妨碍；扰乱
furore	*n.*	群情激愤；骚动
anachronism	*n.*	过时的人（或风俗、思想）
pragmatism	*n.*	实用主义；务实思想
figurehead	*n.*	有名无实的领导人；傀儡
wield	*v.*	拥有；运用
overweening	*adj.*	傲慢的；自负的
divisive	*adj.*	造成不和的；引起分歧的
mawkish	*adj.*	无病呻吟的；自作多情的
afflict	*v.*	折磨；使痛苦
on the line		处于危险中；模棱两可
apathy	*n.*	冷漠；淡漠
scrutiny	*n.*	仔细检查；认真彻底的审查
coax	*v.*	哄劝；劝诱
hemline	*n.*	底边；底缘
obsessive	*adj.*	过分的；着迷的
dwindle	*v.*	（逐渐）减少；变小
scurrilous	*adj.*	恶语毁谤的；用污言秽语谩骂的
obscene	*adj.*	淫秽的；猥亵的
inertia	*n.*	缺乏活力；惰性
diehard	*adj.*	顽固的；因循守旧的
pecking order		社会等级
slimmed-down	*adj.*	（为节省开支或提高效率而）裁员的
marginalize	*v.*	使显得微不足道；使无实权

Exercises

Chapter 7 **Politics—Constitutional Monarchy**

General Election: Who Would Become the Winner of First-Past-The-Post

One of the reasons people hate politics is that truth is rarely a politician's objective. Election and power are.

—Cal Thomas

 Test Your Knowledge

I. Search for relevant information to answer the following questions.

1. How often does Britain have its general election?
2. What are the two major parties in Britain?
3. What's the role of political parties? Why are they important?
4. Do the voters vote for a new Prime Minister? Who chooses the Prime Minister?
5. How many UK Prime Ministers can you name?

II. Match the two major parties in Britain with their ideologies by putting the numbers of the statements in the corresponding box.

	Conservative Party	Labour Party
Ideologies		

1. People should build on the wisdom of past generations, which is embodied in the political institutions and traditions that the present generation has inherited.
2. It emphasizes the values of class solidarity, loyalty to leaders, plain living and plain speaking, and establishing a reserve fund to safeguard the group against unspecified disasters or attacks that the future may bring.
3. Measures should be taken to reduce the inequalities that flow from the economic system and the status system.
4. It favors reducing the influence of trade unions and minimizing expenditures on social welfare.

5. It has belief in an egalitarian economy and the necessity of government provision of a range of public services, such as social welfare, education and public transport.

6. It emphasizes the promotion of private property and enterprise. Human inequality is an inescapable fact of life. Those more fortunate in their birth or more successful in their careers have a social and moral obligation to help fellow citizens who are less fortunate or less successful.

Intensive Reading

Text I How Winston Churchill Lost the 1945 British General Election*

May 1945

The end of World War II in 1945 turned Winston Churchill into the world's most **eminent** statesman. He was **feted** and celebrated everywhere he went and had an approval rating of 83%. Yet three months later, he suffered a **humiliating** election defeat.

Churchill's electoral fate demonstrates that democratic elections are not won on past achievements and personal glory and celebrity status. They are mostly won on a persuasive and realizable program for the contested period of office. Victory means **addressing** the genuine concerns and anxieties of voters. This is why governments in Western countries change so frequently—and why **autocrats** avoid having to hold fair elections.

In 1945 it seemed a **foregone** conclusion that Churchill and his Conservative Party would win the general election. No election had taken place during the war; the last general election was in 1935. Churchill wanted to maintain the wartime coalition until the defeat of Japan, but the Labour Party **demurred**. They left the national government after victory in Europe, sparking an election.

July 1945

Polling day was 5 July 1945, but ballot counting was delayed until the 26th to count votes from soldiers abroad. Churchill **courteously** invited Labour leader Clement Attlee to the "Big Three" conference in Potsdam. The meeting was

---

* Retrieved from The Churchill Project website.

interrupted so that they could go home, wait for the outcome, and form a new government. Stalin assumed that Churchill would "fix" the election result and was astounded when he lost.

Labour won a landslide victory. As soon as the election result was announced, Churchill went to Buckingham Palace to submit his **resignation** to King George VI. **Chauffeured** by his wife in their modest little Austin, Clement Attlee arrived at the Palace within minutes of Churchill's departure to be appointed the new Prime Minister.

The King was distressed at the fall of Churchill, whom he had grown to trust and respect. In the audience room, an uncomfortable silence reigned until Attlee finally spoke up: "I've won the election." The King replied, "I know. I heard it on the Six O'Clock News."

How Churchill Lost

Until the last few days before the vote was held, Churchill and much of the country had been firmly convinced that he and his party would be returned to power with a decent majority. Although his party had conceived of a National Health Service and a vast housebuilding program, it lacked the sweeping fervor of the socialist reformers. Churchill's own focus had been international—on "building the peace" as he called it. When the debate shifted to the people's needs at home, he once reflected, "I have no message for them."

There were three reasons for the loss he and his party experienced:

1. The Conservative Campaign

The six-week election campaign in May–July 1945 largely focused on the future of the country. The progressive reforms proposed by Labour were highly popular. The Conservative program was much more vague, and focused on Churchill's leadership. But after six devastating years of war, voters were more interested in how to bring about a bright future than to dwell upon the past. Most soldiers in the field were fed up with the war and looked forward to a new age of prosperous **normalcy**. To many, a Labour government seemed to hold out the best prospects.

The Conservative campaign was ineffective and poorly thought out. Symbolic of that was Churchill's first campaign broadcast on June 4th, in which he accused Attlee of harboring **dictatorial** ambitions. **Outrageously** to many, Churchill said Labour "would have to **fall back on** some sort of a Gestapo" to enforce its program. Attlee quietly replied that the speech showed Churchill ill-suited to be a leader in times of peace.

2. The Labour Alternative

The Labour Party's **platform** for Britain's future had been carefully worked out. It promised government-supported full employment, a free National Health Service. The Labour **manifesto** included nationalizing key industries: steel, coal, electricity, railways, the Bank of England, civil aviation and road transport. These were new and bright ideas in the eyes of many voters. At least, they thought, Labour had a plan! By comparison, the Tories offered nothing as comprehensive.

Labour also seemed to know how to accomplish all it promised. They were not without experience: Churchill himself had placed many senior Labour leaders in charge of economic ministries during the war. Labour ministers had for the most part done a good job.

British voters agreed with Labour idea of "winning the peace" by creating a **visionary** welfare state. Housing, full employment, social welfare and the health system stood at the top of the list for most voters. Foreign affairs and national security policy, which Churchill emphasized, ranked much lower.

3. The Tories' Poor Image

Despite the nation's tremendous affection for him, Churchill was elderly, with an elite background and, Britons thought, a **paternalistic** Victorian. Many saw him as out of touch with the modern world. His emphatic belief in Empire, and Britain's responsibility thereto, sounded **out of sync** in the new era. India's almost inevitable independence distressed him. The majority of his countrymen didn't care. Churchill called communism "a religion to some people", but Canadian Prime Minister Mackenzie King, who knew him well, said the Empire-Commonwealth was "a religion to him".

Except for the years 1924 and 1929–1931, Britain had been led by Conservative or coalition governments for nearly three decades. With an overwhelming majority after 1935, many Conservatives were viewed as **appeasers** who had **downplayed** the Nazi threat. Under Prime Ministers Baldwin and Chamberlain, Britain had weakly given in to Hitler's territorial demands.

Likewise, the Tories could hardly avoid being seen as responsible for the high unemployment and **threadbare** conditions of prewar years. The war years and **rationing** were reminders of the prewar Depression.

Taking these elements into account, it was little wonder that Churchill and the Tories lost the 1945 election.

Chapter 7 Politics—Constitutional Monarchy

📖 Vocabulary

eminent	*adj.*	卓越的；有名望的
fete	*v.*	欢迎；款待
humiliating	*adj.*	使蒙受耻辱的
address	*v.*	设法解决
autocrat	*n.*	独裁者；独断独行的人
foregone	*adj.*	预知的；预先决定的
demur	*v.*	表示异议
courteously	*adv.*	有礼貌地；亲切地
resignation	*n.*	辞呈
chauffeur	*v.*	为……开车
normalcy	*n.*	常态
dictatorial	*adj.*	独裁的
outrageously	*adv.*	无法容忍地
fall back on		转而使用
platform	*n.*	（政党的）施政纲领
manifesto	*n.*	宣言
visionary	*adj.*	有创见的
paternalistic	*adj.*	专断的；家长式的
out of sync		不协调；不同步
appeaser	*n.*	绥靖者；姑息者
downplay	*v.*	轻描淡写
threadbare	*adj.*	破旧的；陈腐的
rationing	*n.*	（物资紧缺时的）配给量；（常指因紧缺）定量配给

📚 Exercises

I. Decide whether the following statements are true or false, and mark T or F accordingly.

_____ **1.** Winston Churchill had an approval rating of 83% at the end of World War II in 1945.

_____ **2.** Churchill invited Labour leader Clement Attlee and introduced him as his successor to the "Big Three" conference in Potsdam.

_____ **3.** Stalin assumed that Churchill could manipulate the election process and was astounded when he lost.

_____ 4. Winston Churchill and his party had conceived of programs addressing the genuine concerns and anxieties of voters.

_____ 5. Many saw Churchill as out of touch with the modern world and his belief as out of sync in the new era.

II. Read the descriptions of people or organizations and fill in the blanks with their names.

> Churchill   Stalin   The Labour Party   The King   many voters

1. _____ assumed that Churchill would definitely win the election and was astounded when he lost.

2. _____ was distressed when Churchill lost the election for he had grown to trust and respect him.

3. _____ wanted to maintain the wartime coalition government but Labour party as his competitor pined for an election to form a single-party government.

4. _____'s platform for Britain's future had been carefully worked out.

5. Labour manifesto included nationalizing key industries: steel, coal, electricity, railways, the Bank of England, civil aviation and road transport. _____ thought of these as new and bright ideas.

III. Match the statements with the supporting evidence that the author uses in the passage.

1. The Conservative campaign was ineffective and poorly thought out.

2. The Labour Party's platform for Britain's future had been carefully worked out.

A. Churchill was elderly, with an elite background and, Britons thought, a paternalistic Victorian. Many saw him as out of touch with the modern world.

B. The platform promised government-supported full employment, a free National Health Service and nationalizing key industries: steel, coal, electricity, railways, the Bank of England, civil aviation and road transport.

C. Conservative program was much more vague, and focused on Churchill's leadership.

3. The Tories' poor image was another factor that made Churchill lose the election.

D. It also seemed to know how to accomplish all it promised.

E. His emphatic belief in Empire, and Britain's responsibility thereto, sounded out of sync in the new era.

F. British voters agreed with its idea of "winning the peace" by creating a visionary welfare state.

G. In Churchill's first campaign broadcast on June 4th, he accused Attlee of harboring dictatorial ambitions.

IV. Complete the following sentences with the appropriate forms of words and phrases in the box.

| eminent | humiliating | address | courteously | fall back on |
| outrageous | downplay | visionary | platform | vague |

1. The coach is _____ the team's poor performance.
2. An entrepreneur is more than just a risk taker. He is a(n) _____.
3. The party has announced a(n) _____ of political and economic reforms.
4. When necessary, instinct is the most reliable resource you can _____.
5. "Good morning, Pinocchio," said the Fox, greeting him _____.
6. The Democrats have suffered a(n) _____ defeat.
7. Now _____ physicist and mathematician Stephen Hawking argues God was not part of the equation.
8. They have only a(n) _____ idea of the amount of water available.
9. Policymakers are also trying to _____ the problem.
10. By diplomatic standards, this was _____ behaviour.

V. Discuss the following questions with your partner.

1. Should there be some requirements for Prime Minister to meet? If so, what should they be?
2. What factors would contribute to the victory in the election campaign?

Further Reading

Text II Some Arguments Surrounding the Debate over FPTP vs. PR*

For FPTP and Against PR

Farrell has neatly summarised the three main themes in any defence of the British system, as "simplicity, stability and **constituency** representation". These points are worthy of further consideration:

- The First Past the Post (FPTP) system is easy to understand, especially for the voter who marks an "X" on the ballot paper. It has the **alleged** merits of simplicity and familiarity, and, as such, is widely accepted.

- It usually leads to the formation of strong, stable, single-party governments with an overall majority; **coalition** government other than in times of emergency is virtually unknown. Single-party governments **pinpoint** political responsibility. The voters know whom to praise or blame, when things go right or wrong. Such administrations are also said to be capable of providing effective leadership for the nation. This is viewed as more important than achieving a proportional result. In Britain, we know who is to form the government immediately after the election is over. There is no need for private deals to be done by politicians who bargain in smoke-filled rooms, away from the public gaze; it is the voters directly who choose which party is in office.

- Because we have single-member constituencies there is a close relationship between the Member of Parliament (MP) and his or her constituency. The one member alone has responsibility for that area which he or she can get to know well. Once elected, the MP represents all who live in the area, not just those who voted for one particular party; all citizens know whom to approach if they have a problem or **grievance** needing **resolution**. This is very different from what happens under some more proportional systems, in which several elected members represent a broad, geographical area.

In his inquiry, Lord Jenkins himself recognised that FPTP is not without benefits, referring to the "by no means **negligible**" merits of the present

---

* Excerpted from Duncan Watts. *British Government and Politics: A Comparative Guide.* Edinburgh: Edinburgh University Press Ltd., 2006: 338–341.

Chapter 7 **Politics—Constitutional Monarchy**

system. In addition to the points above, the commissioners made the point that it enables the electorate sharply and cleanly to rid itself of an unwanted government; in other words, it is easy to punish those directly responsible for their errors.

Apart from the positive case for FPTP, there are disadvantages associated with Proportional Representation (PR). Among specific criticisms often made, it is suggested that:

PR encourages minor parties to stand for election and makes it more difficult for any one party to emerge victorious. Duverger's observation is often quoted, namely that: "The simple-majority, single-ballot system favours the two-party system; the simple-majority system with second ballot and proportional representation favour multi-partyism."

The primary anxiety of those opposed to an abandonment of FPTP is that it would greatly increase the likelihood of **perpetual** coalition government. As neither has ever **secured** a majority of the votes cast in any election post-war, it is unlikely that single-party government would result.

For Proportional Representation

The case for the use of a proportional scheme of voting in Britain has much to do with the allegedly **adverse** effects of FPTP. Among its **anticipated** benefits, a proportional electoral system:

- would not exaggerate movements of opinion within the electorate and produce landslide majorities that are often based on an **ever-diminishing** proportion of the national vote.

- would not allow a government to exercise power on the basis of minority popular support; e.g., Labour obtained power in October 1974 with the support of only 39% of those who voted, and with under 30% of the backing of the whole electorate.

- would provide greater justice to small parties. Traditionally, it has been the Liberals in their various **guises** who have suffered from FPTP, although in 1997 the Conservatives lost all representation in Scotland in spite of gaining 17% of the vote.

- would yield governments which have the backing of the majority of the electorate, and therefore could claim **legitimacy**; they may be coalition governments, but the parties which voted for them would **in toto** have a broader appeal than is the case at present.

- would avoid the geographical divisions brought about by FPTP. In 1997 the Conservatives were wiped out in Scotland, Wales and the large English provincial cities, just as Labour had suffered badly in the southern half of England back in the 1980s.
- would overcome a problem much emphasised in the Jenkins Inquiry, namely that there are "electoral deserts" under FPTP, areas more or less permanently committed to one party, in which the opposition can make little impact and get even less reward. Many seats in the House of Commons rarely change hands, so that supporters of the minority parties (e.g. Conservatives in Glasgow) have little likelihood of ever securing the election of a representative who supports his or her views. Significant sections of the population are **condemned** to almost permanent minority status.
- would, unlike FPTP, be better at producing parliamentary representation for women and ethnic minorities. For instance, since the introduction of a more proportional system in New Zealand, there has been a marked increase in the percentage of women elected.

In addition, of course, there is a positive case for proportional representation and coalitions. Proportional representation is:

- fair because it produces a close relationship between votes and seats;
- gives minority parties more representation and encourages voters to back them in the knowledge that they will not be wasting their vote;
- makes coalitions more likely. Coalitions can provide government that is stable because it rests on broad backing, legitimate because it has wide popular support and encourages the politics of consensus, cooperation and **moderation**.

Vocabulary

constituency	*n.*	（会支持某政党或政客的）选民阵营；选区
allege	*adj.*	指称（但还未被证实）的
coalition	*n.*	联合政府；联盟
pinpoint	*v.*	准确指出（原因）；给准确定位
grievance	*n.*	委屈；不满
resolution	*n.*	（问题、分歧等的）解决；决议

negligible	*adj.*	微不足道的
perpetual	*adj.*	永恒的；无休止的
secure	*v.*	争取到
adverse	*adj.*	不利的
anticipate	*v.*	预料，预期
ever-diminishing	*adj.*	一直减少的
guise	*n.*	表现形式；伪装
legitimacy	*n.*	合法；合理
in toto		全然，完全
condemn	*v.*	谴责，责备
moderation	*n.*	节制

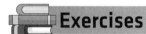

Exercises

Unit 3

Separation of Powers: Would Early Election Do Wonders for Theresa May

A vote is like a rifle: Its usefulness depends upon the character of the user.

—Theodore Roosevelt

 Test Your Knowledge

I. **Search for relevant information to answer the following questions.**

   1. How is the Cabinet formed?
   2. How many elements are there in the Parliament? What are they?
   3. What is the supreme law-making authority in Britain?
   4. Are all the members in the House of Lords hereditary peers?
   5. Does the House of Lords have a special judicial function?

II. **Match the government branches in Britain with their corresponding functions.**

   1. The administration
   2. The legislation
   3. The jurisdiction

   A. It is responsible for the resolution of disputes.
   B. It controls all executive activities of central government.
   C. It initiates some legislation and controls the timing of its entry in Parliament.
   D. It influences future government policy and represents the public and public opinions with the governing process.
   E. It examines all major issues of foreign and domestic policy.
   F. It carries out legislation—to draft new laws.
   G. It administers and interprets the meaning of laws.
   H. It scrutinizes the actions of the government.

Chapter 7 Politics—Constitutional Monarchy

> **Intensive Reading**

Text I Theresa May's Election Announcement: Full Statement*

UK Prime Minister Theresa May announced Tuesday that there will be a snap general election on June 8, 2017. Here is her statement in full.

I have just chaired a meeting of the Cabinet where we agreed that the government should call a general election to be held on June 8. I want to explain the reasons for that decision, what will happen next and the choice facing the British people when you come to vote in this election.

Last summer, after the country voted to leave the European Union, Britain needed certainty, stability and strong leadership. And since I became Prime Minister the government has **delivered** precisely that.

Despite predictions of immediate financial and economic danger, since the **referendum** we have seen consumer confidence remain high, record numbers of jobs and economic growth that has exceeded all expectations.

We have also delivered on the **mandate** that we were handed by the referendum result. Britain is leaving the European Union and there can be no turning back.

And as we look to the future, the government has the right plan for negotiating our new relationship with Europe. We want a deep and special partnership between a strong and successful European Union and a United Kingdom that is free to chart its own way in the world.

That means we will regain control of our own money, our own laws and our own borders. And we will be free to strike trade deals with old friends and new partners, all around the world.

This is the right approach and it is in the national interest. But the other political parties oppose it.

At this moment of enormous national significance there should be unity here in Westminster. But instead there is division. The country is coming together but Westminster is not.

---

* Retrieved from CNN website.

In recent weeks Labour have threatened to vote against the final agreement we reach with the European Union.

The Liberal Democrats have said they want to **grind** the business of government **to a standstill**.

The Scottish national party say they will vote against the legislation that formally **repeals** Britain's membership of the European Union.

And unelected members of the House of Lords have **vowed** to fight us every step of the way.

Our opponents believe, because the government's majority is so small, that our resolve will weaken and that they can force us to change course.

They are wrong. They underestimate our determination to get the job done.

And I am not prepared to let them endanger the security of millions of working people across the country. Because what they are doing **jeopardizes** the work we must do to prepare for Brexit at home. And it weakens the government's negotiating position in Europe.

If we do not hold a general election now, their political game-playing will continue. And the negotiations with the European Union will reach their most difficult stage in the **run-up** to the next scheduled election.

Division in Westminster will risk our ability to make a success of Brexit and it will cause damaging uncertainty and instability to the country.

So we need a general election and we need one now. Because we have, at this moment, a **one-off** chance to get this done while the European Union agrees its negotiating position and before the detailed talks begin.

I have only recently and **reluctantly** come to this conclusion. Since I became Prime Minister I have said there should be no election until 2020.

But now I have concluded that the only way to guarantee certainty and stability for the years ahead is to hold this election and seek your support for the decisions I must take.

And so tomorrow I will move a **motion** in the House of Commons calling for a general election to be held on June 8. That motion as set out by the Fixed-term Parliament Act will require a two-thirds majority of the House of Commons.

So I have a simple challenge to the opposition parties, who have criticized the government's vision for Brexit, who have challenged our objectives, who have threatened to block the legislation we put before Parliament.

This is your moment to show you mean it, to show that you are not opposing the government for the sake of it, to show that you do not treat politics as a game.

Let us tomorrow vote for an election. Let us put forward our plans for Brexit and our alternative programs for government and then let the people decide.

And the decision facing the country will be all about leadership. It will be a choice between strong and stable leadership in the national interest with me as your Prime Minister or weak and unstable coalition government led by Jeremy Corbyn **propped** up by the Liberal Democrats who want to reopen the divisions of the referendum, and Nicola Sturgeon and the SNP.

Every vote for the Conservatives will make it harder for opposition politicians who want to stop me from getting the job done.

Every vote for the Conservatives will make me stronger when I negotiate for Britain with the Prime Ministers, Presidents and Chancellors of the European Union.

Every vote for the Conservatives will mean we can stick to our plan for a stronger Britain and take the right long-term decisions for a more secure future.

It was with reluctance that I decided the country needs this election. But it is with strong **conviction** that I say it is necessary to secure the strong and stable leadership the country needs to see us through Brexit and beyond.

So tomorrow let the House of Commons vote for an election.

Let everybody put forward their proposals for Brexit and their programs for government, and let us remove the risk of uncertainty and instability and continue to give the country the strong and stable leadership it demands.

Vocabulary

deliver	*v.*	实现；履行
referendum	*n.*	公民投票；全民公决
mandate	*n.*	（政府或机构经选举而获得的）授权；委托
grind... to a standstill		……慢慢停滞
repeal	*v.*	撤销；废止（法令）
vow	*v.*	发誓

jeopardize	v.	损害；危及
run-up	n.	前夕
one-off	adj.	一次性的
reluctantly	adv.	不情愿地；嫌恶地
motion	n.	议案；动作
prop	v.	支撑
conviction	n.	坚定的信念

Exercises

I. Decide whether the following statements are true or false, and mark T or F accordingly.

    _____ 1. Since Tereasa May became Prime Minister she had said that they needed a general election and they needed an immediate one.

    _____ 2. It was immediate financial and economic danger that made Tereasa May propose an early general election.

    _____ 3. According to Tereasa May, the only way to guarantee certainty and stability for the years ahead is to hold an early election and seek electors' support for the decisions she had to take.

    _____ 4. Tereasa May's motion of an early general election requires a two-thirds majority of the House of Commons.

    _____ 5. What Labour, the Liberal Democrats and the Scottish National Party were doing jeopardized the preparation for Brexit's negotiation.

II. Read the descriptions and match them with the persons or organizations involved.

1. _____ have threatened to vote against the final agreement we reach with the European Union.   A. The Scottish National Party

2. _____ have said they want to grind the business of government to a standstill.   B. The Liberal Democrats

3. _____ agreed that the government should call a general election to be held on June 8.   C. Labour

Chapter 7 **Politics—Constitutional Monarchy**

4. _____ have vowed to fight every step of the way by Tereasa May's administration.

5. _____ say they will vote against the legislation that formally repeals Britain's membership of the European Union.

D. The Cabinet

E. Unelected members of the House of Lords

III. Complete the following sentences with the appropriate forms of the words in the box.

challenge	certainty	criticize	conviction
exceed	endanger	threaten	jeopardize
remain	reluctance	stability	weaken

1. Last summer, after the country voted to leave the European Union, Britain needed _____, _____ and strong leadership.

2. Despite predictions of immediate financial and economic danger, since the referendum we have seen consumer confidence _____ high, record numbers of jobs and economic growth that has _____ all expectations.

3. I am not prepared to let them _____ the security of millions of working people across the country. Because what they are doing _____ the work we must do to prepare for Brexit at home. And it _____ the government's negotiating position in Europe.

4. So I have a simple challenge to the opposition parties, who have _____ the government's vision for Brexit, who have _____ our objectives, who have _____ to block the legislation we put before Parliament.

5. It was with _____ that I decided the country needs this election. But it is with strong _____ that I say it is necessary to secure the strong and stable leadership the country needs to see us through Brexit and beyond.

IV. Complete the following sentences with the appropriate forms of the words in the box.

| alternative | deliver | jeopardize | motion | mandate |
| one-off | prop | run-up | repeal | reluctantly |

1. We _____ agreed to go with her.

223

2. We oppose any terrorist and violent action that would _____ lives of innocent people.
3. The president and his supporters are almost certain to read this vote as a(n) _____ for continued economic reform.
4. He has promised to finish the job by June and I am sure he will _____.
5. Opposition parties are likely to bring a no-confidence _____ against the government.
6. New ways to treat arthritis (关节炎) may provide a(n) _____ to painkillers.
7. The army is one of the main _____ of the government.
8. Our survey revealed that these allergies were mainly _____.
9. The company believes the products will sell well in the _____ to Christmas.
10. The government has just _____ the law segregating public facilities.

V. Read aloud the following sentences. Pay attention to the rhythm created by the repetition of words and patterns.

This is your moment to show you mean it, to show that you are not opposing the government for the sake of it, to show that you do not treat politics as a game.

Let us tomorrow vote for an election. Let us put forward our plans for Brexit and our alternativeprograms for government and then let the people decide.

Every vote for the Conservatives will make it harder for opposition politicians who want to stop me from getting the job done.

Every vote for the Conservatives will make me stronger when I negotiate for Britain with the Prime Ministers, Presidents and Chancellors of the European Union.

Every vote for the Conservatives will mean we can stick to our plan for a stronger Britain and take the right long-term decisions for a more secure future.

Further Reading

Text II British PM May Calls for Early Election to Strengthen Brexit Hand*

British Prime Minister Theresa May called on Tuesday for an early election on June 8, saying she needed to strengthen her hand in divorce talks with the European Union by **bolstering** support for her Brexit plan.

Standing outside her Downing Street office, May said she had been reluctant to ask Parliament to back her move to bring forward the poll from 2020. But, after thinking "long and hard" during a walking holiday, she decided it was necessary to try to stop the **opposition** "jeopardizing" her work on Brexit.

Some were surprised by May's move—the Conservative Prime Minister has repeatedly said she does not want to be **distracted** by **campaigning**—but opinion polls give her a strong lead and the British economy has so far **defied predictions** of a slowdown.

Growth is faster than expected, consumer confidence is high and unemployment low, but the economy may be **poised** to pass its peak as consumers start to feel the **strain** from rising prices.

Sterling rose to a four-month high against the US dollar after the market bet that May would strengthen her parliamentary majority, which Deutsche Bank said would be a "game-changer" for the pound.

But the stronger pound helped push Britain's main share index to close down 2.3%, its biggest one-day loss since June 27, days after Britain voted to leave the EU.

"It was with reluctance that I decided the country needs this election. But it is with strong conviction that I say it is necessary to secure the strong and stable leadership the country needs to see us through Brexit and beyond," May said.

"Before Easter, I spent a few days walking in Wales with my husband, thought about this long and hard and came to the decision that to provide that **stability** and certainty for the future, this was the way to do it—to have an election," she told ITV news.

---

* Retrieved from Reuters website.

May called US President Donald Trump, German Chancellor Angela Merkel and other European leaders after the announcement, a spokesman said, without giving details of the conversations.

Britain joins a list of Western European countries scheduled to hold elections this year. Votes in France in April and May, and in Germany in September, have the potential to reshape the political landscape around the two years of Brexit talks with the EU expected to start in earnest in June.

May is **capitalizing** on her runaway lead in the opinion polls and she could win around 100 additional seats in Parliament.

A survey conducted after May's announcement put her Conservative Party 21 points ahead of the main opposition Labour Party. The ICM/Guardian poll of 1,000 people showed Conservative support at 46%, with Labour on 25% and the Liberal Democrats on 11%.

May's personal ratings also dwarf those of Labour leader Jeremy Corbyn, with 50% of those asked by pollster YouGov saying she would make the best Prime Minister. Corbyn wins only 14%.

May, a former **interior** minister, was appointed Prime Minister after Britain's vote to leave the European Union forced the **resignation** of her **predecessor** David Cameron. The election will be a vote on her performance so far.

She is counting on winning the support of British voters, who backed Brexit by 52%–48%. Some Britons questioned on social media whether they wanted to cast yet another ballot less than a year after the June referendum and two years after they voted in the last parliamentary poll.

However, the ICM/Guardian poll found that around three in five respondents said May was right to call an election.

Her spokesman said she had the backing of her top team of ministers and had informed Queen Elizabeth of her plans on Monday.

Business groups largely welcomed the move, while expressing concern that the government's focus may **stray** away from the economy, which May said had defied "predictions of immediate financial and economic danger".

Underlining divisions the vote is unlikely to mend, however, Nicola Sturgeon, first minister of the Scottish government, described the decision as a "huge political miscalculation" that could help her efforts to hold a new independence referendum.

The government of the Republic of Ireland also expressed concern that the early election could damage the chances of resolving a political crisis in the British province of Northern Ireland.

Irish Prime Minister Enda Kenny was among the leaders called by May, along with European Council President Donald Tusk.

Tusk, who is running the negotiations with Britain, said in Brussels that the election was a Brexit plot twist worthy of Alfred Hitchcock—the late film director known as the master of **suspense**.

Before holding the early election, May must win the support of two-thirds of the Parliament in a vote on Wednesday, which looked certain after Labour and the Liberal Democrats said they would vote in favor.

Labour's Corbyn welcomed the election plan, but some of his lawmakers doubted whether it was a good move, fearing they could lose their seats. At least two said they would not run.

If the opinion polls are right, May will win a new mandate for a series of reforms she wants to make and also a vote of confidence in a vision for Brexit which sees the country outside the EU's single market.

"The decision facing the country will be all about leadership," May said. "What they are doing jeopardizes the work we must do to prepare for Brexit at home, and it weakens the government's negotiating position in Europe."

Vocabulary

bolster	v.	增强
opposition	n.	强烈的反对；对手
distract	v.	分散（注意力）；使分心
campaign	v.	竞选活动
defy	v.	使不可能（理解或解释）；违抗
prediction	n.	预言
poise	v.	（使）平衡；（使）悬着
strain	n.	压力
stability	n.	稳定（性）；稳固（性）
capitalize	v.	利用
interior	adj.	内政的；内部的
stray	v.	走失

英国社会与文化

underline	*v.*	强调；在……下面画线
suspense	*n.*	悬念

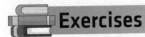

Chapter 7 Politics—Constitutional Monarchy

Product of Ballot and Root of Trouble: Soft Brexit, Hard Brexit or No-Deal Brexit

Sovereignty is not just at the national level; that's the mistake of Brexit that other people make.

—Emmanuel Macron

 Test Your Knowledge

I. **Search for relevant information to answer the following questions.**

   1. Who was the Prime Minister when the EU referendum took place?
   2. What did the Prime Minister do when people voted for Brexit?
   3. Who became the leader of the Conservative Party when the former one resigned after the EU referendum?
   4. Could British people come to the consensus as to how to exit the EU?
   5. Did Theresa May successfully bring the UK out of the EU?

II. **Match each event with the time by filling the corresponding letter in the blank.**

   1. Theresa May announced an early general election _____.
   2. _____ Theresa May said she would step down as UK Conservative Party leader.
   3. _____, Theresa May signed the letter which would start negotiation for the UK to leave the EU.
   4. The EU referendum took place _____.
   5. Boris Johnson became the Prime Minister of the United Kingdom _____.
   6. Theresa May became the Prime Minister _____.

   A. in June 2016
   B. on July 13, 2016
   C. on March 30, 2017
   D. on April 18, 2017
   E. on June 7, 2019
   F. in July 2019

Intensive Reading

Text I Britain and the European Union*

Britain has long had a reputation for being a reluctant European and has developed habit of often being late to join its European partners in new ventures, and of being less than enthusiastic in engaging itself with Europe. **Eurosceptics** see Britain's **reticence** as admirable caution, some even arguing that Britain should never have joined the Community in the first place, and that its key interests continue to lie outside Europe. (One of the more **bizarre** suggestions that have been proffered is for Britain to leave the EU and to join instead the North American Free Trade Area.) For their part, Europhiles argue that Britain's **dilatory** attitude to European integration has prevented it from taking part in the critical planning stages of EU **initiatives**, so denying it the opportunity to mould the process more to its liking and advantage.

The extent to which British public opinion is out of step with that in much (but not all) of the rest of the EU is reflected in the regular polls carried out by **Eurobaronmeter**, the EU polling service. These reveal a low level of psychological attachment to the EU by most Britons, who are also less enthusiastic about the benefit of EU membership than the citizens of almost any other member states. There are several possible explanations:

- Britain's physical separation from the continent has helped make the British feel that they are somehow different from other Europeans, and that they are not really European at all. Even today, many Britons still talk about Europe as something quite **distinct** from Britain.

- At the time that **continental** European leaders were planning the first steps in the process of integration, Britain still had many interests outside Europe: It had an empire, it had strong cultural links with its dominions and colonies (many of which still saw Britain as the mother country), and it had a strong relationship with the United States (in contrast to the distrust with which the French viewed—and continue to view—the US).

- Where nationalism and the nation-state had been **discredited** on the continent by two world wars, they were **vindicated** in Britain by its independence and separation. Where European states concluded that

---

* Excerpted from John McCormick. *Contemporary Britain*. Beijing: China Renmin University Press, 2009: 220–227.

only cooperation and integration could prevent future wars, it was its independence which—in the minds of many Britons—helped Britain avoid becoming caught up in the kinds of conflicts which brought so many changes to the borders of continental European states.

- Many Britons—like many other Europeans—understand neither the EU nor its implications. They are not helped by mass media which often promote myths and misunderstandings about the EU (for example, misrepresenting the powers of the European Commission), and by the fact that even academic specialists on the EU cannot agree on whether it is an international organization or a **nascent** United States of Europe.

The issue of Europe has been at the heart of policy debates within the major British political parties, and indeed has become a cause for much division and disagreement. In the early 1980s, it was the Labour Party policy to withdraw Britain altogether from the Community, a **stance** that helped **prompt** the breakaway of the Social Democratic Party, an event which in turn contributed to Labour's long spell in opposition. By the mid-1990s Labour had **reversed** its policy, arguing that withdrawal would be "disastrous" for Britain, and pushing for a more constructive role in the EU.

Meanwhile, the issue has been even more divisive for the Conservative Party, which ironically was responsible—under the leadership of Prime Minister Edward Heath—for negotiating Britain's entry in 1973. Margaret Thatcher **railed** against what she saw as excessive bureaucratization and regulation by Europe, and argued that EU policies were **undermining** her attempts to free up the British marketplace. "We have not successfully **rolled back** the frontiers of the state in Britain", she famously declared in a speech in 1988, "only to see them reimposed at a European level, with a European superstate exercising a new dominance from Brussels". (This philosophy rather overlooked the fact that "Europe" has few independent powers for making policy, and is still largely the sum of its parts.) Her disagreements with pro-Europeans within her party contributed to her fall from power in 1990, the **split** continued to **dog** the Conservatives under the leadership of John Major, and it has been a key factor in all recent party leadership contests. Some Britons remain hostile to the "federalist tendencies" of the EU, but many misunderstand the notion of federalism and fail to realize that it actually involves the **retention** of often substantial independent powers for the member states. At the same time, though, increasing numbers (particularly professionals and those in their twenties and thirties) are now convinced of the benefits of membership.

Vocabulary

eurosceptic	n.	疑欧派（指反对英国与欧盟关系密切的人）
reticence	n.	沉默；沉默寡言
bizarre	adj.	怪异的
dilatory	adj.	拖拉的
initiative	n.	（重要的）法案；倡议
Eurobaronmeter	n.	欧洲晴雨表
distinct	adj.	有区别的；明显的
continental	adj.	大陆的；内陆的
discredit	v.	使……丧失信誉
vindicate	v.	证明是正确的
nascent	adj.	新生的；初期的
stance	n.	（对某事的）态度，立场
prompt	v.	促使
reverse	v.	使（决定、政策、趋势）转向，逆转
rail	v.	强烈抗议
undermine	v.	逐渐削弱；逐渐动摇
roll back		使退却；削减
split	v.	分开；分裂
dog	v.	（问题、伤病等）长期困扰
retention	n.	保留

Exercises

I. Decide whether the following statements are true or false, and mark T or F accordingly.

_____ 1. It was the habit of often being late to join its European partners in new ventures that denied Britain the opportunity to mould Europe to its liking and advantage, which in turn made it more reluctant to engage itself with Europe.

_____ 2. There is a low level of psychological attachment to the EU by most Britons although they are enthusiastic about the benefit of EU membership.

_____ 3. Britain still had many interests outside Europe when European leaders were planning the process of European integration.

_____ 4. The two world wars made most Britons conclude that cooperation and integration could prevent future wars and

Chapter 7 Politics—Constitutional Monarchy

conflicts.

_____ 5. When the Social Democratic Party broke away from the Labour, it contributed to Labour's long spell in opposition.

II. **Match each statement with its supporting evidence or possible reasons that the author uses in the passage.**

1. There is a low level of psychological attachment to the EU by most Britons.

2. For the Labour Party, the issue of Europe has become a cause for much division and disagreement.

3. The issue of Europe has been divisive for the Conservative Party.

4. Many Britons understand neither the EU nor its implications.

A. They misunderstand the powers of the European Commission.

B. Britain's physical isolation from the European continent makes the British feel that Europe is distinct from Britain.

C. The Social Democratic Party broke away from the Labour Party.

D. They think the notion of federalism involves the deprivation of substantial independent powers for the member states.

E. Under the leadership of Prime Minister Edward Heath, Britain negotiated its entry into the European Community while Margaret Thatcher showed her reluctance to integrate the British economy with it.

F. Britain had many interests outside Europe and it did not value the European integration a lot.

G. The fact that "Europe" has few independent powers for making policy, and still largely the sum of its parts is overlooked.

H. Britain's independence during the two world wars helped Britain avoid involvement in the conflicts which brought so many changes to the borders of continental European states.

I. Thatcher's disagreements with pro-Europeans within her party contributed to her fall from power in 1990.

J. In the early 1980s, the Labour Party opposed the accession of Britain to the European Community and then in the mid-1990s it reversed its policy.

K. The issue of Europe has been a key factor in all recent party leadership contests.

III. Complete the following sentences with the appropriate forms of the words in the box.

| discredit | distinct | initiative | retention | prompt |
| reverse | stance | vindicate | undermine | split |

1. The rejection of such _____ by no means indicates that voters are unconcerned about the environment.
2. He called the success a(n) _____ of his party's free-market economic policy.
3. He _____ my good name with gossip.
4. They have made it clear that they will not _____ the decision to increase prices.
5. Engineering and technology are disciplines _____ from one another and from science.
6. Japan's recession has _____ consumers to cut back on buying cars.
7. Offering advice on each and every problem will _____ her feeling of being adult.
8. There appears to be increasing support for the leadership to take a more aggressive _____.
9. The committee _____ over government subsidies.
10. The Citizens' Forum supported special powers for Quebec but also argued for the _____ of a strong central government.

IV. Complete the following sentences with the appropriate forms of the words in the box.

| conflict | deny | division | develop | integration | heart |
| hostile | notion | engage | prevent | reputation | mould |

1. Britain has long had a(n) _____ for being a reluctant European and has _____ habit of often being late to join its European partners in new ventures, and of being less than enthusiastic in _____ itself with Europe.
2. Europhiles argue that Britain's dilatory attitude to European integration has _____ it from taking part in the critical planning stages of EU initiatives, so _____ it the opportunity to _____ the process more to its liking and advantage.
3. Where European states concluded that only cooperation and _____

could prevent future wars, it was its independence which—in the minds of many Britons—helped Britain avoid becoming caught up in the kinds of _____ which brought so many changes to the borders of continental European states.

4. The issue of Europe has been at the _____ of policy debates within the major British political parties, and indeed has become a cause for much _____ and disagreement.

5. Britons remain _____ to the "federalist tendencies" of the EU, but many misunderstand the _____ of federalism and fail to realize that it actually involves the retention of often substantial independent powers for the member states.

V. Make a 3-minute speech about the possible attitude of the author towards EU. You can pick out relevant sentences from the passage to support your opinion.

Further Reading

Text II Brexit: Pros and Cons*

With Prime Minister David Cameron's government committed to an "in-out" referendum on the UK's membership in the European Union (EU) before the end of 2017, the consequences of a vote to leave the EU (British Exit, or Brexit) need to be considered. This article looks at arguments for and against Brexit, as well as alternative arrangements for trade with the EU.

Brexit Pros

Cost of EU membership: By some estimates, the total economic cost (both direct and indirect) is as much as 11% of annual **gross** domestic product (GDP), or close to £200 billion.

Financial regulation: A particularly sensitive area of regulation for Britain is financial regulation. Brexit **proponents** cite red tape, ill-informed tax initiatives, protectionist policies and high costs of the EU's regulation of financial markets.

Many **commentators** have the general **perception**—rightly or wrongly—that Germany and France are anti-finance and **envious** of the London's position

---
* Retrieved from Nasdaq website.

as Europe's **de facto** financial capital. As a result, they maintain, Brussels is either indifferent to the impact of EU financial regulations on the UK's most crucial industry or is willfully targeting the UK's dominance of Europe's financial industry.

Such regulation and perceived interference has led to calls for leaving the EU so UK financial authorities and Parliament can **formulate** a regulatory framework that is more **accommodating** to London's needs and ensure its continued financial dominance.

Nonfinancial regulation: EU regulations also **hinder** the nonfinancial sector of the UK's economy. For example, regulations designed to **prohibit** dangerous substances and processes are considered extremely costly for businesses, forcing some suppliers to go out of business and others to introduce expensive changes to their business operations or products. These regulations have also raised prices for consumer goods. In total, EU regulations are estimated to cost between 5% and 6% of UK GDP per year.

Common Agricultural Policy (CAP) and protectionist trade policies: Many consider CAP—long a **bugbear** for opponents of British EU membership—hugely wasteful and costly because it fosters an uncompetitive domestic agricultural sector dependent on **subsidies** to survive. Free market supporters are also critical of the EU's protectionist trade policies, such as anti-dumping measures, which the EU imposes when it suspects that unfair subsidies are making imported goods considerably cheaper than their EU-made **equivalents**. The total cost of these trade-**distorting** polices, including CAP and trade protectionism, is estimated at 3% of the UK's GDP.

Immigration and benefit tourism: One of the most emotionally charged issues for Britain is immigration. Due to the EU's founding principle of free movement of people—along with the free movement of goods, services and capital—the UK has no control over immigration from other EU member states. Evidence suggests that migrants from EUA8 (eight Baltic and Eastern European states), employed primarily in low-skilled sectors, have suppressed wage growth in those sectors and increased unemployment levels among the UK-born population.

Figures from January 2012 also show that of a total of 5.5 million welfare **recipients**, 371,000 were foreign-born, and 118,000 were from the European Economic Area (EEA), which provides for the free movement of people through EU states. There is also concern that citizens of EU states with poorer health services will travel to the UK to take advantage of the free services available through the country's National Health Service.

Brexit Cons

Let's take a look at the arguments for the UK to stay in the EU.

Economic benefits: Arguably, the benefits for Britain of staying in the EU are primarily economic. Consider:

- The EU is a large market, accounting for 25% of world GDP, as well as the UK's biggest trading partner—45% of UK exports are to the EU, and 50% of imports are from the EU.

- The UK's attractiveness as a destination for foreign direct investment (FDI) is enhanced by the country's EU membership and access to its markets. In 2012, the UK received FDI amounting to £937 billion while UK firms invested £1,088 billion abroad. Nearly 50% of UK FDI, both inward and outward, is EU-related.

Immigration: Proponents of continued EU membership cite favorable statistics supportive of the principle of the free movement of people, including:

- Immigrants to the UK from the EU are better educated than UK nationals—32% have a degree, compared with 21% of UK subjects—and are less likely to be in the lower education category.

- They tend to be younger than the native UK population, averaging 32.3 years compared with 40.8 years in 2011, a benefit when many countries are struggling with a rapidly aging population.

- Immigrants from the EEA arriving since 2000 have contributed 34% more in **fiscal** terms than they have received.

Alternatives to Full EU Membership

What alternatives would Britain have if it votes to leave the EU?

The EU has entered into three main types of agreements with non-EU countries:

- Membership in the EEA
- Membership in the EU's Customs Union
- Free trade agreements

While it would naturally be in their interest to establish a preferential trade agreement with the UK, it would also not be surprising if the EU member countries sought to **penalize** the UK for leaving the union. The motivation might be to ensure that other member states see a cost to exiting the union. Such a punishment could restrict access for certain sectors, with the financial sector an obvious candidate. Post-Brexit negotiations over an agreement between the UK and EU would be bound to cause risk and uncertainty and could drag on for years.

The Scottish Question

If Britain does decide to leave the EU, what could the consequences be for the union between England and Scotland? The Scottish National Party is emphatically pro-Europe, and if Britain voted to leave the EU, there would doubtless be calls for another referendum on Scottish independence.

Vocabulary

gross	*adj.*	（尤指钱）总的
regulation	*n.*	法规；管理
proponent	*n.*	（某观念或行为的）支持者
commentator	*n.*	（电台或电视的）解说员，评论员
perception	*n.*	理解；看法
envious	*adj.*	羡慕的
de facto	*adj.*	实际上存在的
formulate	*v.*	构想出（计划或提案）
accommodating	*adj.*	乐于助人的；与人方便的
hinder	*v.*	阻碍，妨碍
prohibit	*v.*	（尤指以法令）禁止，阻止
bugbear	*n.*	使人烦恼担忧的事；牵挂
subsidy	*n.*	补贴；补助金
equivalent	*n.*	相等的东西
distort	*v.*	使变形；扭曲
recipient	*n.*	受方；接受者
fiscal	*adj.*	财政的；财政年度的
penalize	*v.*	处罚，惩罚

Exercises

Chapter 8

People—Habit Is Second Nature

Introduction

The British are famous for queuing. They queue up at banks, shop counters, post offices, and sporting events. But queuing in a calm, good-natured manner has not always come naturally. Do you know that even in Britain queuing can be frustrating and tense?

British people complain a lot. They moan about poor service. They moan about a break-down. They moan about bad food. Moaning can be beneficial but constant and excessive moaning is bad for one's physical and psychological health.

British humour is said to be unique. Almost every conversation between Brits has some form of irony, sarcasm, banter, understatement, self-deprecation, teasing or mockery. It is often delivered with a deadpan face. Therefore, getting the British sense of humour is not that easy.

Brits say "sorry" all the time. Saying "sorry" is a way to be polite, but there are other reasons why Brits say "sorry" so much. Text I in Unit 4 will help you get a better understanding of "sorry" said by Brits.

英国社会与文化

Unit 1

Queuing: Queuers and Queue-Jumpers

An Englishman, even if he is alone, forms an orderly queue of one.

—George Mikes

 Test Your Knowledge

Discuss the following questions with your partner.

1. The British are renowned for queuing. Are they better at queuing than people in other countries?
2. How do you feel when you queue up for something?

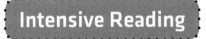

Text I Queuing: Is It Really the British Way?*

It's nearly finals weekend at Wimbledon when thousands of people will be forming an orderly queue to get in. But is queuing politely really the British way?

Queuing, it's what the British are renowned for doing—and doing very well. Better than anyone else in the world, if reputation is to be believed.

Take the Wimbledon queue as an example.

It's held up as a supreme example of Britain's **prowess** when it comes to queuing. The likes of tea, cake and camping chairs often make an appearance. It even has its own code of conduct in case, heaven forbid, anyone doesn't understand how the queue works.

Wimbledon is an exception when it comes to standing in a long line, say social historians. Despite the UK's formidable global reputation, queuing in a calm, good-natured manner has not always come naturally.

---

* Retrieved from BBC website.

Chapter 8 People—Habit Is Second Nature

"We're supposed to be so wonderful at it but really that reputation is built around a whole mythology to do with the British and queuing," says Dr. Joe Moran, a social historian and author of *Queuing for Beginners: The Story of Daily Life from Breakfast to Bedtime*.

The temporary nature of queues makes it hard to trace their history, but key historical events are said to have shaped how the British queue and their reputation for being so good at it. One is the Industrial Revolution.

"The orderly queue seems to have been an established social form in the early 19th century, a product of more **urbanised**, industrial societies which brought masses of people together," says Moran.

People were moving in huge numbers from the countryside into towns changing the patterns of daily life, including shopping.

"More of a **barter** system existed in local markets, the whole way people shopped was more informal," says historian Juliet Gardiner. "Traders started moving from market **stalls** into shops as they moved into towns. In the more formal setting of a shop people had to start to queue up in a more structured way."

Despite the mass expansion of manufacturing not everyone reaped the financial rewards and poverty was **rife**.

"Queuing started to become associated with extreme hardship as the poor had to queue to access handouts and charity," says Dr. Kate Bradley, a lecturer in social history and social policy at the University of Kent.

But what really shaped Britain's reputation as civilised queuers was World War II.

"**Propaganda** at the time was all about doing your duty and taking your turn," says Bradley. "It was a way the government tried to control a situation in uncertain times."

"The queue became loaded with meaning, drawing on notions of decency, fair play and democracy and the myth of the British as patient queuers was forged," says Moran.

"In reality there were arguments and disturbances, often the police had to be brought in to sort things out and restore order. Queuing was exhausting, frustrating and tense."

"Things that weren't rationed would go on sale **spasmodically**, word would go round and long queues would start to form. People often joined the end of a queue without knowing exactly what it was for, they just hoped it would be something useful."

The notion of the orderly queue is a belief that is still cherished today.

"It's a story we still like to tell about ourselves," says Moran. "We like to think it fits in with a particular idea we have of our national character—that we're pragmatic and **phlegmatic**."

Others argue that the British are good at organising themselves into a queue but not so good at waiting in it.

In the post-war years things **flipped** and the queue came to represent everything that was wrong about British society. Politicians and social commentators tried to make capital out of them, like the **dole** queue in the 1980s.

But the nation's reputation for queuing patiently remained **intact**. Wimbledon and other events—from queuing for Glastonbury to the Queen's 60th Jubilee concert—were and still are held aloft as British queuing at its best, but they are not the type of queue people experience in everyday life.

"The queue at Wimbledon is part of the whole ritual. You certainly don't get the same warm glow of togetherness waiting for the bus or standing in a line at the bank," says Moran.

It's the bus queue that is often cited as an example of the **demise** of civilised queuing. In some places it's every man, woman and child for themselves when the bus draws up. But cultural historians say there is little evidence that people behaved any better in years gone by.

"What we do know is that people have been complaining about the disintegration of queue discipline for almost as long as they have been **lauding** the queue as the essence of British decency," says Moran.

What makes standing in a line for a bus problematic is that people have to police the queue themselves.

"The people who push to get on a bus are the same people who wait patiently in other queues," says Dr. Michael Sinclair, a consultant counselling psychologist with City Psychology Group.

"The difference is that in the bus queue people have to enforce the rules themselves. This is when the system can break down. We all want things to be done the way we'd like, the problem is that people have different ideas of what that should be."

"In most other places, like the bank or supermarket, people are shown how to queue so lines are controlled a lot better," says David Worthington, a professor in the department of management science at the University of Lancaster who has researched queues.

Poles with **retractable straps**, numbered ticket machines—developed in Sweden in the 1960s—and electronic called-forward systems, tell people what to do and when.

"People know where they are in the queue and that is important when it comes to keeping things organised," he says.

"Other queue myths have also been picked apart over the years. The notion that other nations can't queue like the British is outdated," says Worthington.

The motives behind the UK's intolerance of queue-jumping have also been questioned.

"When people tackle **breaches** of queue discipline, it's not really the notion of fair play that is driving them, it is protecting their own interests," says Bradley.

Ultimately, if the British can avoid standing in a line, they will, just like everyone else.

Vocabulary

prowess	n.	高超技能
urbanised	adj.	城市化的
barter	n.	物物交换
stall	n.	货摊
rife	adj.	（坏事）普遍的
propaganda	n.	宣传
spasmodically	adv.	断续性地
phlegmatic	adj.	冷静的
flip	v.	变化
dole	n.	失业救济金
intact	adj.	完好的
demise	n.	告终
laud	v.	赞美
retractable	adj.	可伸缩的

| strap | n. | 带子 |
| breach | n. | 违反 |

Exercises

I. Decide whether the following statements are true or false, and mark T or F accordingly.

_____ 1. Queuing in a calm, good-natured manner has always come naturally to the British.

_____ 2. According to Moran, the orderly queue is a product of more urbanised, industrial societies which brought masses of people together.

_____ 3. What really shaped Britain's reputation as civilised queuers was World War I.

_____ 4. The queue at Wimbledon is often cited as an example of the demise of civilised queuing.

_____ 5. According to Bradley, when people tackle breaches of queue discipline, it's not really the notion of fair play that is driving them, it is protecting their own interests.

II. Match the word partners to form collocations.

1. civilised   A. queue
2. established   B. example
3. orderly   C. social form
4. retractable   D. queuer
5. supreme   E. strap

III. Fill in the blanks with the appropriate forms of the words in the box.

| prowess | rife | ration | propaganda |
| demise | laud | breach | phlegmatic |

1. Pakistan recently announced that it was reviving an old system of _____ cards for cheap wheat.

2. The result is that the company is facing substantial difficulties, and even its possible _____.

3. This _____ is false, and its purpose is to confuse you and justify acts of terror.

4. Throughout the Olympics, the physical _____ among the competitors within each event varied little.

5. He was an unassuming man, steady, _____, with a thick brush of white hair and a craggy outdoorsman's face.

6. For generations to come some will _____ him as a saviour of the Serbs.

7. These causes of actions include _____ of contract, intentional interference with contractual relations, and defamation.

8. Yet corruption is so _____ in that country that even the most scandalous allegations surprise nobody.

IV. "The notion that other nations can't queue like the British is outdated." To what extent do you agree with this statement? Write an essay of about 200 words to justify your opinion.

Further Reading

Text II Coronavirus Has Ruined the Great, Orderly British Queue*

A queue forming outside clothes and **gadget** shops used to signal that something exciting was happening: the start of the January sales, the release of the latest iPhone, or the opening of a **trendy** restaurant. Some people even used to camp out in queues for fun. But in the midst of a pandemic queues snaking the length and breadth of storefronts along high streets have not just become an ordinary sight—they're putting people off shopping altogether.

A disorderly queue of people had already formed at the entrance to Sports Direct in Harrow's town centre when 28-year-old Halema walked up, intending to buy some new running gear. But pressed for time, confused about where the queue started, and unsure how long it could take before being let in, she just went back home.

"It didn't seem like anyone was doing the two-metre distancing rule, and

---

* Retrieved from WIRED website.

they were all crowded together which made me think, oh well. I don't want to be waiting there," Halema says. The prospect of standing in line in the **blazing** heat just to get into a store rubbed more salt into the wound.

In Doncaster, supermarket employee Natalie echoed this exact sentiment. Before coronavirus, she would go into town for a bit of retail therapy every other day, but since non-essential shops reopened, Natalie only goes whenever she desperately needs something. "My idea of shopping now is standing outside shops queuing, when before you could walk straight in," she says. "Shopping is just no fun anymore."

Halema and Natalie are a small part of a wider trend: Britons have fallen out of love with queuing. Shopping isn't as fun as it used to be for 64% of Brits, according to a survey from behavioural insights firm Emotional Logic. Aside from fear of the disease, the main reason that put them off shopping was queuing: 22% of **respondents** said they didn't want to stand in line, while a further 21% said that shopping simply wasn't a good experience.

Despite being **dubbed** champions at the dull art of standing in line, the eccentric politeness of British people queuing is mostly fictional. "The thing about the myth of the British as wonderful queuers is that it suggests that queuing is this slightly trivial thing," says Joe Moran, a British cultural historian at Liverpool John Moores University. "You get this sort of celebration of the queues for Wimbledon and people camping out before the January sales, and it becomes a sort of fun thing. Actually, it's not a fun thing."

Contrary to popular belief, Brits in the past have resented queuing and it wasn't actually seen as a polite activity. "Obviously in the war, and even in the rationing after the war, there was just a huge amount of queuing for things that people really needed, like food and fuel," Moran explains. "Queuing would have been quite a difficult, **fraught** activity, a bit like now, actually."

In a 2015 study from Box Technologies and Intel, researchers found that 86% of shoppers would actively avoid a store if they perceived that the queue is too long. Like in the World War II, the times when we are more willing to queue are when we actually need something, which is why queues for the supermarket can often be quite long.

"If we have to get food because there's no other way to get it, we will queue because it's a basic need," says Isabelle Szmigin, professor of marketing and consumer behaviour at the University of Birmingham. "When it comes to things

Chapter 8 People—Habit Is Second Nature

like fashion items or nice-to-haves, the queue is going to put us off."

Adrian Furnham, professor of psychology at University College London, who has researched the psychology of queuing, says that another reason why people are unwilling to queue could be that people simply aren't used to waiting in line in order to get into a shop. "You associate queues with bus stops and tubes, not with local shops of any sort," he explains. "Any type of waiting seems very wasteful."

In a study Furnham conducted, he saw that on average people were willing to wait in line for 5.5 minutes and were less likely to join a queue if there were more than six people already waiting. The feeling that you're wasting your time becomes more **pronounced** when you can't picture how long you're going to be waiting in line for. There aren't any **distractions** to occupy customers' time, for example, unlike the queue to pay which has an **assortment** of goodies lining each side of the queue.

When you're standing in a socially distanced queue to pay, you aren't physically able to see each person in front of you going up to the cashier, you just see someone go into the store and don't know how long they're going to be in there for. "The reason you can cope with the tube is because it tells you when the next tube is coming," Furnham says. "If people get some sense of how fast the thing is moving, that helps."

Restaurants, for example, often tell customers how long the wait could be to help them decide whether they want to wait for a table to become free or not, but currently, customers can't make that decision. Noticing the stress, network operator O2 has implemented virtual technology which puts customers into a virtual queue, so they don't have to physically wait in line. The technology gives customers text message updates on how long the wait could be and when they should come back to the store, so they can enter it without waiting.

Virtual queuing technology could **alleviate** some of the queuing pressures that customers are complaining about. Halema says that the stress of not knowing where to stand in the queue and the anxiety about potentially doing something wrong makes the whole process of shopping a lot less **enticing** than it used to be.

What makes the queuing experience worse is that an etiquette around socially distant queues hasn't been properly established yet. "The shops are different. Some of the shops have one entrance and one exit, others don't," explains Szmigin. "You don't want to do the wrong thing. It puts you into a different frame of mind."

Once you're at the front of the queue, the experience isn't much better. Shop assistants letting people into the stores are adopting a "command and control" position, which Furnham says can be **off-putting** for people who are used to being welcomed into stores. "The people who allow you in sometimes really don't understand their job. They are **brisk** and relatively rude and sort of schoolteacher-like, rather than welcoming. That's equally unpleasant," he says.

Customers can also feel like they are still in a queue once they're inside the shop. Natalie says that she doesn't particularly browse anymore, while Halema says that she isn't able to browse in peace, particularly if there's a one-way system in place. "I like to take my time when I go into a shop, especially when it comes to clothes," she says. "But then I feel like maybe I shouldn't take my time because there are people waiting."

Vocabulary

gadget	*n.*	小玩意；小器具
trendy	*adj.*	时髦的
blazing	*adj.*	炽热的
respondent	*n.*	被调查人
dub	*v.*	把……称为
fraught	*adj.*	令人担忧的
pronounced	*adj.*	明显的
distraction	*n.*	分心的事物
assortment	*n.*	各式各样
alleviate	*v.*	减轻
enticing	*adj.*	诱人的
off-putting	*adj.*	令人不愉快的
brisk	*adj.*	干脆利索的

Exercises

Chapter 8 People—Habit Is Second Nature

Moaning: Workplace Moans and Restaurant Moans

It is worth a reminder here that in all English moaning rituals, there is a tacit understanding that nothing can or will be done about the problems we are moaning about. We complain to each other, rather than tackling the real source of our discontent, and we neither expect nor want to find a solution to our problems—we just want to enjoy moaning about them.

—Kate Fox

 Test Your Knowledge

Search for relevant information to answer the following questions.

1. What are the top ten moans among Brits?
2. Why do Brits complain so much?

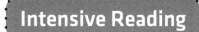

Text I Top 50 Things British People Complain About*

Prolonged Brexit negotiations and **pedestrians** who stare at their phones while they are walking have topped the list of the things British people are most likely to complain about, a survey claims.

Researchers who polled 2,000 adults found that the top 50 list also includes Wi-Fi not connecting, supermarket self-service **tills** and feeling "overworked".

The research also revealed that British people complain three times a day on average.

One in six said they are most likely to complain in the morning, with traffic during their **commute** cited as their main worry.

And one third said they complain less at the weekend.

---

* Retrieved from *The Independent* website.

Geoffrey Dennis of the Society for the Protection of Animals Abroad, which **commissioned** the research, said: "Most people in the UK acknowledge that they complain about trivial matters on a regular basis."

"When we're used to modern conveniences like Wi-Fi, home deliveries and air conditioning, it can be easy to forget that others have to deal with far greater problems every day."

"For people in Britain, everyday problems can seem like the end of the world—and most of us are guilty of complaining about things like bad weather, traffic or people pushing to the front of queues."

The study also found that many British people prefer to complain in private, with 45% waiting until they're home before they voice their concerns.

One in five of the survey's respondents said that there is a stereotype of "moaning British people".

But one fifth said they tend to block out others who moan about their "first world problems".

Around four in ten respondents said they complain more now than they did as children, and half said they feel better after "getting things off their chest".

More than half agreed that there are far more "moaners" today than there used to be.

But some respondents said that complaining works, with four in ten having received money off their restaurant bill after making a complaint.

One in four people agreed that if they complain enough about the price of things, then something will eventually be done about it.

However, almost half of the survey's respondents said they could go a whole day without complaining.

Mr. Dennis added: "These kinds of inconveniences are so minor compared to the problems faced by many people and animals in the world's poorest communities."

"Working animals in developing countries never complain, but they have every right to."

"These horses, donkeys and camels endure incredibly hard lives, carrying **backbreaking** loads in punishing conditions, without the food, water, rest and vital vet care they need."

Chapter 8 People—Habit Is Second Nature

"In developing countries, many working animals have to walk huge distances, pulling heavy loads across difficult terrain, working in temperatures exceeding 40 degrees Celsius."

"These animals often have no **veterinary** treatment available to them when they are sick or injured."

"That's why the work of SPANA (The Society for the Protection of Animals Abroad) is so important—preventing suffering and ensuring these hardworking animals receive the care they so urgently need."

The following are top 50 things British people complain about:

1. Bad customer service

2. Getting **cold called** / calls from unknown numbers

3. People pushing into queues

4. Being too cold

5. Waiting in for a delivery that doesn't turn up

6. Sitting in traffic

7. Wi-Fi not connecting

8. Litter and **fly-tipping**

9. The British weather

10. Being too hot

11. Noisy neighbours

12. Lateness

13. Public transport being late

14. Lack of car parking spaces

15. The behaviour of teenagers and children

16. People who walk along staring at their phones

17. **Spam** emails—including GDPR **opt-ins**

18. Receiving a "we missed you" card from a parcel **courier**

19. Door-to-door salespeople

20. Supermarket self-service tills

21. Brexit negotiations

22. Having no phone signal
23. New shoes that give you **blisters**
24. Never being able to get a doctor's appointment
25. Being hungry
26. People who don't hold doors open
27. Noisy eaters
28. People cancelling plans in the last minute
29. Someone parking outside your house in your "space" / blocking your driveway
30. Having a runny nose
31. The lack of funding for the NHS
32. Hidden charges, such as airline baggage fees
33. Running out of phone battery
34. When a shop doesn't have your size in something you want
35. Discovering you are sitting behind a tall person at a concert
36. Forgetting plastic bags for shopping
37. Returning to work after holiday
38. Being overworked
39. Having to stand on public transport
40. The clocks changing / going to work in the dark in winter
41. Expensive holiday prices during school holidays
42. Getting caught in the rain without an umbrella
43. Bad hair days
44. The price of clothes
45. House prices
46. Arriving at the dentist on time to find out they are running late
47. Leaving home without your phone
48. **Graffiti**
49. Someone spilling something on your carpet
50. Getting a bad haircut

Chapter 8 People—Habit Is Second Nature

Vocabulary

pedestrian	*n.*	行人
till	*n.*	收银台
commute	*n.*	通勤
commission	*v.*	委托
backbreaking	*adj.*	非常辛劳的
veterinary	*adj.*	兽医的
cold call		打陌生推销电话
fly-tipping	*n.*	乱丢垃圾
spam	*n.*	垃圾邮件
opt-in	*n.*	决定参加
courier	*n.*	送快递的人
blister	*n.*	水疱
graffiti	*n.*	涂鸦

Exercises

I. Decide whether the following statements are true or false, and mark T or F accordingly.

_____ **1.** The research revealed that British people complain three times a day.

_____ **2.** One third said they don't complain at the weekend.

_____ **3.** Most British people are guilty of complaining about things like bad weather, traffic or people pushing to the front of queues.

_____ **4.** Four in ten respondents said they had received money off their restaurant bill after making a complaint.

_____ **5.** More than half of the respondents said they could go a whole day without complaining.

II. Match the word partners to form collocations.

1. trivial   *A.* vet care
2. modern   *B.* condition
3. backbreaking   *C.* convenience
4. punishing   *D.* matter
5. vital   *E.* load

III. Fill in the blanks with the appropriate forms of the words and phrases in the box.

> pedestrian commute commission backbreaking
> cold call spam fly-tipping

1. In the countryside the men have the _____ work of farming without mechanisation: Again, fuel is dear, and many powered irrigation systems have broken down.

2. It will _____ a panel to look into why we failed to anticipate the threat.

3. My job was to _____ hot Bay Area technology startups to secure a meeting for my team with the CEO.

4. College grads ranked unreasonable workload as the No. 1 stressor (17%), followed by their _____ (12%).

5. This is not anonymous _____, which actually constitutes the majority of what ails my inbox.

6. _____—the illegal dumping of waste—tends to rise slightly as people try to avoid paying.

7. This movement to legislate distracted walking has a purpose: _____ fatalities are on the rise.

IV. Discuss the following questions with your partner.

1. The Society for the Protection of Animals Abroad commissioned this research on complaining. Geoffrey Dennis pointed out that working animals in developing countries never complain. How do you feel about this research and the comments made by Mr. Dennis?

2. Take a closer look at the top 50 things British people complain about. Do Chinese people complain about the same things? What are the top 10 things that Chinese people complain about on a regular basis?

Chapter 8 People—Habit Is Second Nature

Further Reading

Text II Moaning Is Bad for Your Health*

Having a moan can be a conversational ice breaker. A trouble shared lightens our mental load and facilitates gaining other perspectives. Having a **rant** makes us feel good, especially if we get validated, and it is also a way to bond and connect. In small doses, the verbalisation of **gripes** can be a stress reliever. Some people are heavily burdened with real problems, so who can blame them for moaning?

However, others complain about what seems minor, and moan incessantly on a regular basis. In a survey conducted in the UK, it was revealed that people spend, on average, 10,000 minutes a year moaning. The survey claimed that millennials **whinged** the most. Weather and politics dominated as the leading source of moans, with relationships, work colleagues and rude clients also featuring.

In Ireland, weather-related moans top the polls—it is too windy, too wet and too hot. We also give out about prices, politicians, work, referees, traffic, public transport and feeling tired.

While moaning in short bursts, every now and then, has a positive effect, excessive whining is not good for our physical and psychological health. Chronic complaining induces negativity, rewires the brain and activates the stress hormone **cortisol**. The immune system gets weakened and blood pressure rises, increasing the risk for obesity, heart disease and other **ailments**.

Although we might feel that venting releases **pent-up** pressure, it actually fuels negativity rather than **ameliorates** it. Going on about something or someone **ignites** negative feelings as you relive the scene. And ranting online will not make you feel better. Instead of **blowing off steam**, it fuels the fire. People often complain to gain support, but if it is repetitive and intense, it wears down the patience of others.

Frequent whining becomes habitual and increases the likelihood of feeling negative about other aspects of life. Research has found that complaining triggers anxiety and depression as individuals get stuck in negative emotions.

Psychologist Jeffrey Lohr of the University of Arkansas explains it like this: "People don't break wind in elevators more than they have to. Venting anger

---

* Retrieved from *The Irish Times* website.

is...similar to emotional farting in a closed area."

It is not a pleasant experience for everyone in your line of fire and it is not socially appropriate. Another downside to excessive moaning is that it leads to inaction. It can be astonishing how many hours a person can clock up moaning about a boss, another person, a situation and so forth. And the same stories get repeated over and over with no real changes made.

In the workplace, like the spreading of a yawn, there is an emotional **contagion** effect. The target often gets **demonised**. Negative **cliques** develop based on unhealthy interactions. Whining colleagues have been found to be a leading source of annoyance to colleagues in a survey of office habits.

A negative culture, office **layout**, a lack of structure, unclear roles and too much idle time all can foster moaning on the job. While constructive complaining at work is healthy, constant whining casts a dark cloud over an organisational culture. It exaggerates challenges, is emotionally draining and impacts negatively on morale, creativity and productivity. Over time, it leads workers to hate their jobs.

Are you moaning more than you realise, or would you like to moan less?

Self-awareness is the first step. Monitor yourself for three days and mentally count how many times you whinge. Be aware when you are moaning. Will Bowen founded the movement "A complaint free world" and challenges you to give up moaning for 21 days. Ask yourself—is it reality based and how much does it really matter? Identify the moany themes and triggers.

Rather than dumping all your moans on others, write them down. Pause and assess how it might be impacting the listener. Do they seem bored? Do they look fed up?

Be mindful of body language and social cues. Some people go off on a monologue talking "at" the other person. If you are compelled to have a moan, give it a time limit. Develop a habit of asking the other person about their life and reflect on what has been going on for them. Perhaps they have had a **bereavement**, lost their job, have relationship difficulties. Be aware when it may not be the right time for you to indulge in your moaning. Move from this habitual way of being towards a more solution-seeking position.

If issues arise, aim to address them. Practise daily letting go of minor gripes and **grumbles** to build up your tolerance level. Have a close look at what is really going on with you. The moan often is not the real issue but reflects bigger problems. Perhaps you need therapeutic support? Maybe it is time to change a legacy of moaning you inherited? Cultivate a more positive and optimistic frame of mind and reap the rewards.

What about handling a moan? It doesn't help the other person to facilitate endless ranting and moaning. And prolonged exposure is detrimental to your own wellbeing and you will end up with a moan infection. If you feel comfortable with the other person, try to point it out diplomatically. Be a role model by focusing on solutions and addressing issues.

Ask questions and encourage them to reflect. "This issue has been recurring quite a lot, what do you think is the best way to handle it?" or "What would you like to see happening?"

You can also divert their attention from the moan and discuss neutral or **upbeat** topics. Or throw in some humour to **diffuse** the whining. Try to tactfully give their moan a time limit and highlight **the silver lining**.

In small doses, a good old moan can facilitate bonding, alleviate stress, help to gain a different perspective and generate solutions. Sharing feelings, pointing out if something is not right or instrumental complaining is healthy. However, if it is constant and excessive, it is bad for your physical and psychological health. It drains personal and communal energy. Moaning has a negative impact on others and **impedes** healthy interactions.

Grumbling won't make you happier.

Vocabulary

rant	n.	叫嚷；大声抱怨
gripe	n.	发牢骚
whinge	v.	抱怨
cortisol	n.	皮质醇
ailment	n.	小病
pent-up	adj.	被压抑的
ameliorate	v.	改善
ignite	v.	激起
blow off steam		释放压力
contagion	n.	传染
demonise	v.	使妖魔化
clique	n.	小团体

英国社会与文化

layout	*n.*	布局
bereavement	*n.*	丧亲
grumble	*n.*	抱怨
upbeat	*adj.*	乐观的
diffuse	*v.*	缓解
the silver lining		一线希望
impede	*v.*	阻碍

Chapter 8 People—Habit Is Second Nature

Humour: Understatement and Self-deprecation

Many English people seem to believe that we have some sort of global monopoly, if not on humour itself, then at least on certain "brands" of humour—the high-class ones such as wit and especially irony. My findings indicate that while there may indeed be something distinctive about English humour, the real "defining characteristic" is the value we put on humour, the central importance of humour in English culture and social interactions.

—Kate Fox

 Test Your Knowledge

Discuss the following questions with your partner.

1. Have you watched any British comedy series? Can you get the British sense of humour? Name a few examples of British humour.
2. What is the distinguishing feature of British humour?
3. How can people from other cultures get a better grasp of British humour?

Intensive Reading

Text I   British Humour: What Exactly Is It and How Does It Work?*

Many Brits believe that the British sense of humour is unique, more subtle and more highly developed than other nations.

Popular British playwright Oscar Wilde made this point quite clearly and deliberately when he said, "It is clear that humour is far superior to humor."

Perhaps the most confusing part of British humour however, is that there is no "off" switch. Almost every conversation between Brits is bound to feature

---
* Retrieved from The South African website.

some form of irony, **sarcasm**, **banter**, **understatement**, **self-deprecation**, teasing or mockery.

When every word exchanged between Brits has an **undercurrent** of humour, it becomes difficult to **decipher** when a Brit is joking or being serious.

This is even more problematic considering the delivery of jokes is almost always done with a **deadpan** face.

The **rule of thumb** is therefore, if someone is saying something that makes absolutely no sense with a straight face, he is probably joking.

Core of British Humour: Irony and Sarcasm

The British have a unique **partiality** for irony and are always ready to whip out a sarcastic **quip** when the opportunity presents itself.

An extremely dry example of this would be for a British person to comment on how delightful the weather is when it is pouring outside.

The British make use of irony and its **derivative**, sarcasm, to say the opposite of what they mean in order to make a point.

This typically occurs when a Brit is confronted with a silly question, such as when British actress Cara Delevigne was asked on US television if she had read John Green's book, *Paper Towns*, before starring in the movie.

Delevigne **scoffed** and replied, "No, I never read the book or the script, I just **winged** it."

For the rest of the world, there is a time and a place for irony. For the Brits, that time and place is wherever and whenever.

It is this constant use of irony in conversation which can make the British come across as tiresome and rude to outsiders.

British Fondness for Understatement

In refusing to be overwhelmed by anything, the British resort to rather emotionless statements, such as "Not bad" when they really mean, "That's actually quite good".

British speech is littered with understatement. The Debretts guide to British social skills, etiquette and style notes that British conversations are filled with moderating expressions, such as "quite", "rather", "a bit" and "actually".

A "spot of bother" or "a bit of a pickle" may understate that things are disastrous, in the same way that "Let's go out for a pint" usually means going

Chapter 8 **People—Habit Is Second Nature**

out for many, many more drinks.

A classic example of British understatement can be seen in the "Black Knight" scene from *Monty Python*, where upon having his arm chopped off the Black Knight proclaims, "Tis but a scratch."

Self-deprecation

The British do not parade their achievements and are deeply hostile to **pomposity**.

Instead of boasting and blowing their own trumpets, the Brits tend to make light of their shortcomings by being excessively modest and putting themselves down.

Obvious sources of self-deprecating humour include one's accent, age, physical build, baldness, prominent features, geekiness or strange name.

British comedian and self-proclaimed "language nerd", David Mitchell, is a well-known self-deprecator.

In an episode of *Would I Lie to You?* Mitchell mocks himself by calling his beard a "failure in personal hygiene".

In dealing with the embarrassment of success through such self-mockery, the Brits believe they appear more humble and relatable.

Fellow Brits are able to read beneath the self-deprecation and admire them for their modesty.

It is particularly important for the Brits to not appear too big for their boots when it comes to addressing an audience.

British public speaking website, "Speak like a Pro", emphasises that people who have the ability to laugh at themselves are generally perceived as being secure, confident, and likeable.

Weak people, on the other hand, tend to feel a need to **inflate** themselves.

Comedian Jon Richardson is the perfect example of the extremely likeable self-deprecator.

Sexy Self-deprecation

A recent two-year study on "The Sexual Attractiveness of Self-deprecating Humour" found that self-deprecating humour is the most attractive type of humour.

Participants in the study listened to recordings of men and women who had different levels of status, and who produced different types of humour.

The most desirable mates proved to be men and women of high status who made use of self-deprecating humour.

The study warns that while effective, self-deprecation can be a risky form of humour as it can draw attention to one's real faults and diminish the self-deprecator's status.

Negative Humour: Teasing and Taking the Piss

Besides finding it funny to **self-denigrate**, the British use those around them as sources of humour too.

As Julian Tan argues in an article for the *Huffington Post*, "Why else would you have an extra 'u' in humour if not for the fact that the joke is most often on you?"

A few years back a scientist claimed that typically British "negative humour" which includes biting sarcasm, teasing, ridicule and self-denigration, is linked to genes only found in British men and women.

This claim followed a study conducted on 4,000 twins in the UK and US.

Dr. Rod Martin, one of the researchers, said it is possible that differences exist between the UK and the US in their sense of humour as a result of different genetic and environmental influences.

While classed as "negative humour", for the British, to tease is to show approval and affection.

The same holds true for taking the piss (or taking the mickey), which quite literally means to mock and make fun of someone.

The Brits are also known to "take the piss" in an attempt to **deflate** somebody of their mistaken belief that they are special. Again, this can be seen as affectionate.

Alternatively, negative humour can be used to chip away at **narcissistic** characters who take themselves too seriously.

British Humour Isn't Actually Funny

Much of British humour is not obviously hilarious and does not result in fits of laughter.

According to anthropologist Kate Fox, "At best a well-timed quip only raises a slight smirk."

Chapter 8 People—Habit Is Second Nature

The most difficult part of British humour for foreigners is that it is not often funny across cultures.

But those unaccustomed to British humour need not worry. For the best thing about British humour is that it is not something you can learn, it's something that grows on you.

Vocabulary

sarcasm	n.	讽刺，挖苦
banter	n.	无恶意的玩笑
understatement	n.	低调说法；轻描淡写
self-deprecation	n.	自我贬低
undercurrent	n.	暗流
decipher	v.	辨认；理解
deadpan	adj.	面无表情的
rule of thumb		经验法则
partiality	n.	偏爱
quip	n.	俏皮话；妙语
derivative	n.	衍生物
scoff	v.	嘲笑
wing	v.	即兴创作，即兴表演
pomposity	n.	自大
inflate	v.	夸大，吹嘘
self-denigrate	v.	自我诋毁
deflate	v.	打击；使泄气
narcissistic	adj.	自恋的

Exercises

I. **Decide whether the following statements are true or false, and mark T or F accordingly.**

_____ 1. There are different types of British humour. Almost every conversation between Brits has one type or another.

_____ 2. It is easy for foreigners to tell whether a Brit is joking or not, for the delivery of jokes is almost always done with a grin.

_____ 3. The constant use of irony in conversation makes the British funny and approachable.

_____ 4. The British tend to use emotionless statements and their speech contains a lot of understatement.

_____ 5. "Negative humour", which includes biting sarcasm, teasing, ridicule and self-denigration, is used to show affection and approval.

II. Fill in the blanks with appropriate prepositions to complete these sentences.

1. "We wanted to come across _____ authentic and genuine," says Nationwide spokesman Michael Switzer.

2. It would obviously appear as though the Asian countries have a certain fondness _____ imitating products.

3. Political, diplomatic, legal and economic measures should be tried before any resort _____ arms.

4. History is littered _____ once-dominant institutions that were imperceptibly hollowed out and then suddenly collapsed.

5. In short, reality is beginning to chip away _____ the consensus view of a V-shaped economic recovery.

III. Fill in the blanks with the appropriate forms of the words in the box.

| understatement | deflate | narcissistic | deadpan |
| scoff | decipher | pomposity | sarcasm |

1. Gentle with newcomers, generous in passing on his skills, he would puncture pretension and _____.

2. You must also _____ your sector's operating rules—it might be bound by regulation, or steeped in tradition.

3. If you detect a hint of _____ in my tone this morning, go ahead and give yourself a gold star.

4. Nobody wants to _____, but it is too simple to believe for one minute that debt relief is going to solve this problem.

5. To say the creative Pixar people execute on their ideas brilliantly is a(n) _____.

Chapter 8 People—Habit Is Second Nature

6. The problem with politics in general is that it generally attracts the most _____ and power hungry people in our society.

7. His popularity rating, pumped up before the election, is likely to _____ as discontent spreads.

8. And friends say that, in private, the dolefully _____ look can rapidly give way to a sparkly, sometimes feminine, charm.

IV. Work in a group to create a collage and then fulfill the following tasks.

1. Decide on three English comedians that you want to learn about.
2. Collect their pictures, well-known works and especially examples of their humour.
3. Put them together on a piece of paper. Give it an artistic design.
4. Present your collage to the rest of the class.

Further Reading

Text II The Differences Between American and British Humour*

It's often dangerous to generalize, but under threat, I would say that Americans are more "down the line". They don't hide their hopes and fears. They applaud ambition and openly reward success. Brits are more comfortable with life's losers. We embrace the **underdog** until it's no longer the underdog. We like to bring authority down a peg or two. Just for the hell of it. Americans say, "have a nice day" whether they mean it or not. Brits are terrified to say this. We tell ourselves it's because we don't want to sound insincere but I think it might be for the opposite reason. We don't want to celebrate anything too soon. Failure and disappointment lurk around every corner. This is due to our **upbringing**. Americans are brought up to believe they can be the next president of the United States. Brits are told, "It won't happen to you."

There's a received wisdom in the UK that Americans don't get irony. This is of course not true. But what is true is that they don't use it all the time. It shows

---

* Retrieved from *Time* website.

up in the smarter comedies but Americans don't use it as much socially as Brits. We use it as liberally as prepositions in every day speech. We **tease** our friends. We use sarcasm as a shield and a weapon. We avoid sincerity until it's absolutely necessary. We mercilessly take the piss out of people we like or dislike basically. And ourselves. This is very important. Our **brashness** and **swagger** is laden with equal portions of self-deprecation. This is our license to hand it out.

This can sometimes be perceived as nasty if the recipients aren't used to it. It isn't. It's play fighting. It's almost a sign of affection if we like you, and ego bursting if we don't. You just have to know which one it is.

I guess the biggest difference between the US version and the UK version of *The Office* reflected this. We had to make Michael Scott a slightly nicer guy, with a rosier outlook to life. He could still be childish, and insecure, and even a bore, but he couldn't be too mean. The irony is of course that I think David Brent's dark **descension** and eventual **redemption** made him all the more compelling. But I think that's a lot more **palatable** in Britain for the reasons already stated. Brits almost expect doom and gloom so to start off that way but then have a happy ending is an unexpected joy. Network America has to give people a reason to like you not just a reason to watch you. In Britain we stop watching things like *Big Brother* when the villain is evicted. We don't want to watch a bunch of idiots having a good time. We want them to be as miserable as us. America rewards up front, on-your-sleeve niceness. A perceived wicked **streak** is somewhat frowned upon.

Recently I have been accused of being a shock comic, and cruel and cynical. This is of course almost solely due to a few comments I made as host of last year's Golden Globes. But nothing could be further from the truth.

I never actively try to offend. That's **churlish**, pointless and frankly too easy. But I believe you should say what you mean. Be honest. No one should ever be offended by truth. That way you'll never have to apologize. I hate it when a comedian says, "Sorry for what I said." You shouldn't say it if you didn't mean it and you should never regret anything you meant to do. As a comedian, I think my job isn't just to make people laugh but also make them think. As a famous comedian, I also want a strict door policy on my club. Not everyone will like what I say or find it funny. And I wouldn't have it any other way. There are enough comedians who try to please everyone as it is. Good luck to them, but that's not my game, I'm afraid.

Chapter 8 People—Habit Is Second Nature

I'm not one of those people who think that comedy is your **conscience** taking a day off. My conscience never takes a day off and I can justify everything I do. There's no line to be drawn in comedy in the sense that there are things you should never joke about. There's nothing that you should never joke about, but it depends on what that joke is. Comedy comes from a good or a bad place. The subject of a joke isn't necessarily the target of the joke. You can make jokes about race without any race being the **butt** of the joke. Racism itself can be the butt, for example. When dealing with a so-called **taboo** subject, the **angst** and discomfort of the audience is what's under the microscope. Our own preconceptions and prejudices are often what are being challenged. I don't like racist jokes. Not because they are offensive. I don't like them because they're not funny. And they're not funny because they're not true. They are almost always based on a falsehood somewhere along the way, which ruins the **gag** for me. Comedy is an intellectual pursuit. Not a platform.

As for cynicism, I don't care for it much. I'm a romantic. From *The Office*, and *Extras* to *The Invention of Lying* and *Cemetery Junction*, goodness and sweetness, honour and truth, love and friendship always triumph.

For me, humanity is king.

Oh and for the record I'd rather a waiter say, "Have a nice day" and not mean it, than ignore me and mean it.

Vocabulary

underdog	*n.*	处于劣势的人；失败者
upbringing	*n.*	教养；养育
tease	*v.*	嘲笑，取笑
brashness	*n.*	自以为是
swagger	*n.*	大摇大摆；趾高气扬
descension	*n.*	沉沦；没落
redemption	*n.*	救赎
palatable	*adj.*	可接受的
streak	*n.*	性格特征
churlish	*adj.*	不友善的；不礼貌的
conscience	*n.*	良心
butt	*n.*	笑柄

taboo	*n.*	禁忌
angst	*n.*	焦虑
gag	*n.*	笑话

Exercises

Chapter 8 People—Habit Is Second Nature

Sorry, ...Sorry, ...Sorry, ...What Does It Say About Englishness?

The apology is so habitual and mechanical that we sometimes even say "sorry" when we bump into an inanimate object, such as a door or a lamp-post.

—Kate Fox

 Test Your Knowledge

Discuss the following questions with your partner.

1. In the British culture, saying "sorry" is a way to be polite. Are there any other reasons why Brits say "sorry" so much?
2. How do you feel about Brits saying "sorry" all the time?

Text I Why Do the British Say "Sorry" So Much?*

It is probably the most over-used word in the United Kingdom: Whether they are sorry about the weather or sorry because someone else has bumped into them, chances are that your average Briton has blurted out at least one apology in the past hour or two.

A recent survey of more than 1,000 Brits found that the average person says "sorry" around eight times per day—and that one in eight people apologise up to 20 times a day.

"The readiness of the English to apologise for something they haven't done is remarkable, and it is matched by an unwillingness to apologise for what they have done," wrote Henry Hitchings in his aptly-titled *Sorry!: The English and Their Manners*.

---

* Retrieved from BBC website.

But do the British really apologise more frequently than members of other cultures? If so, what's the reason for this peculiar verbal **tic**...and how bad a habit is it?

Getting reliable data on the frequency of apologies in different countries is harder than you might think. "There's certainly speculation that Canadians and Brits apologise more than Americans, but it's difficult to study in a way that would provide any **compelling** evidence," says Karina Schumann, a psychologist at the University of Pittsburgh who studies apologies and forgiveness.

One approach is to ask people what they'd do in a theoretical situation. For instance, a recent YouGov poll of more than 1,600 British people and 1,000 Americans revealed that there would be approximately 15 British "sorries" for every 10 American ones if they sneezed, if they corrected someone's mistake, or if someone crashed into them.

But the survey found similarities between the British and American respondents, as well: Just under three-quarters of people from either country would say sorry for interrupting someone. And 84% of Brits would apologise for being late to a meeting, compared to 74% of Americans.

However, asking someone what they'd do in a theoretical situation is very different to measuring what they'd do in real life. Take the last example; in the YouGov survey, 36% of British respondents said they would apologise for someone else's clumsiness, compared to 24% of Americans.

But in her book *Watching the English*, social anthropologist Kate Fox describes experiments in which she deliberately bumped into hundreds of people in towns and cities across England. She also encouraged colleagues to do the same abroad, for comparison.

Fox found that around 80% of English victims said "sorry"—even though the **collisions** were clearly Fox's fault. Often the apology was **mumbled**, and possibly people said it without even realising it, but compared to when tourists from other countries were bumped, the difference was **marked**. "Only the Japanese seemed to have anything even approaching the English sorry-reflex," Fox writes.

The origins of the word "sorry" can be traced to the Old English "sarig" meaning "distressed, grieved or full of sorrow", but of course, most British people use the word more casually. And herein lies another problem with studying cultural differences in languages. "We use the word 'sorry' in different ways,"

Chapter 8 People—Habit Is Second Nature

says Edwin Battistella, a linguistics expert from Southern Oregon University and author of *Sorry About That: The Language of Public Apology*. Brits might say sorry more often, but this doesn't necessarily mean they're more **remorseful**.

"We can use it to express **empathy**—so I might say 'sorry about the rain'," says Battistella. "It might be that British and Canadian speakers use that kind of 'sorry' more often, but they wouldn't be apologising, per se. Other researchers have talked about the use of 'sorry' to communicate across social classes, where you're sort of apologising for your privilege."

British society values that its members show respect without imposing on someone else's personal space, and without drawing attention to oneself—characteristics that linguists refer to as "negative-politeness" or "negative-face". America, on the other hand, is a positive-politeness society, characterised by friendliness and a desire to feel part of a group.

As a consequence, Brits may sometimes use "sorry" in a way that can seem inappropriate to outsiders, including Americans. The British will say "sorry" to someone they don't know because they'd like to ask for some information, or to sit down next to them—and because not saying "sorry" would **constitute** an even greater invasion of that stranger's privacy.

"Our **excessive**, often inappropriate and sometimes **downright** misleading use of this word devalues it, and it makes things very confusing and difficult for foreigners unaccustomed to our ways," says Fox. Still, she adds, "I don't think saying "sorry" all the time is such a bad thing. It even makes sense in the context of a negative-politeness culture...Of all the words that a nation could choose to scatter about with such random **profligacy**, surely 'sorry' is not the worst."

There may be other benefits to saying "sorry", too—such as fostering trust. Interestingly, that is true even when people are apologising not for mistakes they've made, but rather for circumstances beyond their control.

In one study, Harvard Business School's Alison Wood Brooks and her colleagues recruited a male actor to approach 65 strangers at a US train station on a rainy day and ask to borrow their telephone. In half the cases, the stranger **preceded** his request with: "Sorry about the rain". When he did this, 47% of strangers gave him their mobile, compared to only 9% when he simply asked to borrow their phone. Further experiments confirmed it was the apology about the weather that mattered, not the politeness of the opening sentence.

"By saying 'I'm sorry about the rain', the **superfluous** apologiser acknowledges an unfortunate circumstance, takes the victim's perspective and expresses empathy for the negative circumstance—even though it is outside of his or her control," says Wood Brooks.

Just how many times you'll need to repeat the apology may vary according to where you live. Wood Brooks and Harvard Ph.D student Grant Donnelly have collected **preliminary** data that suggests that, for a minor **transgression**, the **optimal** number is a single "I'm sorry".

"If the transgression is large, then making two apologies seems to be the magic number for conveying empathy, remorse and restoring trust and liking," Wood Brooks says.

Of course, if you're British, you may need to double that. "A single 'sorry' does not count as an apology: We have to repeat it and **embellish** it with a lot of adjectives," says Fox.

Apologise for the rain while you're at it, too.

Vocabulary

tic	n.	抽搐
compelling	adj.	令人信服的
collision	n.	碰撞
mumble	v.	咕哝
marked	adj.	明显的
remorseful	adj.	懊悔的
empathy	n.	同理心
constitute	v.	构成
excessive	adj.	过多的
downright	adv.	彻头彻尾地
profligacy	n.	挥霍
precede	v.	在……之前
superfluous	adj.	多余的
preliminary	adj.	初步的
transgression	n.	行为失范；越界
optimal	adj.	最佳的
embellish	v.	装饰

Chapter 8 People—Habit Is Second Nature

Exercises

I. **Decide whether the following statements are true or false, and mark T or F accordingly.**

_____ 1. According to a recent survey, the average Brit says "sorry" around 20 times a day.

_____ 2. Solid evidence shows that Canadians and Brits apologise more than Americans.

_____ 3. People use the word "sorry" in different ways. Saying "sorry" doesn't necessarily mean that they are remorseful.

_____ 4. Britain is a positive-politeness society, while America is a negative-politeness society.

_____ 5. Apologising for the rain acknowledges an unfortunate situation and expresses empathy for the negative circumstance.

II. **Match the word partners to form collocations.**

1. reliable   A. evidence
2. compelling   B. difference
3. theoretical   C. data
4. marked   D. transgression
5. minor   E. situation

III. **Fill in the blanks with the appropriate forms of the words in the box.**

| downright | excessive | constitute | superfluous |
| precede | collision | embellish | mumble |

1. Regulators are concerned that SUVs are better than smaller cars when the two are involved in a(n) _____.

2. At the same time not changing the direction of biomedical research may _____ the highest risk.

3. And yet Zarqawi not only managed to survive it but was conscious enough to _____ a few words.

4. For those too young to remember, flying used to be fun and, at times, _____ glamorous.

5. More troubling is that temporary jobs, which usually _____ full-time hiring, did not pick up.

6. This practice exposes women and children to _____ amounts of smoke, endangering their health.

7. Like jazz players, early musicians can _____ melodies and chords within a certain structure.

8. With the PowerPoint slides up on a video screen, Doan's presence was almost _____ for the Democrats.

IV. **Conduct a poll among your classmates asking the following questions. Draw at least two preliminary conclusions about saying "sorry" (or "对不起""不好意思") in China. Compare your conclusions with those about Brits' use of the word.**

Would you say "sorry" if
1. you bump into someone else?
2. you are five minutes late to a meeting or gathering?
3. you accidentally cut in line in front of someone else?
4. you interrupt someone?
5. you make a joke that upsets someone?
6. someone else bumps into you?
7. you sneeze?
8. you correct someone who is wrong?
9. someone interrupts you?
10. someone accidentally cuts in line in front of you?

Further Reading

Text II Terribly Sorry—But Britain's Famed Politeness May Be a Myth*

In 2015, Simeon Floyd, then of the Max Planck Institute for Psycholinguistics, gave a lecture in Antwerp about expressions of gratitude in eight cultures around

---

* Retrieved from *The Guardian* website.

Chapter 8 People—Habit Is Second Nature

the world. I was lucky enough to be there, and have been thinking ever since about the videos he showed. In one, a Cha'palaa (Language of the Chachi people) speaker in Ecuador goes to a hole-in-the-wall shop and asks for some cooking oil. Receiving it, he turns away and leaves. In another, a British student eyes up another's biscuits and asks for one. As he reaches into the **proffered** packet, he smiles and says, "Sweet!"

The **upshot** of the research was that people in general do not express thanks when someone else fulfils a request for them. Of the cultures studied, the most apt to voice appreciation were the two in western Europe: Italy (13.5%) and Britain (14.5%).

This week, *Royal Society Open Science* published Floyd and his colleagues' work, and caused a **flutter**. *The Times* headlined its piece "Britons really do say 'thank you' more than anyone else". *The Independent* referred to Britain's famed **"unrelenting penchant** for politeness".

If Britain is famed anywhere for "unrelenting politeness", it is nowhere more so than in Britain itself, where the national reputation for good manners is treated as a badge of honour. While there's plenty of British self-deprecation in the use of words like "please", "thank you" and "sorry", it comes with some implicit self-congratulation: We use these words because we're so polite, the reasoning goes. The unspoken assumption is that others are less so.

Some **humility** (not the same as self-deprecation or politeness) might be in order here, since the research does not show that the British thank "more than anyone else", but that they thank more (in certain situations) than seven other cultures. Whether British English speakers thank more than people in China, Japan, India or the Middle East is yet unknown—and whether the British thank more than other English speakers is yet another matter. Research for the Longman Grammar of Spoken and Written English, for instance, found that Americans say "thanks" or "thank you" twice as much in conversation as Britons, while Britons say "please" twice as much as Americans.

That doesn't mean Britons make politer requests or that Americans are more grateful. It means that we've acquired different habits. With Rachele De Felice of University College London, I've been trying to dig down into those numbers. If "thank you" is used at different rates in two cultures, it probably means different things to those cultures. Indeed, in our studies of British and American email **correspondence**, we've found that Britons are more apt to begin emails with thanks for the previous message, while Americans are more likely to thank people for their time or interest. We've also found that the lesser American use of "please" is **offset** by more expressions of appreciation in making requests.

British "thanks" comes into its own at the shop till. I was **inducted** into this thanking culture in the early 2000s, when I was a fresh immigrant from the US, and volunteered in a Brighton charity shop. There, to my surprise, I learned that English shop assistants and **patrons** can begin an interaction with "thank you"; the customer who places a box of Christmas cards in front of the shop assistant can use "thank you" to indicate that they are ready to start a **transaction**. The assistant may then say "thank you" as they take the item to ring up. Before the end of the interaction, what with the back-and-forth of credit cards or cash, pin machines or change, **receipts** and bagged goods, there may well be half a dozen more thanks. Do these thanks show gratitude? An alternative reading (made in the 1970s by sociolinguist Dell Hymes) is that the British "thank you" sometimes means "I am asking you to take the next turn in this interaction" or "I am accepting that it is my turn to do something in this interaction".

When we visit other cultures that don't use thanking to manage their interactions in the same way, it can feel off-putting. But to conclude from **ample** "thanks"-giving that "we're more polite" is only to conclude that "we do the things we consider polite more often than other cultures do the things we consider polite". Hardly a surprising finding.

The **prevalence** of thanks in English-speaking cultures doesn't show we care more about others and the **impositions** we make on them. It may instead be a side-effect of our culture's individualism. I have to thank you because I cannot assume that we're close enough for you to naturally be generous towards me. In a more intimate situation or collectivist culture, expressing "thanks" can imply "I hadn't trusted that I could count on you for that".

Anyway, thanks for reading.

Vocabulary

proffer	v.	递上
upshot	n.	结果
flutter	n.	紧张兴奋
unrelenting	adj.	无休止的
penchant	n.	特别的喜好
humility	n.	谦逊

Chapter 8 **People—Habit Is Second Nature**

correspondence	*n.*	信件
offset	*v.*	抵消
induct	*v.*	入门
patron	*n.*	顾客
transaction	*n.*	交易
receipt	*n.*	收据
ample	*adj.*	足够的
prevalence	*n.*	普遍
imposition	*n.*	强加

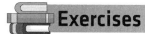

Exercises

Chapter 9

Education—Distinct Educational System and Distinguished Schools

Introduction

In recent years, the trend of studying abroad is increasing at a younger age. Many parents often send their children to study abroad when they are teenagers and enable their children to receive international quality education. Among several well-known overseas study countries, like Britain, Canada and Australia, Britain has undoubtedly become the first choice of many parents for its excellent education quality. However, the education systems of Britain and China are very different, so how to choose a good school has become the concern of many students and their parents.

In this chapter, you can quickly learn about the British education system and its history. We will introduce the different types of schools to you, like grammar schools, public schools and Russell Group Universities as well. Also, we will closely analyze the pros and cons of two different educational routes in Britain: vocational route and academic route. At the same time, we selected two world-famous British universities, Oxford and Cambridge, and made some comparison and contrast. On top of that, you can learn some practical skills like critical argumentation or drafting personal statements, etc.

英国社会与文化

Unit 1

Understanding the UK Education System

No profit grows where is no pleasure ta'en. In brief, sir, study what you most affect.

—William Shakespeare

 Test Your Knowledge

I. Search for relevant information to answer the following questions.

1. Could you list some of the names of famous British schools, including colleges, universities or elementary schools?
2. What do you know about British educational system? In which aspects is it the same as or different from Chinese educational system?

II. Design a PowerPoint and make a 5-minute speech to introduce a university in the UK with detailed description. You can include such subcategories as history, academics, ranking, research, famous faculty, majors for Chinese students, admission requirements and so on. You may attach some pictures, audio or video clips as you like.

Intensive Reading

Text I Academic Route vs. Vocational Route: Which Is Better?*

You stand at a crossroad with two different journeys ahead—which should you choose? The decision of whether to go down the academic route or the **vocational route** is a tough one. Most students will find that they come up

---

* Retrieved from Courses Online website.

Chapter 9 **Education—Distinct Educational System and Distinguished Schools**

against this issue soon after they have completed their GCSEs or A-Levels. Determining what the next steps are is a highly personal decision and should not be taken lightly. Here's what you should know.

What's the difference between the vocational and academic route?

Put simply, vocational pathways include **apprenticeships, internships** and vocational courses. These are usually specific to a certain industry or job role. Young people can gain a higher level of **employability** when they choose to go down this route. What's more, these options are often funded and allow people to earn money as they gain education.

The academic route is usually an undergraduate degree, followed by a master's degree and even a Ph.D. Young people **undertaking** these degree courses can open the door when it comes to graduate jobs and **professional roles**. The career **progression** for people with traditional degrees is often faster than it would otherwise be. At times, having a degree in your arsenal will allow you to "**leapfrog**" to a higher position in your career.

Vocational Route: Pros and Cons

In 2017–2018, more than 814,000 people in England undertook an apprenticeship following new funding from the government. Vocational routes are specific to certain industries and often allow people to train while they also **earn a living**. Here are the pros and cons.

- **Pro: Suited to Specific Sectors**

If you're certain of the career you want, you might find that a vocational course or qualification suits your needs. This route is specifically **tailored** to certain industries. That means that the skills you will gain during your studies will suit the job role that you have chosen. In some cases, this may also mean that you can get a **fast-track** when it comes to your career. Since you are learning the exact traits you need, you may get ahead quickly.

- **Con: Limited Skills**

On the other hand, learning a specific skill set could be somewhat limiting. If you later decide that you would like to pursue a different career, you will likely have to retrain or undertake a completely new qualification. Needless to say, either of these options will prove expensive and **time-consuming** in the long run. For that reason, you should ensure that you consider whether a vocational route suits your future plans well enough.

- Pro: Variety of Assessments

Traditional testing methods don't suit all learners. Intelligent people often find it hard to undertake exams, which can make getting the qualifications they want a difficult **feat**. If that **scenario** sounds familiar, taking on a vocational course could be a good move. When you gain skills in this way, you will be tested in a variety of ways. For example, you may have to undertake practical exams or get graded while you're on the job. If you find it hard to succeed academically, it could be worth looking at vocational options instead.

- Con: Unrecognized Courses

While many of the vocational approaches—such as apprenticeships and courses—will be recognized by their given industries, you have to take extra care here. Since there are seemingly endless options available in this sector, the qualifications and certificates are not always as acclaimed as they first appear to be. When you're looking into your choices, ensure that you research whether the certificates are nationally recognized.

Academic Route: Pros and Cons

Last year, Britons collectively achieved more than 777,000 qualifications in total, marking a 3% increase on the previous year. It's true that more and more people in the UK are seeking out higher education to progress their career. Since there's a broad range of ways in which people can study and a variety of degrees available, choosing this route could be a smart move for your future. Let's take a look at the pros and cons.

- Pro: Recognizable Qualifications

One of the biggest advantages of choosing an academic qualification is the fact that they are nationally—and sometimes internationally—recognizable. For example, if you achieve a 2:1 degree in History or English, a potential employer will understand your qualification completely. You won't have to explain your degree syllabus or its merit.

- Con: Expensive Option

Of course, a higher education degree often doesn't come cheap. If you're studying on-campus at one of the more acclaimed universities in the UK, your annual fees may be around £9,000, according to UCAS (Universities and Colleges Admissions Service). While there are student loans which will cover this amount, that level of debt could be off-putting to some potential students. It's worth considering all the options, including online courses, before making a decision.

Chapter 9 Education—Distinct Educational System and Distinguished Schools

- Pro: Develop Varied Skills

Undertaking an academic degree can unlock key expertise including **analytical skills**, research techniques and debating methods. Each of these can be applied to a whole variety of different careers. That means that you will walk away with a set of transferable skills, which should open up a range of doors for you. When you study a vocational course, the skills that you obtain will be specific to a certain career. However, when you undertake an academic course, you may find that there are more available options.

- Con: Difficult to Obtain

Not everybody has an academic **mindset** or approach to learning. While some people take to this sector of study with ease, many find it hard to follow an academic syllabus. For that reason, it's fair to say that the academic route is not for everyone out there. This type of education involves heavy reading loads, using refined research skills and writing well. Should you struggle in these areas, it could be more beneficial to look at vocational routes.

The choice is yours! There's no right answer when it comes to this question and, of course, it's important to remember that everyone is an individual. When you're making your decision, be sure to weigh up the pros and cons first. Figure out which of these options suits your lifestyle, your learning style and your career **aspirations**.

Vocabulary

vocational route		职业路线
apprenticeship	*n.*	学徒身份；学徒期
internship	*n.*	实习生；实习期
employability	*n.*	就业能力
undertake	*v.*	从事；承担
professional role		职业角色
progression	*n.*	发展；前进
leapfrog	*v.*	跨越；超越
earn a living		谋生
tailor	*v.*	定制，专门制作
fast-track	*n.*	快速道
time-consuming	*adj.*	旷日持久的；耗时的
assessment	*n.*	评估；评价

feat	n.	技艺；壮举
scenario	n.	设想；可能的情况
analytical skill		分析能力
mindset	n.	思维模式
aspiration	n.	志向；渴望

Exercises

I. How much do you know about vocational and academic education? Fill in the blanks with the information given in the passage.

1. What is vocational education?

    Vocational pathways include _____, _____ and _____.
    These are usually specific to a certain _____ or job role. People choosing vocational route can easily find a job and they can _____ as they _____ education.

2. What are the advantages and disadvantages of choosing academic route?

    Advantages include:

    1) An academic qualification is _____ recognizable.

    2) An academic degree can unlock key expertise including _____ _____, which could be applied to a whole variety of different careers.

    Disadvantages include:

    1) A higher education degree is very _____.

    2) The academic route has very hard syllabus and requires heavy loads of _____.

II. Decide whether the following statements are true or false, and mark T or F accordingly.

    _____ 1. If one decides to choose the academic route, he or she will first get an undergraduate degree, followed by a master's degree and even a Ph.D.

    _____ 2. To many students, the biggest advantage of choosing an academic qualification is the fact that they are very reputative on the local and national level.

    _____ 3. People choose the vocational route because they are

Chapter 9 Education—Distinct Educational System and Distinguished Schools

allowed to earn a living while taking training in certain industries.

_____ 4. One of the disadvantages of the vocational route is that learning a specific skill set is expensive and time-consuming.

_____ 5. The academic route is not for everyone, especially those who are not good at heavy book reading and academic writing.

III. Fill in the blanks with the appropriate forms of the following phrases.

go down	when it comes to	earn a living	come up against
needless to say	a set of	a variety of	a range of
weigh up to	figure out		

1. Our school leavers face so much competition that they seldom care what they do as long as they can _____.
2. _____, I felt very embarrassed in assuming he had his dates mixed up.
3. We _____ a great deal of resistance in dealing with the case.
4. If a price, level, or amount _____, it becomes lower or less than it was.
5. She's nobody's fool _____ dealing with difficult patients.
6. It's up to the teacher to provide _____ types of input in the classroom.
7. The savannas are tall and slim and can _____ 9.1 kilograms, making them one of the largest breeds of cats that people can own.
8. I think we should _____ some ways to stop people from polluting the river and call on them to fight against pollution.
9. The slim booklets describe _____ services and facilities.
10. Many literary academics simply parrot _____ impressive-sounding phrases.

IV. Translate the following sentences into Chinese.

1. Needless to say, either of these options will prove expensive and time-consuming in the long run. For that reason, you should ensure that you consider whether a vocational route suits your future plans well enough.
2. Intelligent people often find it hard to undertake exams, which can

make getting the qualifications they want a difficult feat.

3. While many of the vocational approaches—such as apprenticeships and courses—will be recognized by their given industries, you have to take extra care here. Since there are seemingly endless options available in this sector, the qualifications and certificates are not always as acclaimed as they first appear to be.

4. If you're studying on-campus at one of the more acclaimed universities in the UK, your annual fees may be around £9,000, according to UCAS.

5. Each of these can be applied to a whole variety of different careers. That means that you will walk away with a set of transferable skills, which should open up a range of doors for you.

Further Reading

Text II Western Norms of Critical Argumentation*

The development of critical thinking is a stated aim of higher education in Britain, seen in the calls for "rigorous arguments" and "critical analysis" in the Quality Assurance Agency's assessment criteria and **demonstrable** skills at master's level:

> Students should be able to think critically and be creative...organize thoughts, analyse, **synthesise** and critically appraise. This includes the capability to identify assumptions, evaluate statements in terms of evidence, detect false logic or reasoning, and identify **implicit** values.

In Western higher education, academic argumentation and debate are rooted in Socratic/Aristotelian practice of rigorous debate, an aggressive search for truth and a **discerning** of error, bias and contradiction. Andrews describes Western-style **criticality** as "assuming **skepticism** towards given truth, and weighing up different claims to the truth against the evidence". This traditional view of Western critical thinking has been described by Thayer-Bacon as "the battlefield mentality" which results in polarized critiques, with theories and ideas rejected or accepted on the basis of supporting evidence and logical argument. It is based on the **premise** that evidence should be held in doubt and subject to scrutiny

---

* Excerpted from Lixian Jin & Martin Cortazzi (Ed.). *Researching Chinese Learners: Skills, Perceptions and Intercultural Adaptations*. New York: Palgrave Macmillan, 2011: 275–281.

Chapter 9 Education—Distinct Educational System and Distinguished Schools

until it can be proved **legitimate** and truthful. Indeed, this is reflected in the notion of the "Null Hypothesis" used in quantitative data analysis.

The spirit of critical thinking is that we take nothing for granted or as being beyond question. In academic debate, arguments are analysed to find inconsistencies, logical flaws or evidence to the contrary.

So all viewpoints need to be considered and critiqued in a fair-minded manner, and for this a critical thinker has to be prepared to recognize the weaknesses and limitations in his or her own position: When one becomes aware that there are many legitimate points of view, each of which—when deeply thought through—yields some level of insight, then one becomes keenly aware that one's own thinking, however rich and insightful it may be, however carefully constructed, will not capture everything worth knowing and seeing.

Paul's main argument is that critical thinking is a universal skill, ideally to be pursued by all human beings regardless of culture and gender; that it is superior to all other forms of thinking, demanding fairness, discipline and creativity; and that it is the key to full personhood and self-realization. Such thinking demands a deliberate and conscious examination of assumptions and beliefs, which can be an uncomfortable exercise.

Critical thinking is complex because it involves overcoming not only intellectual barriers to progress, but psychological barriers as well. We are comfortable, as a rule, with our ideas, our belief structures, our view of the world. Certainly, if we thought our ideas were flawed, irrational, shallow, or biased in an unfair way, we would have already changed them. When questioned about the **validity** of our ideas or beliefs, particularly the foundational ones, we typically interpret the question to be a challenge to our integrity, often even to our identity.

While many opponents of Paul argue that these notions are culturally biased, they nevertheless agree on one point: that all humans are capable of higher-order cognitive skills. What they disagree on is how thoughts are expressed in the context of a diversity of cultures and across gender.

All humans who are **acculturated** and socialized are already in possession of higher order cognitive skills, though their expression and the practices they are embedded in will differ across cultures.

Street and Gee argue that the type of thinking advocated by the Critical Thinking Movement is narrow and **ethnocentric** and that it represents male-oriented, Western logic. In Hofstede's terms, it reflects the "**masculinity**" and "individualism" of Western cultures. Hofstede's dimension of masculinity versus femininity refers to the distribution of roles between the genders, ranging from very assertive and competitive male values, to modest and caring feminine values. Street and Gee believe that "nurture", that is, the social and cultural context, rather than innate "nature", determines how these higher-order cognitive skills are expressed. In other words, cognitive expression is integrally linked to culture and social communication, and in some cultures the type of logical, explicit reasoning used in the West is not culturally acceptable. It is not that some cultures are incapable of using certain patterns of reasoning, but that they prefer particular patterns above others, such as diffuse thinking above specificity. If Street and Gee are correct, and if Chinese academic discourse patterns fall predominantly outside the dominant Western patterns, then Chinese students can be expected to have different notions from Western academics of how argumentation and debate should operate. As a result, they will employ different communication strategies when expressing disagreement or criticism, or when arguing a point, especially in public discourses.

According to Hofstede and Bond, maintaining harmony and avoiding offence or confrontation in China appear to be of greater value and importance than any search for absolute truth that might result in giving unnecessary offence. Hence, any evaluation of ideas would be based on the premise of first accepting all contributions with a view to conciliatory accommodation and dialogue. Whereas China is a high-context culture, where inference, indirect speech and an avoidance of public disagreement are the norm, British culture has been described as low-context, where explicitness and directness in speech are valued, and where more open disagreement and free expression of one's beliefs and thoughts are acceptable. Teamwork for British students involves brainstorming of ideas, with a readiness to reject any contributions that do not stand up to critical analysis. Teamwork in China, on the other hand, lays an emphasis on listening to others, exposition of accepted fact and restraint in expressing personal opinions, especially when these are contrary to the common consensus or to those in positions of authority. Likewise, relationships among team members are more important than task completion, and critical evaluation of team members' ideas to achieve the best solution carries less weight than maintaining harmony.

This discussion has highlighted aspects of Western-style critical argumentation that may cause adaptation challenges for Chinese students in the UK. It has also

Chapter 9 Education—Distinct Educational System and Distinguished Schools

shown that some recent strands in Western thinking about argumentation stress the value of relationships and a more caring, holistic approach. Further research is needed to explore these challenges in more depth.

Vocabulary

demonstrable	*adj.*	可论证的；显而易见的
synthesise	*v.*	合成；综合
implicit	*adj.*	含蓄的；不直接言明的
discern	*v.*	了解；认识
criticality	*n.*	临界；危急程度
scepticism	*n.*	怀疑态度；怀疑主义
premise	*n.*	前提；假设
legitimate	*adj.*	正当的；合理的
validity	*n.*	（法律上的）有效；合法
acculturate	*v.*	使适应文化；使适应新的文化习俗
ethnocentric	*adj.*	种族优越感的；民族中心主义的
masculinity	*n.*	男子气概；男性

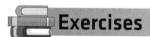
Exercises

英国社会与文化

Unit 2

Public Schools and Independent Schools

As a former high school teacher and a student in a class of 60 urchins at St. Brigid's grammar school, I know that education is all about discipline and motivation. Disadvantaged students need extra attention, a stable school environment, and enough teacher creativity to stimulate their imaginations. Those things are not expensive.

—Bill O'Reilly

I. Search for relevant information to answer the following questions.

1. What is a grammar school?
2. What is a boarding school?
3. What is a public school? What are the top public schools in the UK?

II. Generally speaking, we divide schools into two types: public schools and private schools. What are the types of schools in the UK? What are the differences among them?

III. Do you know the famous alumni from those reputable public schools? Match each of the alumni with the school he or she graduated from.

1. Prince William   A.

2. Winston Churchill   B.

290

Chapter 9 Education—Distinct Educational System and Distinguished Schools

3. Lewis Carroll   *C.*

4. John Locke   *D.*

5. Kate Middleton   *E.*

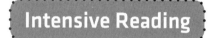

Text I British Education System—Grammar School*

For most people in the UK, grammar schools are associated with the past, belonging to an age of black-and-white TV and children playing with a hoop and stick.

But now there are moves in the English political system to end the ban on new grammar schools and fund their introduction. (This is only the case in England, as education is a devolved matter in Scotland, Wales and Northern Ireland). There are still 164 state-funded grammar schools in the UK, but that's compared to nearly 1,500 in their heyday. Whether or not grammar schools should be reintroduced is now being hotly debated across British politics. While the Conservatives and UKIP (UK Independence Party) are broadly in favor, and Labour, the Liberal Democrats and the Greens are broadly opposed, there are many dissenting voices on both sides. In this article, we look at why the issue is so controversial, and what the possible outcomes mean for parents, students and teachers across England.

What Is a Grammar School?

A grammar school in the sense that it's being used in the current debate is a selective state school for students aged 11 to 18. At the age of 10, students who

---
* Retrieved from Oxford Royale website.

wish to apply for the grammar school sit an exam called the 11-plus, and those who pass are accepted into the grammar school. A typical 11-plus exam consists of Maths, Verbal Reasoning and Non-verbal Reasoning questions, the latter two types of questions resembling IQ test questions. The pass rate varies depending on the grammar school in question; some grammar schools will calculate who is accepted depending on how close they live to the school and how many applicants they've had that year as well as the raw score that the applicant gets on the test.

When what's usually referred to as the "grammar school system" was at its height, from the 1940s to the 1970s, grammar schools existed in a three-part structure alongside technical schools and secondary moderns. The idea of a technical school was to focus on training for science and industry, but the idea never really caught on, and at most 3% of secondary school students in the UK attended one. Secondary moderns were much more widespread, taking in the vast majority of students who had been rejected by grammar schools. They offered fewer opportunities for students to take exams, and traditionally only taught pupils from 11 to 15, as after that age, secondary modern students were expected either to go to a grammar school for sixth form education (the final two years of secondary education), or go out to work.

Going further back, the reason why they're called grammar schools in the first place dates to medieval times, where they were schools (usually attached the monasteries) in which the main focus was the teaching of Latin. The earliest schools along these lines date back to the 6th century, though they weren't referred to as grammar schools until the 14th century. While the curriculum widened from its focus on Latin to cover subjects such as logic and rhetoric as well, Latin remained priority. Following the reformation, the desire to be able to understand **scripture** in the original languages caused Greek and Hebrew to be added to the curriculum of some grammar schools.

From the 18th century onwards, the desire for an education in classical languages **waned**. Good teachers of the Classics became harder to come by, and schools began to add subjects such as **arithmetic** and English. And alongside grammar schools, a huge variety of other schools were established; no nationwide system of education existed until 1947, so schools were set up along a variety of different lines in a system that served some areas and some groups of students much better than others. Yet the existing grammar schools, some of which had medieval origins, were seen as a model of good educational practices when the 1947 reforms to education were designed, leading to their name being

Chapter 9 **Education—Distinct Educational System and Distinguished Schools**

retained for the new nationwide system.

Why Do Some People Want the System Back?

A key argument made in favour of grammar schools is that they aid social mobility. Because they are supposed to select students solely on the basis of academic merit, rather than on the basis of family wealth, religion or anything else, bright students from poorer backgrounds get a chance to succeed. The proponents of grammar schools believe that they give students from disadvantaged backgrounds a better chance of succeeding than an equivalent comprehensive (i.e. non-selective) school would do. But it's worth noting that this claim has been strongly contested—see later in this article for the opposing perspective.

What is not usually disputed is that the students (poor or otherwise—more usually otherwise) who are selected into grammar schools do better there than they would do in an equivalent comprehensive school. This makes logical sense; brighter students are usually better behaved, and a school full of bright, well-behaved students is naturally going to end up with good results. Grammar schools fill the top places of most league tables of school results, including against private schools that may also operate their own form of selection. As Theresa May noted in her speech, 80% of existing selective schools are rated outstanding, compared with 20% of state schools overall.

Looking at the Prime Minister offers a neat case study in what people hope grammar schools will achieve. Of the five Prime Ministers who went to school after 1947, one attended a comprehensive (Gordon Brown), two attended private schools (Tony Blair and David Cameron) and two attended grammar schools (John Major and Theresa May). It's long been argued that the **dominance** in leadership positions of people who went to private school can only be beaten by grammar schools, which act to propel the most **promising** pupils to the top in the same way that private schools enable access to an outstanding education for those who are lucky enough to be able to afford it.

Put bluntly, for some advocates of grammar schools, it seems as if the **elite** in British society can either be private-school educated (there because of their parents' wealth) or grammar-school educated (there because of their own academic ability). Many people support grammar schools on the basis that the latter seems more **meritocratic** than the former. It's worth noting that at the same time as Theresa May announced her support for more grammar schools, she also threatened the funding of private schools by suggesting that they would have to meet much more **stringent** requirements to obtain **charitable** status.

Vocabulary

scripture	*n.*	经文
wane	*v.*	衰落
arithmetic	*n.*	算数
dominance	*n.*	控制
promising	*adj.*	有希望的
elite	*n.*	社会精英
meritocratic	*n.*	精英领导的
stringent	*adj.*	严格的，严厉的
charitable	*adj.*	乐善好施的

Exercises

I. Decide whether the following statements are true or false, and mark T or F accordingly.

_____ 1. Students could apply for a grammar school at the age of 8, and they have to pass an exam consisting of grammar and maths.

_____ 2. Even though the grammar school is an invention of the past, as the figure shows that there are only 164 stated-funded grammar schools in the UK, both Conservatives and the Liberal Democrats strongly supported the idea of reintroduction of grammar schools.

_____ 3. The pass rate of entrance examination of the grammar school varies depending on the applicants' scores only, the subjects being tested including Maths, Verbal Reasoning and IQ test.

_____ 4. The fundamental reason raised by some people who would like to bring back the grammar school system is that it aids brilliant students with academic success to accomplish their social mobility regardless of their poor family background.

_____ 5. It is said that only graduates from private schools are the future leaders of the country because both Tony Blair and David Cameron graduated from private schools.

Chapter 9 Education—Distinct Educational System and Distinguished Schools

II. Complete the following table with the descriptions of famous British Prime Ministers according to the passage.

	Attitudes towards grammar schools	Parties he/she belongs to	Schools attended
Theresa May			
Tony Blair			
Gordon Brown			
David Cameron	N/A		

III. Translate the following sentences into Chinese.

1. Whether or not grammar schools should be reintroduced is now being hotly debated across British politics.
2. When what's usually referred to as the "grammar school system" was at its height, from the 1940s to the 1970s, grammar schools existed in a three-part structure alongside technical schools and secondary moderns.
3. The pass rate varies depending on the grammar school in question; some grammar schools will calculate who is accepted depending on how close they live to the school and how many applicants they've had that year as well as the raw score that the applicant gets on the test.
4. What is not usually disputed is that the students (poor or otherwise—more usually otherwise) who are selected into grammar schools do better there than they would do in an equivalent comprehensive.
5. From the 18th century onwards, the desire for an education in classical languages waned.

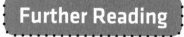

Text II Best of British as Elite Public Schools Tap up Chinese Pupils*

The early evening dinner rush has hit Windsor's most popular Chinese restaurant, 1423 China Kitchen, situated in a small **cobbled** lane off the bustling High Street.

---

* Retrieved from Evening Standard website.

Owner Ying Wang is busy seating two groups of tourists, dishing out Chinese-language menus and taking orders in Mandarin.

Ying, who **hails from** Dalian in northern China and has also been a tour guide in the UK for 12 years, opened the restaurant four months ago to **cater** for the busloads of Chinese visitors who descend on the **picturesque** town every week to visit Windsor Castle and, increasingly, Eton College, the public school founded by Henry VI in 1440.

"They know Eton is unique and number one in the rankings," he says during a break in service. "One of the big reasons they come also is Prince William and Harry, they known they've been there."

Chinese parents Lily Wu and her husband, who live in Shanghai and did their masters in the UK, plan to enroll their 10-year-old at an independent school in the UK next September, and said British boarding schools were known for their "outstanding quality and a tradition of innovation".

"In the UK, the courses of study focus on developing students with strong thinking. Children need to be taught to become active members of society and also be **socialized**," Wu says.

"However, most schools only teach textbook knowledge in China, the so-called 'innovation and creativity' are the most different points between Chinese and UK education systems."

Names such as Eton, Harrow, Winchester and Westminster resonate with China's **affluent** middle class, who are prepared to spend big on their child's education.

Images of Eton-educated Olympian **equestrian** sportsman Alex Hua Tian, a British citizen who has represented China, have helped bolster the **"aristocratic"** reputation of boarding schools.

Chinese mainland is already the largest source of foreign-born pupils at British boarding schools, with numbers rising 10% last year to nearly 8,000, according to the latest figures.

"Before 2000, nobody had heard of British independent schools in China," says Barnaby Lenon, a former headmaster at Harrow and chairman of the Independent Schools Council, which compiled the figures.

Four in five students from China attend full time at UK boarding schools, where average fees are nearly £10,800 a term (Eton charges £12,900). That

Chapter 9 **Education—Distinct Educational System and Distinguished Schools**

means Chinese pupils are worth about £220 million annually to British boarding schools.

However, the bigger draw for some schools, perhaps, is **leveraging** their name and setting up **franchises** in China.

There are 15 campuses there run by UK independent schools, including a Harrow **offshoot** in Beijing. Eton has resisted a similar move although it did launch EtonX, an online tuition course for Chinese children.

Yet these are not huge boosts for the **bursar**. Eton's net fee income for the year ending August 2016 rose to £40.4 million, up from £38.8 million, but EtonX brought in just £142,000 and profits were flat (the project has since closed).

Harrow's international schools' franchise, which also has sites in Shanghai, Hong Kong and Bangkok, generated turnover of £2.3 million and profits of £277,429.

That is compared with net school fees of £39.3 million.

"They can develop pupil exchanges, it's great for global citizenship and you can develop a global alumni network," says Colin Bell, chief executive of the Council of British International Schools. "They want to future-proof themselves."

Some also see this Chinese-British love in boosting the wider UK economy as it tries to forge new trade and cultural links post-Brexit.

"It's a phenomenally good export; it doesn't just take revenues for itself, it also creates revenues for everything else in the economy," said William Vanbergen, founder of BE Education, which is exploring a London float.

It helps place Chinese children at schools such as Harrow and Eton, where he was a pupil. "There's nothing better to sell than education—it beats Burberry hands down."

The enrolment boom has also helped London property and retail—with wealthy parents buying digs for their children and splashing out in the West End.

But there are questions over the long-term benefit to the UK, with many Chinese students leaving Britain for top US universities and ultimately heading back to China.

However, Vanbergen says Chinese children growing up here might also be more disposed to pro-British **sentiment** as they know the culture. "They can act as a bridge between the two countries going forward," he adds.

If this looks like a **rose-tinted** view of UK schools, think again; the families who choose to send their offspring abroad are increasingly **savvy** about their choices, visiting schools and meeting headmasters, who regularly tour China.

So why come here then?

One theory for public schools' popularity in China cites the extra-curricular activities on offer such as music and sports—and the lack of an excessive focus on exam results.

"The Chinese system is focused to an even greater degree than our system on exams and tests. The British education system is broader," says ex-Harrow headmaster Lenon.

Back at the 1423, the rush has died down.

Ying says he sees no reason for a slowdown in Chinese demand for British education:

"When they get the money they will look at what is most important to them and the number one thing is education."

Vocabulary

cobbled	v.	铺有鹅卵石
hail from		诞生于
cater	v.	提供餐饮服务
picturesque	adj.	风景如画的
socialize	v.	使适应社会
affluent	adj.	富裕的；富足的
equestrian	adj.	马术的
aristocratic	adj.	贵族的
leverage	v.	充分利用（资源、观点等）
franchise	n.	（公司授予某人的）特许经营权
offshoot	n.	分支机构
bursar	n.	财务部门；财务主管
sentiment	n.	感情

Chapter 9 Education—Distinct Educational System and Distinguished Schools

| rose-tinted | *adj.* | 希望的；乐观的；玫瑰色的 |
| savvy | *adj.* | （非正式）有见识的；懂实际知识的；通情达理的 |

Unit 3

How to Apply for a British University

The gratification of wealth is not found in mere possession or in lavish expenditure, but in its wise application.

—Oscar Wilde

 Test Your Knowledge

I. **Discuss the following questions with your partner.**

1. What are the key factors in composing a successful personal statement?
2. If you are the admission interviewer, what sorts of questions will you ask the applicants of a British university?

II. **Translate the following mottoes of world-famous universities into Chinese.**

1. The wind of freedom blows. (Stanford University)
2. Mind and hand. (Massachusetts Institute of Technology)
3. Let Plato be your friend, and Aristotle, but more let your friend be Truth. (Harvard University)
4. The Lord is my light. (University of Oxford)

Text I The Personal Statement That Got Me a Large Scholarship to Cambridge*

When I submitted my application for the master's program in Latin American Studies at Cambridge University, I was a bit lost in life. I was what they call a "**super-senior**" at UCLA, taking my last three General Education

---

* Retrieved from Accepted website.

Chapter 9 **Education—Distinct Educational System and Distinguished Schools**

requirements during Fall quarter of a fifth year. I had already walked for graduation the June before and the future was oddly wide open, and incredibly empty to me.

Like many students who are "good at school", I thought that a graduate program seemed like a reasonable idea, especially because I graduated during an economic crisis and the job search was difficult. I opened a number of applications for PhD programs in the United States and, on the advice of a professor, I applied to Cambridge because of the opportunity to focus exclusively on Latin American Cinema and a chance to be considered for the Gates Cambridge Scholarship.

My Gates Cambridge Personal Statement

While the application to Cambridge's Latin American Studies program did not differ greatly from that of most global graduate schools, in order to be considered for funding opportunities like the Gates Cambridge award I was required to submit an additional personal statement.

The prompt was daunting: "In not more than 500 words, please describe below how your interests and achievements, both academic and extra-curricular, demonstrate a capacity for leadership, commitment to using your knowledge to serve your community and to applying your talents to improve the lives of others."

I was 22, and I had never really tried to articulate how my curiosity about foreign languages, Latin American literature, culture, and film could demonstrate "a capacity for leadership", or the ability to "serve my community". But I gave it a go.

How I Was Shocked During My Gates Cambridge Interview

During my 25-minute interview with the Gates committee in February, I was completely stunned by a question that one of the British members posed as a research question. It was something like: "Given that you propose to study Latin American film as part of your research, what do you think of the footage of Oscar Grant's death?"

I was pretty much speechless when this question was asked, and I had a hard time composing myself. Footage of Oscar Grant's killing was impossible to avoid in Oakland. The cell phone recordings of Oscar Grant's death were also the first **reel** of raw film images that I had ever seen to **depict** the end of an actual person's life. I had seen *American History X*, a movie in which a white man brutally commits racist and fatal hate crimes, but those were fictional images. Most of the films that I studied regarding Latin America were also made of fictional images. The footage of Oscar Grant dying was a **visceral** reality for me, and it came with weeks of rioting in my hometown, a series of incredibly tense conversations with neighbors and family, feelings of guilt about my whiteness, and a deep sense of helplessness about the world around me.

None of those words came out in my interview. Overwhelmed with emotions, I just wasn't able to express myself in that moment, and I tried to move on as quickly as possible. But since then, I've thought a lot about that question.

What I Learned from Writing My Personal Statement for the Cambridge College Scholarship Application

In **hindsight**, the question that the committee asked me was a genuine response to my personal statement, which means that the statement had been effective even before it became timely. Remember, I was selected for the shortlist before Oscar Grant was shot, but the setting that I created by observing my own surroundings in the personal statement is what allowed for the committee to connect with a reality that was (and still is) unfolding around me.

When I first wrote this statement, I was afraid it didn't say enough about my achievements, past leadership experiences, or meaningful accomplishments. I wasn't ready to discuss obstacles overcome, I acknowledged my privilege, and I didn't know anything about what the essay was supposed to be like. In fact, I didn't share any of my applications materials with advisors or friends before submitting (a horrible idea!).

However, after my many years of working with students from a variety of backgrounds on diversity statements and scholarship applications, I understand why this was a successful statement. All I did was to observe myself in the world, genuinely and honestly at that stage of my life. I described my relationship to Oakland from an insider's eyes, and an outsider's eyes, and that allowed the committee to learn about me within the context of where I grew up. Because I described Oakland from the eyes of someone just off a plane from Rio de Janeiro, I gave the committee concrete insights that they couldn't have **surmised** from the first sentence: "I grew up in Oakland, California."

This is an issue that comes up a lot when I work with people on personal statements. Oftentimes the things that you know about yourself and your surroundings are so obvious to you that you forget to describe these insights to

Chapter 9 Education—Distinct Educational System and Distinguished Schools

your audience. In a personal statement it is your job to explain who you are, what drives you to accomplish your goals, why your current course of study matters to you and how it can impact others.

How to Write a Compelling Personal Statement

If you're working on a statement like this and you start to wonder what it's supposed to be, or what you're supposed to talk about, tell yourself to stop asking that question. Instead ask yourself, what do you know intuitively about how you move in the world? How can you observe yourself so that someone else gets a glimpse of how you think, what you care about, and why you want to do the things that you want to do?

I didn't end up getting the Gates Cambridge Scholarship, which felt like a blow at the time.

As a result of the same application materials and essays, however, I was awarded a Cambridge Overseas Trust Scholarship for £10,000 ($17,000) which covered most of my tuition. Because of this funding, I ended up going to Cambridge and studying Latin American film. I also took away some incredible lessons from Gates Cambridge interview, and those personal insights made the whole process worth it.

Attachment

The statement of purpose to Cambridge:

I grew up in Oakland, California, one of the most violent and disparate urban communities in America. While I knew this as a child, I only knew it in a distant sense. I caught glimpses of newspaper headlines with phrases like "gang violence" and "high **homicide** rate". I heard rap songs on the radio that referred to the infamous "O-town of the West", or the area code "510". Those were always funny references to my hometown, but they were words and sayings; they never felt like realities to me as I grew up.

To my great surprise, these newspaper articles, statistics, and song lyrics only became real to me when I left Oakland and America to spend my junior year abroad in Rio de Janeiro, Brazil, and then return home.

Before I arrived there, Brazil only existed on paper, in books like *Peter Winn's Americas*, and on screen in films like *City of God*. The **mesmerizing** topography and diverse population of Rio de Janeiro were realities that I approached with **trepidation**. But after a year, I abandoned my preconceptions about the city and was even comfortable using unofficial vans, or **kombis**, to navigate my way through the chaotic and **sprawling** city. I overcame my fears and learned how to assert myself appropriately in difficult situations. Just as I had become comfortably aware of the realities of Oakland, I became **inured** to the violence and class conflicts that had frightened me before arriving in Rio.

With regards to this experience, the most educational and enlightening moments of shock came to me as I drove through Oakland on my way home from the airport. I had not been home for a year, my eyes were glued to the car window, and I saw everything differently. Though the **terrain** between the Oakland airport and my home is relatively flat, that day the socio-economic inequality was as clear to me as the diverse topography of Rio de Janeiro. To put it simply, there were houses with fences and window guards, and houses with large driveways and beautifully landscaped gardens. Through subtle markers and contexts, the issues and conflicts that had surprised and scared me in Rio were suddenly applicable to the scenery and media of my hometown.

Both of these experiences, of arriving in Brazil and returning to Oakland, are powerful instances of where academic or literary knowledge solidifies through the experience of real events. I want to know more about issues of urban Latin America because they are directly related to urban American issues. Emotional and analytical access to these socio-economic issues through literature and film is a bridge that I passionately want to extend towards students. Every person who enters a college classroom is profoundly privileged with the opportunity to see herself and her surroundings differently. It is my dream to inspire others to see education as an opportunity to travel, to experience difference, and to return home with critical points of view, and the desire to create positive change.

Vocabulary

super-senior	*n.*	大四学生
reel	*n.*	一卷胶卷；卷轴
depict	*v.*	描述；描绘
visceral	*adj.*	出于本能的；发自肺腑的
hindsight	*n.*	后见之明
surmise	*v.*	猜测，推测
homicide	*n.*	杀人，谋杀
mesmerizing	*adj.*	施催眠术的；迷住的
trepidation	*n.*	恐惧，惊恐；颤抖

Chapter 9 Education—Distinct Educational System and Distinguished Schools

kombi	*n.*	康比小客车（可乘坐约十人）
sprawling	*adj.*	蔓延的；杂乱无序伸展的
inured	*adj.*	习惯的
terrain	*n.*	地势；地形

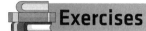 **Exercises**

I. **Answer the following questions briefly.**

1. Why did the writer apply for a master program?
2. How did the writer make the decision of applying for University of Cambridge?
3. Why did the writer submit an additional personal statement?
4. According to the passage, the writer had a 25-minute interview. How did the interview change her attitude towards her personal statement?
5. Could you summarize the writer's experience of a successful personal application?

II. **Translate the following Chinese phrases into English.**

1. _____ (被情绪淹没了), I just wasn't able to express myself in that moment, and I tried to move on as quickly as possible. But since then, I've thought a lot about that question.
2. I had seen *American History X*, a movie in which a white man brutally commits racist and fatal _____ (仇恨犯罪), but those were fictional images.
3. The President is _____ (决心从事) reforming health care.
4. All I did was observe myself in the world, _____ (真诚地和诚实地) at that stage of my life.
5. I caught glimpses of newspaper headlines with phrases like "gang violence" and "_____ (高凶杀率)."
6. The mesmerizing topography and _____ (多样化的人口) of Rio de Janeiro were realities that I approached with trepidation.
7. With regards to this experience, the most _____ (有教育意义的和受启发的) moments of shock came to me as I drove through Oakland on my way home from the airport.
8. Both of these experiences, of arriving in Brazil and returning to Oakland, are powerful instances of where academic or literary knowledge _____ (使变得坚定) through the experience of real events.

III. Suppose you are going to apply for a master program of a foreign university. Please write an outline of your proposal for or personal statement of your dream university.

Further Reading

Text II What Is a Collegiate University?*

A **collegiate** university can come in all shapes and sizes, but it's the sense of community within a big environment that's the common feature.

The clue is in the name—if a university is described as being "collegiate", it means that it is made up of a mixture of colleges. The most famous of these are Oxford and Cambridge, each comprising of over 30 colleges, every one having its own **quirks** and traditions, while other collegiate establishments include: Lancaster University, the University of York and Durham University.

Not only does a college dictate your type of accommodation—you'll all live in the same building, share the same kitchens and line-up in the same shower queue—it offers a close-knit community within a bigger university establishment. And for some, this provides just the right amount of coziness in what can be a sprawling city campus.

Inter-college Sport

So, what happens when you divide a university into sections? Inter-college sport of course! Not quite dedicated enough to set aside three evenings a week to train, on top of matches? College sport offers people an alternative to the **ultra-competitive** university teams, providing as varied a selection of teams as varsity, but with a more chilled out (but no less competitive) attitude. **Netball**, rugby, swimming, table tennis, badminton, rowing, tennis, **kayaking**, chess club—you name it, they've got it.

And because you all live in the same college, post-match celebrations (and commiserations) are regularly **lodged in** the college bar. That's right—a dedicated in-house bar. Most collegiate universities have one and it's, inevitably, the hub.

---

* Retrieved from Independent School Parent website.

Chapter 9 **Education—Distinct Educational System and Distinguished Schools**

Students usually live in college in the first year, then **branch out** into private accommodation to let in the **newbies** in second year. That is unless you go to Oxbridge, where they often cater for students throughout their degree.

Will a Collegiate University Suit You?

It's worth thinking about whether a collegiate-style university will suit your personality. It's very different to a big city-centre campus. You're a big fish in a small pond, rather than a little fish in a vast ocean. There are benefits to both environments, if you're used to a small school then perhaps throwing yourself into a non-collegiate university is the push you need to spread your wings.

Different Styles of Collegiate Universities

Don't assume, however, that there's a one-size-fits-all approach to the collegiate system. When you imagine a collegiate university, traditional buildings and lush green quads may spring to mind. In contrast, the University of York, comprising nine colleges, is only 53 years old.

In the sixties, the campus was built in the grounds of Heslington Hall, on the outskirts of Heslington Village. Colleges were built around a man-made lake and university departments and accommodation are in the same buildings—yes, you can literally fall into your 9:15 am seminar, toast in hand, post-9 am alarm.

Further north, the 14 colleges making up Durham University are a mixture of more modern halls just outside the city centre and traditional colleges in what is known as the Bailey—where Durham Cathedral will become your daily wake-up call.

Like all collegiate universities, Durham's halls inevitably have distinct stereotypes: Tervis is keen on music, St. Hild and St. Bede are rich kids' stomping grounds, Van Mildert likes to give something back with DUCK (charity committee), St. Chad's is, well, tiny, and University College is highly sought after for its Hogwarts-esque atmosphere.

Make Sure to Visit a Collegiate University Open Day

Royal Holloway is a college under the umbrella organization of the University of London. It's vital that you visit all the colleges you're interested in at university open days. And ensure you do the walk to your lecture halls (imagining it in the worst weather conditions even if it's glorious sunshine).

And you may be surprised to learn that well-known institutions like UCL, King's College London, Goldsmiths, Royal Holloway, Queen Mary and the Royal

Academy of Music are all "colleges" under the umbrella organization of the University of London. Commonly referred to as universities, these 17 colleges benefit from shared facilities. However, you apply to, and graduate from your college, not the University of London.

How to Apply to Oxbridge

If you've got your sights set on Oxbridge, be aware that due to their collegiate system you'll apply to a specific college as well as for a particular course. This does not indicate that you won't get into the university if a college is full, there is a "pool" system which means if you're accepted by a department then a college with space will **pluck** you out of the pool and give you a home.

And if all else fails, some of the best-formed friendships have been born out of a mutual dislike of halls! Admissions tutors know what they're doing, and often having the decision taken out of your hands is the spontaneity that you need to make the most of your university life.

Vocabulary

collegiate	*adj.*	学院的
quirk	*n.*	怪癖
inter-college	*adj.*	学院间的
ultra-competitive	*adj.*	高度竞争的
netball	*n.*	篮网球
kayaking	*n.*	皮艇运动
lodge in		固定停留在
branch out		扩展范围；长出枝条
newbie	*n.*	初学者
pluck	*v.*	拔去；挖掘

Exercises

Chapter 9 Education—Distinct Educational System and Distinguished Schools

Different Types of British Universities and Their Strengths

Education is not the filling of a pail, but the lighting of a fire.

—William Butler Yeats

 Test Your Knowledge

I. Besides Oxford and Cambridge Universities, are there any other top universities that you know? Please make a brief introduction of the top universities in the UK according to your knowledge, including the names, the locations, as well as other useful information.

II. When talking about higher education, what factors would come to your mind first? Please discuss with your partner the relevant aspects like access to higher education, tuition and living cost, education equality, scientific research level, and so on.

Intensive Reading

Text I Differences Between Oxford and Cambridge*

It's a summer's day. People are eating strawberries in punts on the river. Students cycle past, their **panniers** overloaded with books, and narrowly avoid crashing into a large group of tourists who were concentrating more on their map than on the traffic. There's a lively market in the square not far away, and you are surrounded by beautiful, historic buildings on all sides.

---

* Retrieved from Oxford Royale website.

That's a scene that immediately brings to mind only two places: Oxford and Cambridge (though residents of Bath and Canterbury might argue that it could also take place there). But it's **nigh-on** impossible to say which one it might be. They have plenty of other similarities as well; roughly equal **proximity** to public transport links, including a fast train to London and a good range of airports nearby. Suggestions that Oxford is better for the humanities and Cambridge for the sciences (or vice versa) are soon proven to be outdated. And there's no **perceptible** difference in teaching quality between the number one and number two universities in the UK, either.

So, whether you're planning on attending a summer school, or you're figuring out what to put on your UCAS form, the choice between the two can be a challenge given that they are so very similar. To save you from tossing a coin, here's our look at what separates them.

Oxford Is Bigger and Livelier; Cambridge Is Smaller and Quieter

As differences go, this one is still not all that significant. Oxford has a population of 150,000; Cambridge has a population of 124,000. An additional 26,000 people is unlikely to feel that different if, for instance, you are also considering studying in London (population: 8.7 million). Both Oxford and Cambridge are small cities that feel like they sit on the intersection between being small cities and large towns; if you've come from London, Manchester or Birmingham, say, both will feel small. They are also both of a size that means you can cycle across them in about half an hour (in Oxford, we've defined this as Summertown to Rose Hill; in Cambridge, as the Science Park to Grantchester Road).

All the same, if you're seeking differences, rather than similarities, this is one of the more noticeable ones. **Gentrification** has progressed further in Cambridge than in Oxford, so that the lively area of Mill Road in Cambridge is distinctly quieter and more middle-class than its equivalent in Oxford, Cowley Road. In Cambridge, the nightlife is more student-orientated, as the students make up a greater percentage of people going out.

This difference is sometimes expressed as "Oxford is bigger and livelier; Cambridge is smaller and prettier", which is unfair to Oxford. Whether you prefer the delicate spires of King's College, Cambridge, to the grand surroundings of Radcliffe Square, Oxford, is very much a matter of taste, and both cities have an equal number of **stunning** buildings and memorable views. Oxford's architecture is more uniform, as it's mostly built from the same Headington

Chapter 9 Education—Distinct Educational System and Distinguished Schools

stone, while as Cambridge has no local stone, its buildings are more diverse. But there's certainly no consensus as to which city is therefore more beautiful.

One side-effect of Oxford being larger is that it has two main bus companies, rather than just one, and the competition between the two means that bus travel is easier in Oxford than Cambridge. However, if you're planning on walking or cycling, there's no noticeable difference between the two; both are extremely friendly to pedestrians and cyclists.

Cambridge and Oxford Universities Offer Different Subjects

That's not to say that they offer completely different subjects, of course; but you certainly shouldn't assume that every subject will be offered by both universities, and, if offered, it will be taught in the same way.

For instance, Cambridge offers a course in Architecture, which Oxford doesn't. Oxford offers Fine Art, which Cambridge doesn't. Celtic courses at Oxford are currently under review, and can't be studied until at least 2018, while Cambridge's celebrated Anglo-Saxon, Norse and Celtic course (ASNC— or "az-nack") is still going strong. Cambridge offers a Natural Sciences degree that covers a wide range of areas within science, allowing students to choose their **specialism** later, while Oxford students have to choose their focus at the point at which they apply to the university. Oxford also doesn't offer a course in Veterinary Medicine, while Cambridge does.

Beyond these differences between the subjects that are offered at each university, there are also differences in what is taught within the specific subject. For instance, both universities offer English courses (in Cambridge called simply "English", and in Oxford, "English Language and Literature"). But in Oxford, in your first year, you will study "early medieval literature, Victorian literature and modern literature up to the present day", while being introduced to "the conceptual and technical tools used in the study of language and literature, and to a wide range of different critical assumptions and approaches". At Cambridge, in your first two years, the only **compulsory** papers are "English Literature and Its Contexts 1300–1550" and "Shakespeare". You can choose to avoid "Practical Criticism and Critical Practice" (that's the same thing as Oxford's "Critical Assumptions and Approaches") altogether if you prefer, and the earliest literature you will study dates from 1066 onwards. Oxford's definition of first-year "early medieval literature" is from 650 onwards, whereas in Cambridge this is assigned to Anglo-Saxon, Norse and Celtic.

You can see that while the two courses have more in common with each other than they might do with many other English courses elsewhere (Lancaster's first-year English literature course, for instance, focuses on the late 16th century to the present, and **modules** to be taken in later years are also mostly about modern literature), they also have significant differences, especially if you're interested in early medieval literature. You'll see the same sorts of differences in almost any subjects, as what's included will depend on the choices of the particular faculty—so it's worth looking carefully in case one university or the other doesn't cover your particular interests.

Vocabulary

pannier	*n.*	驮篮；肩筐
nigh-on	*adv.*	差不多；几乎
proximity	*n.*	接近；邻近
perceptible	*adj.*	可察觉的，可感知的
gentrification	*n.*	中产阶级化
stunning	*adj.*	极好的；极吸引人的
specialism	*n.*	专业
compulsory	*adj.*	必须做的，义务的，强制的
module	*n.*	（大学课程）组成单元

Exercises

I. **Match the information with the two universities respectively.**

A. The lively area of Mill Road is distinctly quieter.

B. There are fewer middle class in Cowley Road.

C. The nightlife is more student-oriented.

D. The buildings are more diverse.

E. Gentrification has progressed further.

F. Its architecture is more uniform.

G. It offers a course in Architecture.

H. It offers Fine Art.

I. Its celebrated Anglo-Saxon, Norse and Celtic course is still going strong.

J. It offers a course in Veterinary Medicine.

K. Its definition of "early medieval literature" is from 650 onwards.

Chapter 9 Education—Distinct Educational System and Distinguished Schools

1. Oxford: _____
2. Cambridge: _____

II. Choose the best answer to each question.

1. Which course is **NOT** offered in Cambridge?

   A. Architecture.

   B. Veterinary Medicine.

   C. ASNC.

   D. Critical Assumptions and Approaches.

2. Which course is provided in Oxford?

   A. Fine Art.

   B. Shakespeare.

   C. ASNC.

   D. Practical Criticism and Critical Practice.

3. Which one is **NOT** a place in Oxford?

   A. Rose Hill.

   B. King's College.

   C. Cowley Road.

   D. Radcliffe Square.

4. Which of the following is **NOT** true about what is taught in the two universities?

   A. Both universities offer English courses.

   B. In Cambridge, the earliest literature you will study dates from 1066 onwards.

   C. Oxford's definition of early medieval literature is from 650 onwards.

   D. Oxford offers courses like Fine Art, Architecture and Veterinary Medicine.

III. Fill in the blanks with the appropriate forms of the words in the box.

approach	equivalent	proximity	assumption
compulsory	specialism	stunning	perceptible

1. In the new curriculum, some courses are _____, while others are optional for middle school students.

2. Yunnan Province is located in southwest China, enjoying geographical _____ to Myanmar, Laos and Vietnam.

3. With _____ speed, the Internet is profoundly changing the way we work, shop, do business, and communicate.

4. In most of the world the climate changes to date are barely _____ or hard to pin on warming.

5. Steamed dumpling contains low calorie, _____ to only 70% of the rice, and lower fat and carbohydrate than the latter.

6. His _____ is game theory, a branch of maths that studies how people negotiate with each other.

7. Traditional economic analysis is premised on the _____ that more is better.

8. So what are the benefits of this _____ and how do they help resolve the debate?

Further Reading

Text II Why Should You Study at a Russell Group University?*

The Russell Group universities are some of the best universities in the UK and they are all an excellent choice for your future career plans. Let's take a look at some of the reasons why you should opt to study your postgraduate program at a Russell Group university.

- **Location, Location, Location**

Most Russell Group universities are close to or in the centre of major cities of the UK, making transportation easy for international students as well as for British students. For example, London School of Economics and Queen Mary's University London—which are both members of the Russell Group—are located in London, which makes it very easy to access any part of the world using London's excellent connections. Other major cities, such as Leeds, Manchester, Liverpool, Newcastle, Cardiff, Edinburgh and Glasgow are all bases for Russell Group universities and the UK's excellent transportation networks allow easy travel.

---

* Retrieved from Postgrad website.

Chapter 9 Education—Distinct Educational System and Distinguished Schools

- Area of Expertise

Choosing a Russell Group university is a perfect choice for anyone considering a future within **academia** or as a researcher. The Russell Group universities all produce large **volumes** of published research every year and this means that it is a good idea to choose a Russell Group university for your postgraduate studies if you want to publish work as well. Some universities, for example the University of Manchester, have an excellent reputation in the field of Science, and other universities, such as the University of Edinburgh and University of Leeds are particularly well respected in the worlds of Medicine and Law. The London School of Economics and Durham University both have great reputations in Business and Finance and the University of Cambridge and the University of Oxford are both members of the Russell Group with world-class reputations in almost any field you can think of.

Table 9.1 **illustrates** some of the various subject areas the different Russell Group universities are well known for **excelling** in:

Table 9.1

Subject Area	Russell Group University
Medicine	University of Glasgow University of Oxford University of Edinburgh Queen Mary's University London University of Cambridge
Agriculture	Queen's University Belfast Newcastle University University of Nottingham
History	University of Cambridge University of Oxford Durham University University College London University of Exeter
Sports Science	University of Glasgow University of Edinburgh University of Exeter Durham University University of Birmingham

- Prestigious Qualifications

The Russell Group universities all rank highly and have long histories of excelling in academic teaching. This is part of the attraction of the Russell Group for many students, and as the entry qualifications vary across the group, even if you do not have the necessary grades for one Russell Group university you might find that you can gain a place with the same grades at another one. The Russell Group universities also offer online learning opportunities for postgraduate students so it is worth checking these out too.

- **Career Advancement**

The Russell Group universities pride themselves on their contacts within local, national and international governments, organisations, industry and business. These contacts will make up a vital part of the network that you could form whilst undertaking your postgraduate studies and these will **propel** your career forwards, especially in its early years. The experiences you can gain and learn from at a Russell Group university will make you all the more attractive to potential future employers. The networking events that you attend while studying at a Russell Group university combined with the power of your alumni network will help you for the rest of your career.

The Russell Group universities have some great choices of courses for postgraduate study and research, but are they the key to success?

Well, the short answer is "no", you are in fact the key to your success. However, undertaking your postgraduate studies at a Russell Group university will certainly help you on your way. Here's why:

- **Remarkable Research**

If you're considering research in the form of an MRes (Master of Research) or a Ph.D, then you can't really go wrong by choosing a Russell Group university. The 24 members of the Russell Group have one main thing in common and that's research quality. They dominate the academic research publications in the UK and if you think that being part of published academic work will be important for your future career—for example as a researcher or an **academic**—then you'll want to be at a Russell Group university for your postgraduate research degree.

- **Networking Opportunities**

The Russell Group universities work together to connect and **lobby** the UK government to ensure that their universities have the right conditions to work well. This means that the Russell Group has extensive contacts in

Chapter 9 Education—Distinct Educational System and Distinguished Schools

government and across different industries. They also have amazing networking opportunities for their students. It's not always about what you know, knowing and meeting the right people will always help, so get out and join those alumni clubs or networking sessions while you are studying.

- **Clubs & Societies**

The facilities available at the Russell Group universities are all considered excellent and this transfers across to the facilities available for student activities. Joining in with the associations and clubs both in **conjunction** with your course and those clubs that have nothing to do with your career will help you. We all know that taking some time away from your studies can be a valuable use of time and will help you to focus afterwards. So get out there and join some of the great clubs and societies on offer—it will broaden your mind and enhance your learning experience.

- **Fantastic Funding**

One big advantage to the Russell Group universities is funding. They have a great deal of negotiating power and links with the different UK Research Councils to get funding for their projects. This means that they are more likely to be able to offer postgraduate students positions like funding PhD studentships or offering scholarships and **bursaries**. It's worth having a good look through their lists of scholarships while you are researching courses to see what is available.

- **Excellent Rankings**

Ranking lists can be a little tricky and confusing to interpret. Each list will use different data to rank the universities, but it's safe to say that if a university is regularly in the top group of institutions across many different subject areas and rankings, then you know that it's probably a well-respected choice. That's the big benefit to studying a postgraduate course at a Russell Group university, they are all well-respected universities with excellent facilities and always perform well in league tables.

- **You'll Be in Good Company**

Plenty of students choose to study at Russell Group universities. Table 9.2 shows the numbers of postgraduate students who studied at some of the Russell Group universities in the academic year 2018/19.

Table 9.2

Russell Group University	Number of PG Students
University of Birmingham	12,505
Cardiff University	9,230
University of Edinburgh	11,525
University of Liverpool	6,960
University of Manchester	13,395

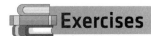 Vocabulary

expertise	n.	专业知识；专门技能；专长
academia	n.	学术环境；学术界
volume	n.	（成套书籍中的）一卷，一册
illustrate	v.	（用例子、故事或图表）阐明
excel	v.	精通，擅长；超过，胜过
prestigious	adj.	有威望的，有声望的
advancement	n.	晋升，升迁
propel	v.	推动，驱动，推进
academic	n.	大学教师；学者
lobby	v.	游说（政治家或政府）
conjunction	n.	结合；同时发生
bursary	n.	奖学金

Exercises

Chapter 10 Feminine Culture in Britain

Introduction

The final chapter of the course focuses on the culture of women in Britain. Like other parts of the world, gentleness, empathy, sensitivity, caring, sweetness, compassion, tolerance, nurturance, etc., are traits that have traditionally been cited as feminine. But in the land that has produced some outstanding queens and three female Prime Ministers, we may infer that British women enjoy equal rights as men. Is that true? Through the study of this chapter, we'll get the answer.

英国社会与文化

Unit 1

Women's Movement in Britain

It's not about supplication; it's about power. It's not about asking; it's about demanding. It's not about convincing those who are currently in power; it's about changing the very face of power itself.

—Kimberle Williams Crenshaw

 Test Your Knowledge

Discuss the following questions with your partner.

1. Do you know the word "suffragette"? What does it mean? How did it come from?

2. This anti-suffrage artwork *Looking Backward* shows a woman leaving behind love, marriage, children, and home for suffrage and loneliness. This message—that women who had the vote would be miserable—was not uncommon in anti-suffrage messages. Do you agree with the message conveyed by the picture? What's your opinion?

Chapter 10 Feminine Culture in Britain

> **Intensive Reading**

Text I The Lives of the Suffragettes*

It was on 8 June 1913 that the most infamous moment in the history of the suffragette movement occurred in front of spectators at the Derby horse race. Emily Davison, a former governess and academic, stepped out onto the course and was hit by King George V's horse. Her injuries proved fatal, making her an enduring **martyr** to the cause, even though newspapers at the time condemned her as "malignant", "grotesque" and "miserable".

That last adjective was accurate, at least. Davison had suffered the pain and anguish of being force-fed by authorities while on **hunger strike** in prison, and had previously attempted suicide. Another famous suffragette subjected to this kind of cruelty was Emmeline Pankhurst, the leader of the movement, who spoke of the "civilised torture of solitary confinement", and described Holloway Prison as a "place of horror and torment".

But, while the likes of Emily Davison and the Pankhurst dynasty are still synonymous with the suffragettes, the reality is that the movement encompassed countless women whose names have been lost in time. In fact, many of us **delving into** our family trees on Ancestry may be surprised to discover unsung suffragettes among our ancestors.

The movement had its roots in the Victorian era. An early **champion** of votes for women was the philosopher and politician John Stuart Mill, who published a famous essay advocating female suffrage in 1869. Even before that, though, an amateur scientist called Lydia Becker established herself as an influential activist, writing "if it be granted that women may, without offence, hold political opinions, on what ground can the right be withheld of giving the same expression or effect to their opinions as that enjoyed by their male neighbours?"

One of her associates was Dr. Richard Pankhurst, a lawyer, socialist and advocate of women's rights. His wife, Emmeline Pankhurst, would go on to form the Women's Social and Political Union in 1903. Eventually dubbed the "suffragettes", Pankhurst and her activists **were committed to militant** action and civil disobedience. Their guiding principle was "deeds not words", which

---
* Retrieved from Sky History website.

distinguished them from the rival suffragist movement, which believed in bringing change only through peaceful, political campaigning.

The suffragettes achieved **notoriety** through acts of **arson** and **vandalism**. Home-made bombs were planted at various sites across the country, including numerous churches, leading many to dub them terrorists. They were careful not to harm life, however. As one suffragette later said in an interview, "Mrs. Pankhurst gave us strict orders...there was not a cat or a **canary** to be killed: no life."

The suffragettes also had a respectable public **profile** that ran parallel to the explosive activism. They had their own branding and merchandise—department stores like Selfridges sold ribbons and clothes with the white, green and purple suffragette colours, and they even raised funds with sales of a **board game** called "Pank-a-Squith", referencing Emmeline Pankhurst and the Prime Minister Herbert Asquith.

People from all backgrounds and social classes joined the movement. Some deeply privileged women even reinvented themselves in the name of social justice. Take the example of Lady Constance Bulwer-Lytton. Uncomfortably aware of how well she was treated compared to other suffragettes, simply because of her aristocratic status, she took on an alternative identity by posing as an "ugly London **seamstress**" called Jane Warton, and **was subjected to** force-feeding while on hunger strike.

One of her opposites on the social **spectrum** was Annie Kenney, who worked in a Yorkshire cotton mill as a child and rose up to become one of the most senior suffragettes from a working class background. Proud of leading "fishwives, East End women, laundresses, teachers, nurses" to meet politicians, Annie Kenney found infamy in 1905 after disrupting a speech given by a young MP, Winston Churchill, and demanding to know his **stance** on women's rights.

A particularly fascinating figure who unfairly fell into obscurity over time was Edith Garrud, who was one of the first female **martial arts** instructors in British history. "Physical force seems the only thing in which women have not demonstrated their equality to men," she once said, and did her bit to change that by teaching **jujutsu** to suffragettes. She trained the "Bodyguard"— a special group of suffragettes who were tasked with protecting members of the movement and carried **clubs** hidden in their dresses.

Another name which deserves to be better known is Evaline Hilda Burkitt, who had the **morbid** distinction of being the first suffragette to be force-fed in prison. Hunger striking time and time again, she is thought to have been force-fed close to 300 times, yet remained stubbornly committed to the cause. She wrote a powerful letter to the Home Office asserting that she was willing to die "to bring about the freedom of my sex". Fortunately, she survived and went on to make a living as a "**confectioner** and cake maker".

As for Emily Davison, her death at the Derby is still a subject of much debate. Did she deliberately take her own life? Known for direct action such as arson, and described by Sylvia Pankhurst as "one of the most daring and reckless of the militants", Davison had certainly regarded suicide as a political weapon, and had once tried to kill herself by leaping from a prison balcony. "I felt that by nothing but the sacrifice of human life would the nation be brought to realise the horrible torture our women face," she wrote.

However, many have argued that her death at the Derby was accidental, suggesting her aim had actually been to attach a suffragette flag to the king's horse. Whatever the truth of her motivations, her act turned out to be a final, dramatic **flourish** for the suffragette movement. With the outbreak of the Great War in the following year, the suffragettes suspended their activism to join the patriotic war effort. The radical social changes of those turbulent years led to a change in the law in 1918, with some (but not all) women being given the vote. It would be another decade before equal voting rights were finally granted.

Vocabulary

martyr	*n.*	殉道者；烈士
hunger strike		绝食抗议
delve into sth		探究；考查
champion	*n.*	斗争者；捍卫者
be committed to		致力于；以……为己任
militant	*adj.*	好战的；激进的
notoriety	*n.*	臭名昭著，声名狼藉
arson	*n.*	纵火；纵火罪
vandalism	*n.*	故意破坏公共财物罪
canary	*n.*	金丝雀
profile	*n.*	印象；形象
board game		棋盘游戏
seamstress	*n.*	女裁缝
be subjected to		受到……；经受……

spectrum	n.	范围；层次
stance	n.	观点；立场
martial arts		武术
jujutsu	n.	柔术
club	n.	棍棒
morbid	adj.	病态的
confectioner	n.	糖果制造人；甜食商
flourish	n.	惊人之举

Exercises

I. Decide whether the following statements are true or false, and mark T or F accordingly.

_____ 1. After disrupting a speech given by a young MP, Winston Churchill, in 1905, Annie Kenney ruined her past good reputation.

_____ 2. Many of our ancestors may be suffragettes though they did not leave their names in the movement.

_____ 3. The "suffragettes" Emmeline Pankhurst and her activists believed in bringing change only through peaceful, political campaigning.

_____ 4. The author agreed that the newspapers' condemnation at the time on Emily Davison's death was accurate.

II. Choose the best answer to each question.

1. The newspapers at the time thought of Emily Davison at the Derby horse race all the following EXCEPT _____.

   A. noble and great

   B. strange and unpleasant

   C. harmful and evil

   D. unhappy and uncomfortable

2. From what Lydia Becker wrote, we may infer the following EXCEPT _____.

   A. women did not have the same right as men due to some political reasons

   B. if women were given right to express political opinions, this would be likely to upset a lot of people

C. there is no reason to refuse women's political rights

D. men enjoyed the right to freedom of speech

3. The example of Lady Constance Bulwer-Lytton showed that some high-bred women joined the movement to _____.

A. realize that they live better than other lower-class women

B. present themselves in a new image for social justice

C. pretend to be underprivileged women

D. conceal their aristocratic background

4. According to the passage, which of the following is true about Emily Davison?

A. She took her own life deliberately and recklessly.

B. Davison committed suicide because she regarded it as a political weapon.

C. The truth of her death is still a subject of much debate.

D. She wanted to bring the nation to realise the horrible torture of women through the sacrifice of her own life.

5. What led to a change in the law in 1918 giving some women the vote according to the passage?

A. The outbreak of the Great War.

B. The suffragettes' persistence with their activism and efforts.

C. The suffragettes' patriotic war effort.

D. The need for thorough changes by the society after the Great War.

III. Match the names of activists with their relevant information according to the passage.

1. Annie Kenney

2. Edith Garrud

3. Evaline Hilda Burkitt

4. John Stuart Mill

5. Emmeline Pankhurst

A. teaching martial arts to suffragettes to demonstrate women's equality to men in physical strength

B. who published a famous essay to support suffrage movement

C. being force-fed by authorities while on hunger strike repeatedly

D. ordering her members not to harm life in action

E. one of the most senior suffragettes from a working class background

Further Reading

Text II Woman as Other*

The category of the Other is as **primordial** as consciousness itself. In the most primitive societies, in the most ancient mythologies, one finds the expression of a duality—that of the Self and the Other. This duality was not originally attached to the division of the sexes; it was not dependent upon any **empirical** facts. It is revealed in such works as that of Granet on Chinese thought and those of Dumézil on the East Indies and Rome. The feminine element was at first no more involved in such pairs as Varuna-Mitra, Uranus-Zeus, Sun-Moon, and Day-Night than it was in the contrasts between Good and Evil, lucky and unlucky **auspices**, right and left, God and **Lucifer**. Otherness is a fundamental category of human thought.

Thus it is that no group ever sets itself up as the One without at once setting up the Other over against itself. If three travellers chance to occupy the same compartment, that is enough to make vaguely hostile "others" out of all the rest of the passengers on the train. In small-town eyes all persons not belonging to the village are "strangers" and suspect; to the native of a country all who inhabit other countries are "foreigners"; Jews are "different" for the **anti-Semite**, Negroes are "inferior" for American racists, aborigines are "natives" for colonists, **proletarians** are the "lower class" for the privileged.

Lévi-Strauss, at the end of a profound work on the various forms of primitive societies, reaches the following conclusion: "Passage from the state of Nature to the state of Culture is marked by man's ability to view biological relations as a series of contrasts; duality, alternation, opposition, and symmetry, whether under definite or vague forms, constitute not so much phenomena to be explained as fundamental and immediately given data of social reality." These phenomena would be incomprehensible if in fact human society were simply a **Mitsein** or fellowship based on **solidarity** and friendliness. Things become clear, on the contrary, if, following Hegel, we find in consciousness itself a fundamental hostility towards every other consciousness; the subject can be posed only in being opposed—he sets himself up as the essential, as opposed to the other, the inessential, the object.

---

* Excerpted from Simone de Beauvoir. *The Second Sex*. (Constance Borde & Sheila Malovany Chevallier, Trans.). Vancouer: Vintage Books, 2009: 26–28.

Chapter 10 Feminine Culture in Britain

But the other consciousness, the other ego, sets up a **reciprocal** claim. The native travelling abroad is shocked to find himself in turn regarded as a "stranger" by the natives of neighbouring countries. As a matter of fact, wars, festivals, trading, treaties, and contests among tribes, nations, and classes tend to deprive the concept Other of its absolute sense and to make manifest its relativity; **willy-nilly**, individuals and groups are forced to realize the reciprocity of their relations. How is it, then, that this reciprocity has not been recognised between the sexes, that one of the contrasting terms is set up as the sole essential, denying any relativity in regard to its correlative and defining the latter as pure otherness? Why is it that women do not dispute male sovereignty? No subject will readily volunteer to become the object, the inessential; it is not the Other who, in defining himself as the Other, establishes the One. The Other is posed as such by the One in defining himself as the One. But if the Other is not to regain the status of being the One, he must be **submissive** enough to accept this alien point of view. Whence comes this submission in the case of woman?

There are, to be sure, other cases in which a certain category has been able to dominate another completely for a time. Very often this privilege depends upon inequality of numbers—the majority imposes its rule upon the minority or **persecutes** it. But women are not a minority, like the American Negroes or the Jews; there are as many women as men on earth. Again, the two groups concerned have often been originally independent; they may have been formerly unaware of each other's existence, or perhaps they recognised each other's **autonomy**. But a historical event has resulted in the **subjugation** of the weaker by the stronger. The scattering of the Jews, the introduction of slavery into America, the conquests of imperialism are examples in point. In these cases the oppressed **retained** at least the memory of former days; they possessed in common a past, a tradition, sometimes a religion or a culture.

The parallel drawn by Bebel between women and the proletariat is valid in that neither ever formed a minority or a separate collective unit of mankind. And instead of a single historical event it is in both cases a historical development that explains their status as a class and accounts for the membership of particular individuals in that class. But proletarians have not always existed, whereas there have always been women. They are women in virtue of their **anatomy** and **physiology**. Throughout history they have always been **subordinated** to men, and hence their dependency is not the result of a historical event or a social change—it was not something that occurred. The reason why otherness in this case seems to be an absolute is in part that it lacks the **contingent** or **incidental** nature of historical facts. A condition brought about at a certain time can be abolished at some other time, as the Negroes of Haiti and others have proved: But it might seem that natural condition is beyond the possibility of change. In truth, however, the nature of things is no more **immutably** given, once for all, than is historical reality. If woman seems to be the inessential which never becomes the essential, it is because she herself fails to bring about this change. Proletarians say "We"; Negroes also. Regarding themselves as subjects, they transform the **bourgeois**, the whites, into "others". But women do not say "We", except at some congress of feminists or similar formal demonstration; men say "women", and women use the same word in referring to themselves. They do not **authentically** assume a subjective attitude. The proletarians have accomplished the revolution in Russia, the Negroes in Haiti, the Indo-Chinese are battling for it in Indo-China; but the women's effort has never been anything more than a symbolic **agitation**. They have gained only what men have been willing to grant; they have taken nothing, they have only received.

Vocabulary

primordial	*adj.*	原始的
empirical	*adj.*	经验主义的；经验的
auspice	*n.*	预兆
Lucifer	*n.*	撒旦；魔鬼
anti-Semite	*n.*	反犹太主义者
proletarian	*n.*	无产阶级者；无产者
Mitsein	*n.*	共同存在
solidarity	*n.*	团结一致；相互支持
reciprocal	*adj.*	相互的
willy-nilly	*adv.*	不管愿不愿意
submissive	*adj.*	顺从的；服从的
persecute	*v.*	迫害
subjugation	*n.*	征服；镇压
retain	*v.*	保持；保留
anatomy	*n.*	（动植物的）结构；解剖
physiology	*n.*	生理学；生理机能
subordinate	*v.*	使从属于；把……置于次要地位
contingent	*adj.*	偶然（发生）的

incidental	*adj.*	附带的；次要的
immutably	*adv.*	不变地；永恒地
bourgeois	*n.*	资产阶级
authentically	*adv.*	真正地；确实地
agitation	*n.*	骚动；煽动

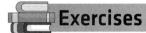

Exercises

Unit 2

Great Women Leaders in British History

To be a king and wear a crown is a thing more glorious to them that see it than it is pleasant to them that bear it.

—Queen Elizabeth I

 Test Your Knowledge

I. Before you read Text I, look at its title. What may the word "jubilee" mean? Can you discover any figure of speech in the title? The combination of the two seemingly contradictory words "twilight" and "splendor" is called oxymoron. What can you infer from the use of oxymoron?

II. What do you know about Queen Victoria? Please pick out the facts about her.

    A. She inherited the throne after her father's three elder brothers died without surviving legitimate issue.

    B. She is the longest-reigning monarch in British history.

    C. She's the second daughter of her king father.

    D. She's the only child of her father.

    E. She became Queen when she was 18.

    F. She has been credited with starting the tradition of white weddings and white bridal gowns, although she was not the first royal to be married in white.

    G. She never married and died childless, known as the Virgin Queen.

    H. She's mother to nine children with her husband. Her children's marriages with Europe's royal families earned her the nickname "the grandmother of Europe".

    I. After her husband's death, she entered a state of mourning and wore black for the remainder of her life. Her seclusion earned her the nickname "widow of Windsor".

Chapter 10 **Feminine Culture in Britain**

III. What else do you know about Queen Victoria and her reign?

Intensive Reading

Text I Twilight of Splendor: The Court of Queen Victoria During Her Diamond Jubilee*

In the early summer of 1897, respected society photographer A. J. Downey stood in the middle of a richly appointed room, its **gilt-ornamented** walls hidden behind screens and a large backdrop. Within the same building, in the privacy of a room hung in green and gold, a young woman crisply uniformed in black and white moved quickly yet carefully, conveying pieces of jewelry to a dressing table. Here sat a seventy-eight-year-old woman, half-crippled with **rheumatism** and **arthritis**, growing blind, and increasingly suffering from ill health. Despite this, the old lady exuded a sense of majesty. Barely five feet tall, with a rotund figure resembling a **squat** little ball with legs, she had long ago lost the traces of her youthful attraction. Even at age eighteen, she had been plain rather than pretty; now her **protuberant** eyes, receding chin, and small mouth seemed lost against the fleshy face.

The **diminutive** old lady wore a black silk gown, her habitual mourning attire since the death of her beloved husband nearly forty years earlier. But the **stark visage** was enlivened with delicate **embroidery** of sparkling jet and **offset** by layers of contrasting white lace.

When all was ready, a bell brought an Indian servant, attired in an exotic robe and brilliantly white **turban**, who assisted the aged woman into her wheelchair and pushed her through the **labyrinth** of passages to the room where Downey stood waiting. All around him were the accoutrements of his profession: **tripods** and cameras, lenses and lights, and assistants standing ready with fragile glass plates. Settled in a gilded armchair, the elderly woman waited patiently as Downey prepared to take her photograph. Politely whispered instructions alternated with powder flashes as her portrait was captured for **posterity**, her gaze directed to the side, the fan of white lace in her hands

---

* Excerpted from Greg King. *Twilight of Splendor: The Court of Queen Victoria During Her Diamond Jubilee*. Maitland: Wiley, 2007: 15–17.

held firm. The lens took it all in: The sharp black of the gown, the contrasting white of the lace, the **poignant** display of the wedding veil as a reminder of happier times long past. In his studio, Downey worked his magic in an effort to transform the woman into the very visage of imperial glory: Subtle retouching erased the wrinkles from her aged face, the girth of her waist, and the stockiness of her arms. The resulting image, **redolent** of majestic splendor, soon appeared on postcards and **lithographs**, commemorating Queen Victoria's sixty years on the British throne.

As June 21, 1897, came to a close, London sweltered in the heat of summer. In the East End, impoverished workers **shambled** through the dank street, passing desperate prostitutes plying their trade in rancid alleys. The wharfs and dockyards were alive with activity as ships were unloaded and goods carted along the **quays**. In the city, lamplighters moved from post to post, leaving a trail of **flickering** gaslights as a few carriages rumbled through the streets. In the glow of a crimson sunset that washed over the leafy, tree-filled parks and broad, **magisterial** buildings reflecting in the Thames, some three million people began to crowd its streets. They stood behind ranks of **sentries** and uniformed police, watching as troops from the immense British Empire trained: Scarlet-coated Canadians, turbaned Sikhs, Australians in khaki, Egyptians in red fez, and Bengal **Lancers** armed with shining pikes rode back and forth in a vivid display of pageantry and power. As bands practiced, London **slumbered** restlessly, anticipating the pageantry of the following day's Diamond Jubilee.

The Victorian era was at its height that summer. For sixty years, the queen had presided over a time of unprecedented growth and technological advancement. While the government portrayed the Diamond Jubilee as a celebration of empire, it meant something different to most of the queen's subjects. For most people, Victoria was the only sovereign they had ever known. The accomplishments of literature, science, and industry were all uniquely tied to her reign, and lent to the queen an aura of greatness beyond her own personal accomplishments.

When Victoria acceded to the throne in 1837, Britain was the most powerful country in the world, commander of the seas, and the center of finance and industry. The British Empire, at the height of its power, stretched across a quarter of the globe, encompassing some four hundred million people. Decades of territorial acquisitions had transformed both the empire and the attitudes that drove its conquests; in the process, as one historian noted, "the image of Victoria lost its home-and-hearth quality, and became a transnational and

transcendental absolute equivalent to that once projected by Judeo-Christian religion. The charismatic image of Victoria overwhelmed and finally obliterated the old image of the melancholy widowed Queen."

The developments of the industrial age placed the distant city on the Thames at the center of this empire. Railways and steamships, telegraphs and telephones all made communication possible, expanding its sphere of influence rapidly across the globe. The London of 1897 was secure and complacent in its domination. Its 4.5 million inhabitants lived amid its vivid contrasts of enshrined power and aristocratic privilege, and slums swollen with the dispossessed and the debauched.

Vocabulary

gilt-ornamented	*adj.*	镀金装饰的
rheumatism	*n.*	风湿病
arthritis	*n.*	关节炎
squat	*adj.*	矮胖的
protuberant	*adj.*	鼓出的，凸起的
diminutive	*adj.*	小的
stark	*adj.*	普通的
visage	*n.*	容貌，外表
embroidery	*n.*	刺绣品
offset	*v.*	抵消；补偿
turban	*n.*	（穆斯林或锡克教男教徒等用的）包头巾
labyrinth	*n.*	迷宫
tripod	*n.*	三脚架
posterity	*n.*	子孙；后代
poignant	*adj.*	令人沉痛的；酸楚的
redolent	*adj.*	使人想到
lithograph	*n.*	平版印刷画
shamble	*v.*	蹒跚地走；摇晃不稳
quay	*n.*	码头
flickering	*adj.*	闪烁的；忽隐忽现的
magisterial	*adj.*	权威的；官吏的
sentry	*n.*	哨兵
lancer	*n.*	长矛轻骑兵

| slumber | *v.* | 睡眠 |
| transcendental | ***adj.*** | 先验的；卓越的 |

Exercises

I. Learn the following knowledge about context clues.

Context clues are hints that an author gives to help define a difficult or unusual word. The clue may appear within the same sentence as the word to which it refers or it may follow in the next sentence.

Generally, a context clue can be categorized into one of four types:

1) Synonym (or a repeat context clue): An author will use more than one word that means the same thing.

   Examples:

   As June 21, 1897, came to a close, London **sweltered** in *the heat of summer*.

   The charismatic image of Victoria *overwhelmed* and finally **obliterated** the old image of the **melancholy** *widowed* Queen.

2) Antonym (or a contrast context clue): The text may include a word or words that have the opposite meaning, which can reveal the meaning of an unknown term.

   Examples:

   Its 4.5 million inhabitants lived amid *its vivid contrasts of enshrined power* and *aristocratic privilege*, and slums swollen with **the dispossessed** and **the debauched**.

   As bands practiced, London *slumbered* **restlessly**, anticipating the pageantry of the following day's Diamond Jubilee.

3) Explanation (or a definition context clue): An unknown word is explained within the sentence or in the sentence immediately after.

   Examples:

   ...*scarlet-coated Canadians, turbaned Sikhs, Australians in khaki, Egyptians in red fez, and Bengal Lancers armed with shining pikes rode back and forth in a vivid display* of **pageantry** and power.

   The diminutive old lady wore *a black silk gown*, her habitual mourning **attire** since the death of her beloved husband nearly forty years earlier.

4) Specific example (or an example context clue): The text provides one or

more examples used to define the term.

Example:

All around him were the **accoutrements** of his profession: *tripods and cameras, lenses and lights*, and assistants standing ready with fragile glass plates.

Now use the context clues to figure out the meanings of the boldfaced words in the sentences above. Then match the correct word with its definition.

1. suggestive or expressive of sadness or depression of mind or spirit _____
2. people who have had property taken away from them _____
3. without real rest or sleep _____
4. to remove all signs of something, either by destroying or covering it completely _____
5. people who behave in a bad or immoral way, such as drinking too much alcohol, taking drugs, or having sex with many people _____
6. impressive and exciting events and ceremonies involving a lot of people wearing special clothes _____
7. to be very hot in a way that makes you feel uncomfortable _____
8. clothes _____
9. the equipment needed for a particular activity or way of life _____

II. **Fill in the blanks with the appropriate forms of the words in the box.**

display	portray	sovereign	expand	encompass
unprecedented	barely	secure	resemble	convey

1. In March 1889, she became the first British _____ to set foot on Spanish soil.
2. Why do fossils most closely _____ living animals appear only in the highest and youngest layers of rock?
3. Our tiny apartment, it is true, is _____ suited for two people, and certainly not for four.
4. Robyn was well aware that clothes do not merely serve the practical purpose of covering our bodies, but also _____ messages about who we are, what we are doing, and how we feel.

5. The depression that started in mid-1929 was a catastrophe of _____ dimensions for the United States.

6. From Melbourne to Seoul, intraregional trade and investments were rapidly _____.

7. In that role, Prince Philip, who met nearly every post-war US president, sought to _____ himself as working tirelessly in support of his wife.

8. The Hindu religion _____ many widely differing forms of worship.

9. The authors of the book argue that human sentence processing _____ both structural and statistical characteristics and therefore requires the integration of the two views.

10. As women joined men in _____ higher education, the average age of marriage increased.

III. Choose the best answer to each question.

1. We can get the information from the description of the seventy-eight-year-old woman at the very start **EXCEPT** _____.

    A. she had been rather pretty and attractive when she was young

    B. she's in deteriorating poor health

    C. she's short and fat like a little ball

    D. the old lady appeared to be impressive and dignified despite her plain looking

2. In the sentence "…and became a transnational and transcendental absolute equivalent to that once projected by Judeo-Christian religion", the word "project" probably means _____.

    A. to plan an activity, a project, etc., for a time in the future

    B. to estimate what the size, cost or amount of something will be in the future based on what is happening now

    C. to try to make other people have a particular idea about somebody

    D. to make light, an image, etc., fall onto a flat surface or screen

3. Which of the following is **NOT** true about the Victorian era?

    A. The progress of society and technology had never happened before in history.

    B. The empire reached its peak during the era.

C. Great accomplishments of literature, science, and industry were made under her reign.

D. All the greatness and accomplishments were hardly comparable with the Queen's personal accomplishments.

4. Which of the following is **NOT** true about the transformation of Queen Victoria's image sixty years after she ascended to the throne?

    A. The Queen ruled over an Empire that covered a quarter of the globe with 400 million subjects, so her symbol was beyond national boundaries.

    B. During Queen Victoria's reign, she displayed a kind of femininity centred on the family, motherhood and respectability.

    C. Victoria's towering presence as a symbol of her Empire can be compared with that of Christianity.

    D. With the British Empire at the height of its power, the Queen's new image replaced her old image as a widow.

5. In June 1897, her proud and prosperous nation marked her sixtieth year on the throne of England with the most lavish display of pomp, circumstance, wealth, and affection in its history. What can you infer about the East End of London from the passage?

    A. The East End was as prosperous and wealthy as other parts of London.

    B. There was neither poverty nor women prostitution in the East End.

    C. While the British Empire was expanding its sphere of influence rapidly across the globe, the slums of London were expanding with poor people.

    D. Parts of the East End were, without doubt, lawless ghettoes where the people lived in appalling conditions.

Further Reading

Text II Slums in Late-Victorian London*

Between 1800 and 1850 the population of England doubled. At the same time, farming was giving way to factory labour: In 1801, 70% of the population lived in the country; by the middle of the century only 50% did. Cities **swelled** as people **flocked** from the countryside to find work. This was exacerbated by

---

* Retrieved from British Library website.

migration (especially from Ireland during the famine years in the middle of the century). As a result, cities only big enough to contain 18th-century populations were under pressure to house their new residents.

Previously, the rich and poor had lived in the same districts: the rich in the main streets; the poor in the service streets behind. Now, the prosperous moved out of town centres to the new suburbs, while much of the housing for the poor was demolished for commercial spaces, or to make way for the railway stations and lines that appeared from the 1840s. Property owners received **compensation**; renters did not: It was always cheaper to pay off the owners of a few **tenements** than the houses of many middle-class owners. Thus the homes of the poor were always the first to be destroyed.

"Improvements"

The reshaping of the city was always referred to as making "improvements". In 1826, when the process was just beginning, one book boasted that "Among the glories of this age, the historian will have to record the conversion of dirty alleys, dingy courts and squalid dens of misery...into stately streets...to palaces and mansions, to elegant private dwellings."

Yet few worried what was to happen to those whose houses—and neighbourhoods—vanished. These people could not afford to live in the nice new streets. Instead, they ended up just moving into other already crowded districts, which therefore became even worse—and even more expensive. Many couldn't even afford that, and ended up instead moving endlessly from place to place, without a home.

For the "improvers", this was not a problem, since it was easier to think of the inhabitants of the slums as being, not hard-working but impoverished people, but only drunkards and thieves. Field Lane, in Clerkenwell, for example, was said to have been "occupied entirely by receivers of stolen goods, which...are openly spread out for sale". The police frequently excused their lack of oversight of the slums by saying they were too dangerous to enter, but Dickens, for one, knew better, and that insomniac author frequently walked these areas, learning about the other London: "I...mean to take a great, London, back-slums kind of walk tonight, seeking adventures in **knight errant** style", he wrote to a friend. And the author Anthony Trollope's younger brother claimed that, aged eight, he had wandered peacefully through the Clerkenwell slum, having heard the adults speak of its "wickedness".

"Indescribable Filth"

In 1838, Dickens described the horrible slum called Jacob's Island, in south London. It was, he wrote, a place of "crazy wooden galleries...with holes from which to look upon the **slime** beneath; windows, broken and patched...rooms so small, so filthy, so confined, that the air would seem too tainted even for the dirt and squalor which they **shelter**...dirt-besmeared walls and decaying foundations". Although this description was in *Oliver Twist* (ch. 50), a work of fiction, journalist and campaigner for better housing, Henry Mayhew, described it in almost exactly the same way: "The water of the huge ditch in front of the houses is covered with a **scum**...and **prismatic** with grease...Along the banks are heaps of indescribable filth...the air has literally the smell of a graveyard."

Much slum-housing was down narrow alleys, the passageways that had originally been designed to give access to **stables**. Built around dead-end courtyards, the houses therefore could have windows on just one side. Sometimes courts had even more buildings **erected** behind them, in what had been the yards of the houses behind; these buildings had no windows at all. In *Bleak House*, the orphaned 12-year-old Charley lives in a room with her baby brother and sister and, she notes with pride, "When it comes on dark, the lamps are lighted down in the court, and they show up here quite bright—almost quite bright"(ch. 15). "Almost quite bright" made their room not a slum at all, but ordinary working-people's lodgings.

Charley was, like many slum-dwellers, a hard worker. She and her **siblings** were only three in a room, but often a single room was home to a family of five or six, who might even take in "lodgers", to share the cost. Different rooms in each house had different rents. The cheapest of all were the **cellars**, which at best were just damp and dark; in particularly bad lodgings, the liquids from the **cesspools** beneath **seeped** up through the floor.

Sanitation and Disease

Sanitation was a **pervasive** problem. Few houses had **drainage**, and there were few privies. Usually an entire court, several hundred people, shared one standpipe—a single outdoor tap—for all their water supplies, and had one, or at most two, privies (toilets in a shed outside) for everyone.

In 1849 a letter was published in the *Times*, giving a rare voice to the slum-dwellers themselves:

> Sur—May we beg and beseach your proteckshion and power, We are Sur, as

it may be, livin in a Willderniss, so far as the rest of London knows anything of us, or as the rich and great people care about. We live in muck and filthe. We aint got no priviz, no dust bins, no drains, no water-splies, and no drain or suer in the hole place. The Suer Company, in Greek St., Soho Square, all great, rich and powerfool men, take no notice watsomedever of our cumplaints. The Stenche of a Gully-hole is disgustin. We all of us suffur, and numbers are ill, and if the Colera comes Lord help us.

This was in St Giles, steps away from Tottenham Court Road, and written after the area had been "improved"—in fact the courts' single privy had been removed to make way for "improvements".

When the *Times* followed up this letter, they found one room filled with the living and the dying side-by-side: a woman with **cholera**, two boys with fever, and their families. As Dickens addressed the authorities directly, after the homeless boy crossing-sweeper Jo dies in *Bleak House* of a similar fever: "Dead, your Majesty. Dead, my lords and gentlemen…Dead, men and women, born with heavenly **compassion** in your hearts. And dying thus around us every day."

Vocabulary

swell	v.	（使）增大；扩大
flock	v.	群集；蜂拥
compensation	n.	补偿金
tenement	n.	经济公寓；廉租公寓
knight errant		游侠骑士
filth	n.	污物，污秽
slime	n.	黏液；污泥
shelter	v.	庇护；遮蔽
scum	n.	浮渣；泡沫
prismatic	adj.	棱镜的；五光十色的
stable	n.	马厩
erect	v.	（使）竖立；建造
sibling	n.	兄弟姐妹
cellar	n.	地窖；地下室
cesspool	n.	污水池；化粪池
seep	v.	（液体）渗漏；渗透
sanitation	n.	公共卫生；卫生设备

pervasive	*adj.*	普遍的
drainage	*n.*	排水系统
cholera	*n.*	霍乱
compassion	*n.*	同情；怜悯

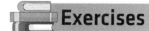

Exercises

Unit 3

The Crazy Hat

If you want something said, ask a man. If you want something done, ask a woman.

—Margaret Thatcher

 Test Your Knowledge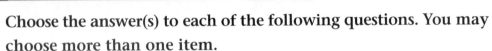

I. Choose the answer(s) to each of the following questions. You may choose more than one item.

1. The following are keywords of Great Britain EXCEPT _____.

    A. Washington, D. C.

    B. fish and chips

    C. baseball

    D. Winston Churchill

    E. Margaret Thatcher

    F. Thanksgiving Day

    G. Brexit

    H. Franklin D. Roosevelt

    I. Trooping the Colour

2. Foremost as the first female British Prime Minister, Margaret Thatcher was very aware of her image and used clothing as a tool of power. Like many politicians, she created a personal style to project _____ values.

    A. political

    B. social

    C. moral

3. What are the three elements that accurately define the style of Margaret Thatcher?

    A. The brooches.

    B. The pearls.

C. The pussy-bow blouse.

D. The pantsuits.

E. The handbags.

4. A symbol of the past reflecting a more _____ femininity, the pussy-bow blouse clashed with the _____ power suits.

   A. soft; hard

   B. aggressive; conservative

   C. conservative; aggressive

Intensive Reading

Text I Margaret Thatcher: Fashion Rebel?*

It is a **cringeworthy** moment: high-priced **frocks**, dashed by **ad-hoc** and chains, parading as punk at The Metropolitan Museum of Art, of all places. But let's set that aside. Walking through the museum's exhibition, *PUNK: Chaos to Couture*, which opened in New York on May 9th, I was struck less by who and what was there—Vivienne Westwood and Sid Vicious, on video; clothes by Balenciaga and Givenchy, zipped, slashed, and pinned up like posers—than I was by what was not. An absence, which, during the late 1970s and early 1980s, was one of the very things that London's **avant-garde** had fashioned itself against: the former Prime Minister of England, Margaret Thatcher, and her **indomitable** two-piece suits.

Fashion is a temporal language of lines and volumes, of nuance and gesture. It lives best in the moment. When placed beneath a retrospective lens, burdened by the question of its current meaning today, even a moment as **vibrant** and ad-hoc as punk can run pale; in the hands of Andrew Bolton, Curator in The Costume Institute, punk is reduced to a **trussed** up example, a thinly drawn story, a spirit in **pastiche**. Faced with **mannequins** in spiky wigs and a recreation of CBGB's graffiti-wrecked bathroom, I couldn't help but wonder if Thatcher's look has suffered a similar fate. Even after her death, Thatcher's aesthetic was as **polarizing** as her politics, and remains symbolic of her neoliberal agenda, the death of British collectivism.

---

* Retrieved from The Point website.

At least that's one way to read it. But **plumbing** that two-piece suit for intrinsic political truth seems as risky as turning a painting into a Rorschach test for an artist's state of mind—or **rehashing** the story of punk within the framework of corporate couture. It wasn't the meaning of Thatcher's clothes that mattered, so much as their visual effect—and the way she carried them off. If we looked at the lines and volumes of Thatcher's clothes, the historical contexts that shaped them, and also the way she wore them, can we discern something new, maybe even radical, in Thatcher's sense of style?

Trends in fashion evolve in conversation with the past, so that every shape affirms, distorts, or **subverts**, a shape that came before (at The Met, a Moschino dress with a shopping bag skirt may want to affirm a DIY spirit, but its price and production most surely distort it). In this light, Thatcher's shapes—those British-made suits, conservatively tailored, adorned with pockets, buttons and a signature brooch—can be seen as a confirmation of something **quintessentially** "British": the Queen, colonial enterprise, leisure sports, boarding schools and, of course, a rejection of all that was punk. The fact that, initially, Thatcher's look was fashioned by a man, political strategist Gordon Reece, represents another kind of confirmation of the past. Reece **dispensed with** Thatcher's dowdy hats (too middle-class mom), while counseling her to make her coif bigger and brighter. Reece also enrolled Thatcher in **elocution** lessons. By the time she was elected Prime Minister, her voice was low and deep, like the call of a ram. All of this stands to confirm that for a woman to be in power she had to resemble a man.

But in the continuum of fashion, this resemblance is also a kind of distortion. Since the Middle Ages, fashion has been a marker of gender difference (prior to that, both sexes wore long, flowing robes). During the Renaissance, men wore plate armor suits and tights—the shape of an Iron Gentleman, with externalized legs and **genitals**, empowered to work and fight. Meanwhile, women wore high, elaborate collars and full, impenetrable-looking dresses—a baroque, ornamental shape that concealed the body while simultaneously evoking its mysterious presence. These gendered patterns extended through Victorian England, when women wore wide skirts, layers of petticoats, and fitted bodices, while men of all classes wore suits—then a recent innovation in fashion. Compared to corsets and hoop skirts, the lines and volumes of the suit seemed radically modern: linear, efficient and functional, a locomotive in textile form. In at least this regard, one can argue that men's fashion has always

Chapter 10 **Feminine Culture in Britain**

been more cutting edge and progressive than women's. In her book, *Sex and the Suit*, Anne Hollander writes, "the 'gradual modernizations' in female costumes since 1800 have mainly consisted of trying to catch up with the male ideal more closely".

This catching up has engendered some of fashion's most **provocative** moments. In 19th-century Victorian England, the sight of a woman **galloping** across the countryside, wearing a flowing skirt, a fitted waist and a masculine, double-breasted collar (and presumably wielding a whip), piqued a puzzling, erotic question: What exactly is underneath? Similarly, in the Jazz Age, bobbed haircuts, trousers and vertical flapper dresses—so reminiscent of Art Deco architecture—evoked a seductive androgyny. By the 1980s, the power suit was a form of **antagonistic** expression, the aesthetic of doing battle in the office. The shoulder pads, the pencil skirts, the pointy-toed pumps, could be read as armor for women, helping them to assimilate into a man's world while simultaneously communicating the subversive sexual charge of female power.

Thatcher was not the first woman to rock the power suit (Katherine Hepburn, Coco Chanel), but she was the first woman to walk the halls of Parliament as Prime Minister in it. Her contemporary fashion referents included the Queen and Nancy Reagan, yet these women occupied very different political spaces. The Queen, **ostensibly**, can wear whatever she wants, although Elizabeth II has always stuck to the royal script: Feminine but conservative, her aesthetic seems like the **sartorial** version of afternoon tea. Nancy Reagan favored **ruffles** and couture (her favorite designer was the extravagant James Galanos), often in a pink- and red-hued palette. Always gazing lovingly upon Ronnie, she was **decorous** and **demure**, the socialite lady who lunched. One had the bloodline, the other the man.

Thatcher, of course, had neither. What she did have was steely-eyed confidence, combined with a keen appreciation for elegant fabrics and well-made clothes (her mother had been a dressmaker). Indeed, as a grocer's daughter from Grantham, who made it to Oxford by the **valor** of her wits and determination, one assumes she was also keenly aware of the power of clothes to signify. There may have been a vacuum of female shapes to confirm or distort within her particular political sphere, but male shapes were plentiful: Parliament practically brimmed with blue and gray suits. In this narrow context, Thatcher's suits can be looked at anew.

Vocabulary

cringeworthy	adj.	令人感到尴尬（或不舒服）的
frock	n.	女装；连衣裙
ad-hoc	adj.	特别的；专门的
couture	n.	高级时装设计制作
avant-garde	n.	前卫派（艺术家等）
indomitable	adj.	不屈不挠的
vibrant	adj.	充满活力的
truss	v.	捆紧；缚牢
pastiche	n.	东拼西凑；混杂
mannequin	n.	人体模型；服装模特儿
polarize	v.	（使）两极分化
plumb	v.	探索；钻研，探究
rehash	v.	只作轻微改动；换汤不换药
subvert	v.	颠覆，推翻；破坏
quintessentially	adv.	典型地；标准地
dispense with		摒弃；不再用
elocution	n.	演讲技巧；演说术
genital	n.	生殖器
provocative	adj.	挑衅的；煽动性的
gallop	v.	骑马疾驰
antagonistic	adj.	敌对的；对抗性的
ostensibly	adv.	表面上
sartorial	adj.	服装的，衣着的
ruffle	n.	（领口、袖口等的）褶饰；花边
decorous	adj.	端庄稳重的
demure	adj.	端庄的；娴静的
valor	n.	英勇，勇气

Exercises

I. Decide whether the following statements are true or false, and mark T or F accordingly.

_____ 1. The author was more surprised by what he saw at the museum's exhibition, *PUNK: Chaos to Couture* than by anything else.

Chapter 10 **Feminine Culture in Britain**

_____ **2.** In the hands of Andrew Bolton, Curator in The Costume Institute, punk lost its past life and energy.

_____ **3.** From the two-piece suits Thatcher wore, we can find out the political truth underneath.

_____ **4.** The Queen, Elizabeth II, tried on varied styles of clothing because she could wear whatever she wanted.

_____ **5.** Thatcher gained much sense of fashion from her two contemporaries—the Queen and Nancy Reagan.

II. **Choose the best answer to each of the following questions.**

1. At the Met, a Moschino dress may want to affirm a DIY spirit, but its price and production most surely distort it. Which of the following description is **NOT** true?

    A. People can make such a Moschino dress with a shopping bag skirt by themselves.

    B. The Moschino dress exhibited was to express the punk concept of "do-it-yourself".

    C. The price of a Moschino dress is usually high.

    D. The spirit deliberately conveyed through the Moschino dress is actually against its haute couture nature.

2. Which of the following best reflects the relation between males and females in the continuum of fashion?

    A. Before the Middle Ages, there was no gender difference because both sexes wore the same robes.

    B. Trends of men's wear always go in advance of women's wear in modern times.

    C. Women don't need to mold themselves into masculine looks anymore.

    D. Women's fashion has been more modern than men's.

3. Which of the following best discribes a power suit?

    A. It is a British-made suit.

    B. An outfit that can give a woman power.

    C. Katherine Hepburn introduced the first power suit.

    D. Giving women dominant and dynamic look has always been the idea behind the power suit.

4. Which of the following is true of Thatcher?

   A. Her success in politics owed much to her privileged birth.

   B. She learned public speech skills all by herself.

   C. She made it to the top of the Parliament by her confidence, wits, determination and probably the use of fashion as a political tool.

   D. Parliament is particular because everyone should wear blue or gray suits.

III. Translate the following terms from Chinese into English or vice versa.

1. 权力套装
2. 政治领域
3. 视觉效果
4. 性别差异的标志
5. 对典型的"英国式"的确认
6. the shoulder pads, the pencil skirts, the pointy-toed pumps
7. It (fashion) lives best in the moment.
8. a temporal language of volumes and lines
9. the sartorial version of afternoon tea
10. empowered to work and fight

IV. Fill in the blanks with the appropriate forms of the words in the box.

follow	femininity	conservative	assert	image
signature	project	match	fierce	sexist
aggressive	tool	paradox	setter	

Jane Tynan, a lecturer in fashion history at Central St. Martin's School of Art in London, says that our tendency to scrutinise what women wear is a reflection of a(n) **1.** _____ society that draws attention away from the real work they do in politics. Nevertheless, she argues that Thatcher was very aware of her **2.** _____ and used clothing as a(n) **3.** _____ of power. But a trend **4.** _____ she was not. Instead, the former Prime Minster adopted the **5.** _____ "power-dressing" style of the 1980s. "Like many politicians, she created a personal style to **6.** _____ political values. She **7.** _____

trends to some extent but **8**. _____ this with style references to emphasise her **9**. _____ values," explains Dr. Tynan. "With 'power dressing' she could tap into the image of a career woman but her reputation as a(n) **10**. _____ leader then drove her to wear clothes that might 'soften' her image, which was why she wore pussy-bow blouses." A symbol of the past reflecting a more conservative **11**. _____, the pussy-bow blouse clashed with the **12**. _____ power suits. "This was the **13**. _____ of the Thatcher image: At once she sought to embody conservative values while also seeking to **14**. _____ her right to power as a woman."

Further Reading

Text II History of Women Wearing Men's Clothing*

Figure 10.1   Contemporary women wear

Today most people wouldn't **bat an eye** at a woman wearing pants or a **bow tie** (in the Western world) (see Figure 10.1), but it wasn't always this way. In fact, prior to the late 19th and early 20th century, social customs were very strict regarding women's clothing, with women wearing dresses, underskirts and painfully tight corsets.

In the 1850s, women's rights activist, Amelia Bloomer, started to shake things up. She advocated for women to **ditch** the tight corsets and heavy

---

* Retrieved from Kirrin Finch website.

petticoats worn under their skirts. Initially inspired from Turkish dress, the wide loose fitting pants worn under a knee length skirt, were aptly named the "Bloomer" (see Figure 10.2). The Bloomer became a symbol of women's rights in the early 1850s and was worn by famous feminists, like Susan B. Anthony, and Elizabeth Cady Stanton.

Figure 10.2 The Bloomer

Then in the 1920s, there was another big shift in women's clothing with women entering the workforce during World War I and gaining the right to vote. They had to think more practically about their **outfits**, and demanded less restrictive, more casual **attire**. Although women continued to wear skirts, their clothing became more masculine, loose and sporty.

One of the most influential fashion icons of the 1920s was Coco Chanel. She rebelliously dismissed the feminine styling of her day and embraced androgynous style. She accelerated the already growing movement towards female empowerment and paved the way for menswear-inspired clothing, designing elegant suits, tweed **blazers** and simple everyday-wear for women. She was best known for wearing **nautical stripes**, trousers, and **chunky** knit sweaters (see Figure 10.3).

The 1930s brought menswear-inspired fashion to the forefront, with actresses such as

Figure 10.3 CoCo Chanel's best known outfit

Chapter 10 **Feminine Culture in Britain**

Marlene Dietrich, Audrey Hepburn and Katharine Hepburn sporting suits and bow ties in popular movies (see Figure 10.4).

Figure 10.4   Left image: Marlene Dietrich. Right image: Katherine Hepburn

Although Coco Chanel, Marlene Dietrich and Katharine Hepburn rocked trousers before the 1930s, it was only considered socially acceptable for women to wear pants in specific situations, like sports or during the wars when they took over many of the men's jobs. With their husbands away at war, women took on what were previously male dominated roles such as farm or factory work. Since traditional women's attire wasn't appropriate for the more physically demanding work, they raided their husbands' closets and altered them to fit.

In 1939, *Vogue* illustrated a woman in a pair of pants on the cover of its May issue (see Figure 10.5). The editors wrote, "Our new slacks are **irreproachably** masculine in their tailoring, but women have made them entirely their own by the colors in which they order them, and the **accessories** they add." However, the article goes on to depict when, where and how these slacks may be worn, stating "One iron rule is that they are well-cut and well-**creased** to appear properly 'feminine' and stresses the necessity to avoid the 'mannish accessories' that characterised the 'early, experimental days' of trouser wearing." So women could be free to wear whatever they wanted as long as they still looked like a stepford housewife and looked pretty for their husbands!

After the war ended, women returned to their role as housewife and mother, and with that they went back to dresses and skirts. The 1950s was subsequently hyperfeminine

Figure 10.5   Woman in pants on the cover of *Vogue*

with clothing made to **accentuate** a women's hips and bust with tight waisted dresses, and curved jackets. However there were still pockets of women breaking free from the trends. For example, there was a group of women in London called Teddy Girls who rejected the traditional notions of femininity, dressing in jackets, rolled up jeans and flat shoes (see Figure 10.6).

Figure 10.6　The Teddy Girls

Although there were instances of women wearing men's clothes throughout the 20th century, it really wasn't until the 1960s and 1970s that menswear-inspired fashion was no longer considered a rebellious political statement. In the 1960s women made large **strides** toward equality with the passing of Equal Pay Act and Title VII of the Civil Rights Act, which both gave women more rights in the workplace. In 1961 Audrey Hepburn wore black capris in the movie *Breakfast at Tiffany's*, inspiring a new resurgence of women breaking away from traditional feminine clothing.

Yves Saint Laurent took menswear-inspired styling to new heights with his "Smoking" **Tuxedo** Jacket (see Figure 10.7), **hailed as** the alternative to the Little Black Dress. As he said himself, "For women, the tuxedo is an indispensable outfit, which they

Figure 10.7　Yves Saint Laurent's "Smoking" Tuxedo Jacket

feel comfortable with, so they can be who they are. This is style, not fashion. **Fads** come and go, style is forever."

Another influence was credited to the 1977 movie *Annie Hall* starring Diane Keaton, where Diane Keaton's menswear-**clad** character **donned** bowler hats, vests, wide ties and button-up shirts (see Figure 10.8).

Figure 10.8   Menswear-clad character in *Annie Hall*

Then the 1980s was all about the power suit, which included a tailored jacket with large shoulder pads and a knee length skirt (see Figure 10.9). A recent article from *Vice* magazine about the evolution of the pant suit stated, "These big shouldered jackets and pants disguised a women's figure and took the focus off her gender, creating a feeling of authority as the traditional sex roles continued to blur." UK Prime Minister, Margaret Thatcher, always wore a suit, saying that "she was in a man's world, and she had to look the part".

Figure 10.9   The power suit

英国社会与文化

In the last twenty years, menswear-inspired fashion has increased in popularity from sculptural shoulders, buttoned vests, **plaid** patterns, classic **fedoras** and **trench coats** to **slouchy** boyfriend jeans and suit sets. But, until recently it has still had a feminine element with **cinched** waists, addition of ribbons or lace, and pastel colors.

In the last five years this trend for menswear-inspired fashion has continued to grow, but there has also been a growing demand for women's clothing that is masculine without the feminine touches; so no longer just inspired from menswear, instead it is actual menswear designs fitted to the female body. This style has been given many names, but most commonly referred to as androgynous fashion, tomboy style, or menswear-inspired fashion.

Vocabulary

bat an eye		眨一下眼睛（表示惊讶）
bow tie		蝶形领结
ditch	v.	摆脱；丢弃
outfit	n.	全套服装
attire	n.	服装；盛装
blazer	n.	轻便短上衣
nautical	adj.	航海的；船员的
stripe	n.	条纹；线条
chunky	adj.	厚实的
irreproachably	adv.	无过失地；不可非难地
accessory	n.	（衣服的）配饰
creased	adj.	有折痕的；有皱纹的
accentuate	v.	强调；使突出
stride	n.	进展；进步
tuxedo	n.	男士无尾半正式晚礼服；无尾礼服
hail as		称赞……为……
fad	n.	时尚；一时流行的狂热
clad	adj.	穿……衣服的
don	v.	穿上；戴上
plaid	n.	格子花呢；格子图案
fedora	n.	一种男式软呢帽

Chapter 10 **Feminine Culture in Britain**

trenchcoat	*n.*	军用式雨衣；风衣
slouchy	*adj.*	懒散的；没精打采的
cinch	*v.*	用带子系（衣服）

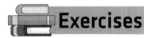

Unit 4

Weddings: The Carrier of British Culture

Since I can do no good because a woman, reach constantly at something that is near it.

—*The Maid's Tragedy: Beaumont and Fletcher*

Test Your Knowledge

I. Choose the answer to fill in the blanks about British customs and traditions of marriage and wedding.

1. Marriage is usually initiated by a _____ of marriage, simply called "a _____".

   A. wedding; wedding   B. proposal; proposal   C. ritual; ritual

2. In a heterosexual relationship, the man traditionally proposes to the woman and the actual proposal often has a ritual quality, involving the presentation of _____ and the formalized asking of a question such as "Will you marry me?"

   A. a bouquet   B. a gift   C. a ring

3. The man may even go down on _____ before proposing.

   A. one knee   B. two knees   C. stairs

4. If the proposal is accepted, the couple become _____.

   A. proposed   B. married   C. engaged

5. In the United Kingdom, the engagement ring is worn by the woman on the _____ finger of the left hand (the ring finger).

   A. pinky   B. third   C. middle

6. In the UK the 29th of February (in a(n) _____ year) is said to be the one day (coming round only once every four years) when a woman can propose to her partner.

   A. common   B. leap   C. even

II. Match the following titles with their explanations.

A. ringbearer

B. maid of honour

C. flower girl

D. father of the bride

E. groomsman

F. bridesmaid

G. ushers

H. best man

1. one or more female attendants who support the bride
2. a close male friend or relative of the groom, given a place of honour
3. helpers, usually men, who assist with the organization
4. a close female friend or relative of the bride, given a place of honour
5. an attendant, often a young boy, who carries the wedding rings
6. a young girl who scatters flowers in front of the bridal party
7. one or more male attendants who support the groom
8. one who symbolically "gives away" the bride; if her father is deceased or otherwise unavailable, another male relative, often an uncle or brother, will give the bride away

Intensive Reading

Text I Miss Brooke*

It was hardly a year since they had come to live at Tipton **Grange** with their uncle, a man nearly sixty, of **acquiescent** temper, **miscellaneous** opinions, and uncertain vote. He had travelled in his younger years, and was held in this part of the county to have contracted a too **rambling** habit of mind. Mr. Brooke's conclusions were as difficult to predict as the weather: It was only safe to say that he would act with **benevolent** intentions, and that he would spend as little money as possible in carrying them out. For the most **glutinously** indefinite minds enclose some hard grains of habit; and a man has been seen lax about all his own interests except the **retention** of his snuff-box, concerning which he was watchful, suspicious, and greedy of clutch.

---

* Excerpted from George Eliot. *Middlemarch*. London: Penguin Books, 2003: 10–15.

In Mr. Brooke the hereditary **strain** of Puritan energy was clearly **in abeyance**; but in his niece Dorothea it glowed alike through faults and virtues, turning sometimes into impatience of her uncle's talk or his way of "letting things be" on his estate, and making her long all the more for the time when she would be of age and have some command of money for generous schemes. She was regarded as an heiress; for not only had the sisters seven hundred a-year each from their parents, but if Dorothea married and had a son, that son would inherit Mr. Brooke's estate, presumably worth about three thousand a-year—a rental which seemed wealth to provincial families, still discussing Mr. Peel's late conduct on the Catholic question, innocent of future gold-fields, and of that gorgeous **plutocracy** which has so nobly exalted the necessities of **genteel** life.

And how should Dorothea not marry?—a girl so handsome and with such prospects? Nothing could hinder it but her love of extremes, and her insistence on regulating life according to notions which might cause a **wary** man to hesitate before he made her an offer, or even might lead her at last to refuse all offers. A young lady of some birth and fortune, who knelt suddenly down on a brick floor by the side of a sick laborer and prayed **fervidly** as if she thought herself living in the time of the Apostles—who had strange whims of **fasting** like a Papist, and of sitting up at night to read old **theological** books! Such a wife might awaken you some fine morning with a new scheme for the application of her income which would interfere with political economy and the keeping of saddle-horses: A man would naturally think twice before he risked himself in such fellowship. Women were expected to have weak opinions; but the great safeguard of society and of domestic life was, that opinions were not acted on. Sane people did what their neighbors did, so that if any **lunatics** were at large, one might know and avoid them.

The rural opinion about the new young ladies, even among the cottagers, was generally in favor of Celia, as being so amiable and innocent-looking, while Miss Brooke's large eyes seemed, like her religion, too unusual and striking. Poor Dorothea! compared with her, the innocent-looking Celia was knowing and worldly-wise; so much subtler is a human mind than the outside tissues which make a sort of **blazonry** or clock-face for it.

Yet those who approached Dorothea, though prejudiced against her by this alarming hearsay, found that she had a charm unaccountably reconcilable with it. Most men thought her **bewitching** when she was on horseback. She loved the fresh air and the various aspects of the country, and when her eyes and cheeks glowed with mingled pleasure she looked very little like a devotee. Riding was an indulgence which she allowed herself in spite of **conscientious qualms**; she felt that she enjoyed it in a pagan sensuous way, and always looked forward to **renouncing** it.

She was open, **ardent**, and not in the least self-admiring; indeed, it was pretty to see how her imagination adorned her sister Celia with attractions altogether superior to her own, and if any gentleman appeared to come to the Grange from some other motive than that of seeing Mr. Brooke, she concluded that he must be in love with Celia: Sir James Chettam, for example, whom she constantly considered from Celia's point of view, inwardly debating whether it would be good for Celia to accept him. That he should be regarded as a suitor to herself would have seemed to her a ridiculous irrelevance. Dorothea, with all her eagerness to know the truths of life, retained very childlike ideas about marriage. She felt sure that she would have accepted the **judicious** Hooker, if she had been born in time to save him from that wretched mistake he made in **matrimony**; or John Milton when his blindness had come on; or any of the other great men whose odd habits it would have been glorious piety to endure; but an amiable handsome Baronet, who said "Exactly" to her remarks even when she expressed uncertainty—How could he affect her as a lover? The really delightful marriage must be that where your husband was a sort of father, and could teach you even Hebrew, if you wished it.

These peculiarities of Dorothea's character caused Mr. Brooke to be all the more blamed in neighboring families for not securing some middle-aged lady as guide and companion to his nieces. But he himself dreaded so much the sort of superior woman likely to be available for such a position, that he allowed himself to be dissuaded by Dorothea's objections, and was in this case brave enough to defy the world—that is to say, Mrs. Cadwallader the Rector's wife, and the small group of gentry with whom he visited in the northeast corner of Loamshire. So Miss Brooke presided in her uncle's household, and did not at all dislike her new authority, with the **homage** that belonged to it.

Vocabulary

grange	*n.*	农庄；庄园
acquiescent	*adj.*	顺从的
miscellaneous	*adj.*	混杂的；各种各样的
rambling	*adj.*	冗长而含糊的

benevolent	adj.	慈善的，仁慈的
glutinously	adv.	如胶一样黏地
retention	n.	保存，存放
strain	n.	个性特点；性格倾向
in abeyance		归属待定；悬而未决
plutocracy	n.	富豪统治
genteel	adj.	上流社会的
wary	adj.	小心翼翼的，谨慎的
fervidly	adv.	激情地，热情地
fast	v.	斋戒，禁食
theological	adj.	神学的
lunatic	n.	疯子
blazonry	n.	纹章图案
bewitching	adj.	迷人的
conscientious	adj.	凭良心的，与良心有关的
qualm	n.	疑虑；不安
renounce	v.	宣布放弃（信仰、行为方式）
ardent	adj.	热烈的，热切的
judicious	adj.	审慎而明智的；有见地的
matrimony	n.	婚姻
baronet	n.	从男爵；准男爵
homage	n.	敬意，尊敬

Exercises

I. Choose the best answer to each of the following questions.

1. How could Dorothea not be married?

   A. She should marry, with all her qualifications of beauty, birth and wealth.

   B. She usually had some sudden wish to do something unusual.

   C. She constantly considered from her sister Celia's point of view.

   D. Owing to her extreme love of religion, she wished that her husband could be a sort of father or tutor, which was not common in life.

2. Who was the last man Dorothea would accept as a husband?

   A. Hooker.

   B. John Milton.

   C. Any great man with unusual habits.

D. An agreeable young aristocrat.

3. Which of the following is **NOT** true about Mr. Brooke?

   A. He did not have any definite or decided opinion.

   B. He was very likely to change his idea.

   C. There was nothing he cared about in life.

   D. His mind consisted of many different kinds of things that were difficult to put into a particular category.

4. Why did the author describe Mr. Brooke's character in details?

   A. To introduce the family where the sisters live.

   B. To contrast sharply with that of Miss Brooke.

   C. To explain for his not having a lady as guide and companion to his nieces.

   D. To illustrate what his way of "letting things be" was like.

5. What did the author think of Dorothea's views on marriage?

   A. As simple as a child.   B. Childish.

   C. Admiring.   D. Ridiculous.

II. Fill in the blanks with the appropriate forms of the words in the box.

idealistic	apart	disinherit	ultimately	provision
pursue	error	allege	wish	jealous
commit	seek	earnest	senior	involve

Dorothea is a(n) **1.** _____ intelligent woman who makes a serious **2.** _____ in judgment when she chooses to marry Edward Casaubon, a pompous scholar many years her **3.** _____. Dorothea hopes to be actively **4.** _____ in his work, but he wants her to serve as a secretary. She comes to doubt both his talent and his **5.** _____ masterpiece. Furthermore, the controlling Casaubon becomes **6.** _____ when she develops a friendship with Will Ladislaw, his **7.** _____ cousin. Although disappointed, Dorothea remains **8.** _____ to the marriage and tries to appease her husband. After Casaubon has a heart attack, Dorothea is clearly devoted to him, but he bars Ladislaw from visiting, believing that his cousin will **9.** _____ Dorothea when he dies. Casaubon subsequently **10.** _____ her promise that she will follow his **11.** _____ even after his death. She delays answering but

12. _____ decides that she should agree to his request. However, he dies before she can tell him. Dorothea later discovers that his will contains a(n) **13.** _____ that calls for her to be **14.** _____ if she marries Ladislaw. Afraid of scandal, Dorothea and Ladislaw initially stay **15.** _____. However, they ultimately fall in love and marry.

III. Complete the comparison chart between Celia and Dorothea according to the passage.

	Celia	Dorothea
Appearance	**1.** _____ and **2.** _____	**6.** _____; Her large eyes seemed too **7.** _____ and **8.** _____.
Opinion About Her	The opinion was generally **3.** _____ her.	She had a(n) **9.** _____ and most men thought her **10.** _____.
Character	She was **4.** _____ and **5.** _____.	She was **11.** _____, **12.** _____ and not in the least **13.** _____.
To Her Sister		Her imagination **14.** _____ her sister Celia with **15.** _____ her own.
Author's Opinion		She was **16.** _____ against by rumour.

Further Reading

Text II Marriage Therapy in the 1960s: Marriage as a Platform for Personal Growth*

Over the course of the 1960s, during the same years that British divorce law reformers were bringing attention to the emotional distress caused by **dysfunctional** marriages, marriage therapists reconsidered the value of

---

* Excerpted from Chettiar T. 2015. Treating marriage as "the sick entity": Gender, emotional life, and the psychology of marriage improvement in postwar Britain. *History of Psychology*, 18(3): 270–282.

spouses' personal "adjustment" to marriage and the preservation of marriage for its own sake. Therapists, counselors, and **caseworkers** increasingly came to view marriage as a necessary platform for psychological growth, with the spousal relationship seen as closely **rivaling** the mother–child relationship in developmental importance. In marriage, caseworker Lily Pincus maintained, "the past is **recapitulated**", giving this important relationship the dual function of supporting both "the self-realization of husband and wife, and the social development of their children". Explaining the centrality of marriage to the completion of an individual's social and psychological development in adulthood, Tom Main, director of the Cassel Marital Clinic, explained that, "within the marital relationship the self-realization of each partner is achieved through the other by the steady reality testing of the partner against the fantasies derived from earlier conflicts". The aim of marriage therapy was thus, "not so much to produce changes in the personalities of the individual partners as to enable them together to make use of the potentialities for growth and self-realization which are inherent in the marital union".

Anthony Giddens argues that intimate life underwent a steady process of **democratization** during the second half of the 20th century. He maintains that whereas marriage had been anchored in public duty earlier in the century, it became a "pure relationship" during the post-World War II decades, "entered into for [its] own sake…[and] continued only in so far as it is thought by both parties to deliver enough satisfactions for individuals to stay within it". Although marriage therapists increasingly understood marriage as performing a crucial task for personal growth and self-realization in the 1960s, Lily Pincus noted that "confusion about sexual roles" remained "fundamental themes in marriage problems". Case reports from Britain's marriage therapy services offer a more **nuanced** perspective on what Giddens describes as a loosening of moral restrictions on intimate life in the 1960s. For example, although the Family Discussion Bureau caseworkers noted that Mr. and Mrs. Smith had made progress "integrating within themselves the **hitherto** denied parts of their personalities" as a result of a few months of marriage therapy, their case report's demonstration of therapeutic success focused on spouses' acceptance of their distinctly family oriented masculine and feminine **marital** roles. Proof of the improvement of their marriage was evidenced in the fact of Mr. Smith having secured a stable job after three months of unemployment, and Mrs. Smith having become "more feminine in appearance, and more able to enjoy her feminine tasks in house and kitchen".

The persistent focus on gender roles and identities in marriage therapy is especially striking given that counselors and caseworkers claimed not to believe that the gendered division of labor in families was rooted in biological differences between men and women. By 1960, FDB caseworkers had openly **lamented** that clients' "conceptions of masculinity and femininity are invariably somewhat unrealistic" and thus a major cause of emotional conflict. Distinguishing between biologically determined sexual differences (especially those related to reproduction) and the numerous social expectations of adult men and women, Lily Pincus emphasized that many gender-differentiated behavioral attributes and family duties were rooted in cultural stereotypes. Despite the new possibilities that the widely respected ideal of companionate marriage presented for **dismantling** the **asymmetrical** marital roles associated with Victorian "separate spheres", caseworkers emphasized that most marital conflict stemmed from spouses' anxieties about gender performance:

The client will often strive to bring them together in a picture of marriage "as it ought to be", in which the husband has authority, makes decisions in every sphere and is the **initiator**, provider, protector—and **invulnerable**; while the wife is dependent, sexually attractive and **yielding**, but at the same time a competent housewife and devoted mother.

Rather than challenging clients' expectations as unrealistic, caseworkers repeatedly presented the arc of marriage improvement in case reports as a progressive movement toward spouses' gender-differentiated maturity.

Therapists' **attribution** of psychological meaning to marriage **resonated** beyond the marriage therapy clinic in the 1960s. After close to a decade of heated debate in Parliament and the popular media, the 1969 Divorce Reform Act made "breakdown" of marriage rather than **matrimonial** "offense" the legal basis for divorce. Outlining the meaning of breakdown, a group of church leaders appointed by the **Archbishop** of Canterbury to investigate divorce procedures explained that "frequently, if not always, the failures in adjustment that lead to the divorce court come of failure to deal successfully with the **legacy** of **infantile** experience". This **watershed** moment in the history of Britain's divorce law sought to remove the **stigma** from marital breakdown and make divorce by mutual consent possible: No longer would each spouse be considered either an innocent "victim" or guilty "offender" when a marriage was brought to an end. Instead, marriage was presented as a relationship that both parties were equally involved in strengthening and **stabilizing** or, alternatively, causing to fall apart: "Indeed it is widely accepted that matrimonial offenses or separation are generally a symptom not a cause of breakdown." As part of their argument in favor of liberalizing the divorce law, the Archbishop's group advocated further expansion of Britain's marriage services, claiming that they helped spouses to "learn how to accept in the other, as well as in himself (or herself), some of the deepest elements of early infantile relationships. If both succeed in doing this, a new and more creative relationship may emerge". At the heart of the passage of Britain's 1969 Divorce Reform Act was an acceptance of the expert-driven psychologically informed view that marriage was a mutually created and sustained relationship.

Vocabulary

therapy	n.	治疗，疗法
dysfunctional	adj.	机能失调的；功能障碍的
spouse	n.	配偶
caseworker	n.	社会工作者；个案工作者
rival	v.	与……相匹敌，比得上
recapitulate	v.	重述；概括
democratization	n.	民主化
nuanced	adj.	微妙的；具有细微差别的
hitherto	adv.	迄今
marital	adj.	婚姻的
lament	v.	对……表示失望；抱怨
dismantle	v.	（逐渐）废除，取消
asymmetrical	adj.	不对称的
initiator	n.	发起人，创始人
invulnerable	adj.	不会受伤害的；打不败的
yielding	adj.	柔软的；顺从的
attribution	n.	归因；属性
resonate	v.	引起共鸣
matrimonial	adj.	婚姻的；与婚姻有关的
archbishop	n.	大主教
legacy	n.	遗留问题
infantile	adj.	婴儿的；幼儿的
watershed	adj.	标志转折点的

英国社会与文化

| stigma | *n.* | 耻辱，羞耻 |
| stabilize | *v.* | （使）稳定，稳固 |

Exercises

(Keys to all exercises of this book)